ANCHORS IN THE SKY

Lieutenant Theodore Gordon Ellyson, United States Navy, in
January 1911.

ANCHORS IN THE SKY

Spuds Ellyson, the First Naval Aviator

George van Deurs

PRESIDIO PRESS
SAN RAFAEL, CALIFORNIA
LONDON, ENGLAND

Published by Presidio Press
of San Rafael, California, and
London, England
with editorial offices
at 1114 Irwin Street
San Rafael, California

Library of Congress Cataloging in Publication Data

Van Deurs, George, 1901-
    Anchors in the sky.

        Bibliography: p.
        Includes index.
        1.   Ellyson, Theodore Gordon, 1885-1928.
2.   Air pilots, Military — United States — Biography.
3.   United States.   Navy — Biography.   I.   Title.
V63.E44V36   358.4'13'320924 [B]   78-74
ISBN 0-89141-034-1

    In publication with the cooperation of the Admiral and
Mrs. DeWitt Clinton Ramsey Fund which is administered by
the Smithsonian Institution National Air and Space Museum,
for "the increase and diffusion of knowledge pertaining to
United States Naval Flight History."
Printed in the United States of America
Book Designed by Joe Roter

To the thousands of naval aviators who have soloed
since Spuds Ellyson led the way

Contents

Contents

List of Illustrations

Preface

When, in 1915, the United States Navy Department began to issue gold wings and designations to its naval aviators, Theodore Gordon "Spuds" Ellyson, first lieutenant of the battleship *South Carolina*, was awarded the number one wings and designation. Glenn Curtiss, a mechanical genius and the first licensed flier in America, had taught Ellyson to fly in 1911.

Ellyson was headlined as "*the* Navy flier" early in his career. He had become a legend while still a young lieutenant; then, convinced that a Navy flier had to know a naval officer's basic trade, he had returned to sea duty in 1913. Eight years later, he returned to flying until, in 1928, an air crash ended his life at the age of forty-three.

Those who knew Spuds Ellyson shortly before his death remember a solid, husky man with lively eyes. A few purple veins lined his flushed cheeks. The tilt of his cap over his starboard eye revealed a fringe of close-cropped reddish hair above the opposite ear. On his crisply pressed blue uniform he wore the number one gold wings above ribbons for the Navy Cross, the Mexican Campaign, and World War I. Three gold stripes ringed each cuff. The hands beyond the cuffs trembled as they raised a coffee cup but were steady enough at flying and at the rough fun he never entirely outgrew.

As one of the earliest submarine skippers and the first naval aviator, Ellyson devoted his energies to making submarines and airplanes into effective Navy tools. In the days before aeronautical engineering had become a science, more men got off the ground than ever learned to fly. Ellyson and his teammate Lieutenant junior grade John Henry Towers were among the few who became expert pilots. Nevertheless, despite his skill, some of Ellyson's most important contributions to the art of flying were unexpected and unplanned.

After World War II, Ellyson was largely forgotten outside the Navy; even among the thousands of pilots who now wore replicas of his number one wings were many who could not identify Spuds Ellyson. But the story of his career emphasizes a characteristic that raised Spuds above the average: *He stuck his neck out.*

Aviators and submariners have been following his lead ever since, voluntarily taking on extra study, extra tests, extra work, and extra personal risks. Spuds Ellyson's story shows us that genius is not the only requirement for making lasting contributions to the welfare of one's country.

Acknowledgments

For help in finding the man behind the legend of Spuds Ellyson, I am indebted to two pioneer aviation mechanics, Dale Sigler and Charles Wiggin; to Ellyson's surviving *South Carolina* shipmates; and to some of the pilots he commanded in the twenties. All provided me with anecdotes and personal recollections, and the manner of their telling revealed widespread affection for the Navy's first flier.

Helen Ellyson answered many of my questions, authorizing my access to the Navy record of her late husband and allowing me to share some of his many letters to her. Ellyson was a copious letter writer, but only scraps of his correspondence have been found. Besides those letters in his wife's fragmentary collection, others were included among the papers of Capt. Washington Irving Chambers; a few, directed to Richmond relatives, and preserved in the Ellyson family archives. Wherever possible, the conversations in this book have been quoted directly from letters. Other dialogue is, of necessity, fictionalized, but, given the situation and the characters involved, approximates what must have been said at the time.

I wish to thank especially Mrs. Terrell Andrew Nisewaner, the daughter of Capt. Kenneth Whiting, and three Navy Department historians—Rear Adm. Ernest McNiel Eller, USN (retired), Adrian O. Van Wyen, and Lee M. Pearson—for their patient assistance, valuable criticism, and many suggestions.

CHAPTER ONE

Family Life in Richmond:

Waiting

*W*hen he was born on 27 February 1885 in the big house at 814 Park Avenue, Richmond, Virginia, Henry Theodore and Lizzie Ellyson named their third son Theodore Gordon. Like his brothers, the new baby was redheaded. His world held no automobiles, record players, radios, television sets, movies, Kodaks, or flying machines. Telephones had been invented nine years before his birth, but few homes had them. Edison's six-year-old electric light was even rarer. The safety bicycle with two wheels of the same size was so new that none had been seen in Richmond.

Theodore Gordon's cousin, Styles Ellyson, saw his Aunt Lizzie as a "staunch soul, full of pep, courage, humor, and good sportsmanship, and a beautiful woman with red hair." Tall, forceful, energetic, Lizzie Ellyson endowed her seven children with lusty, aggressive natures and a set of positive values. She saw everything as either right or wrong; though she admitted no middle ground, she did not expect perfection. If anyone had suggested that a son of hers might someday fly, she would have retorted, "If the Lord had intended my boys to fly, they would have wings, but they'll not be angels." She would have been correct; her flying son was no angel.

Gordon's father left most of the family's decisions to Lizzie. She never suspected that her slight, meek husband was a wild dreamer.

1

Henry Theodore Ellyson sought in religion a release from a life which little matched his dreams, leading his family in daily prayers and walking them to the Second Baptist Church each Sunday. The Reverend Doctor W.W. Landrum's long sermons bored young Gordon, who learned, before he was old enough for school, to duck the church parade. Punishments made no difference in his attendance. When his father asked for him as the church hour drew near, the maid would say, "Went out back with a fish pole," or "Ain't seen him since breakfast."

Henry and Douglas, Gordon's older brothers, ruled the neighborhood. Gordon learned to fight, as he learned to avoid church. During most of his boyhood, he wanted to "lick Henry"; he never quite made it, but the practice he got in trying hardened him. Years later, schoolmates remembered Gordon as "the redhead who was always fighting someone bigger than himself." Sometimes he battled for a cause; sometimes he fought only to see if he could win.

Schoolmaster John Payten McGuire, who believed in rugged character, encouraged such aggressive spirits. His ungraded private school filled the upper floor of a store building. It had no gym, no athletic teams, no frills. At recess his boys ran across the street for noisy, rough fun in Monroe Park. In class they were orderly and decorous, knowing that McGuire applied a strap when it was deserved. Each boy studied an assigned subject for as long as it took him to finish it and then took a stiff examination. Unless he scored 90 or better, he repeated the entire subject—perhaps two years' work. While McGuire forced Gordon to master fundamentals, the boy also learned how to absorb information from a printed page—and that girls could be more fun than any printed page.

While Gordon studied for McGuire, Marconi demonstrated wireless telegraphy, Langley flew his unmanned machine over the Potomac, and the Spanish-American War left the United States in need of a deep-sea navy. Highly colored reports of naval victories at Manila and Santiago and pictures of new men-of-war being built for the fleet fired Gordon's imagination. Other members of the Ellyson family took little interest in battleships until June 1900, when Gordon graduated from McGuire's.

The husky fifteen-year-old, who parted his curly red hair on the center line, told his family he wanted to go into the Navy, and he wanted to begin his career at the Naval Academy. Lizzie Ellyson was jolted. She believed Ellysons belonged in Richmond, knew them to be freshwater folk with no seagoing traditions. She had chosen Virginia colleges for all her boys. Henry and Doug were already enrolled, according to plan. She never understood why her third son rebelled, asking to live on an ocean he had never seen.

Gordon's father might have enlightened her, but she gave him no chance to do so; she had no reason to suspect that he might understand his son's desire. But Henry Theodore sensed the feelings of his pugnacious son, for he shared them, in secret. He had always been overshadowed by a famous father and ambitious brothers, all of whom walked tall in city, state, and Baptist organizations. He hated their competition, stifled his inner yearnings, and settled for his position as treasurer of the *Richmond Despatch,* the family newspaper. Lizzie never forgave him for slipping into that comfortable rut. Better even than Gordon, his father understood the lad's instinct to want to escape from everlasting family comparisons, wanting to avoid the trails blazed by Henry, Doug, and his cousins and uncles. The father was eager for his son to escape the life that had trapped him.

A young man was appointed to the United States Naval Academy by a senator, a congressman, or the president. Whenever a midshipman graduated or flunked out, the official who had appointed him would nominate a principal to fill the vacancy, and a first, second, and third alternate. All candidates took the written examinations held at the same time all over the country in February and again in April of each year. After passing the written examination, a candidate had to pass a physical examination at the Naval Academy. If the principal failed either, the senior alternate who passed both got in. An appointment was never final until a man passed both examinations, held up his hand, and swore to defend the Constitution. Since a candidate must be between sixteen and twenty years old when sworn in, Gordon had a year to wait.

Henry Theodore looked for a politician with an Annapolis vacancy to fill. He sent Gordon to spend the year at "Bobby's War College," as generations of Navy men called Werntz's Annapolis Preparatory School. Robert Lincoln Werntz, a Naval Academy alumnus, had resigned from the Navy Engineer Corps in 1890 to spend his next forty years coaching boys for entrance into the service academies. Office and storerooms filled the lower floor of his brick building on Maryland Avenue in Annapolis. The upper story was the classroom where he and his brother Jimmy alternated as instructors. These tall, lanky brothers were serious men who dressed always in the same chalk-impregnated jackets—Bobby's of black alpaca, Jimmy's of tweed.

Bobby collected fees in advance, made no refunds, and told each new boy, "We know what you need to get into the Academy — and to stay in. We'll show it to you. The rest is up to you. We give an examination each Saturday morning. It allows you to get used to taking tests against the clock, and tells me how you are doing. If you don't learn, we drop you from the school."

Bobby used no strap. His candidates were eager to prove their grown-up independence; they dressed like beatniks, chewed tobacco, smoked, and talked aloud in class. The Werntz brothers, ignoring the pretensions, began each day with a formal roll call of surnames and home states. Gordon, with a battered derby on the back of his head and a new pipe between his teeth, answered to "Ellyson, Virginia." He also paid close attention; he wanted very much to become a naval cadet.

On his third day he tilted his chair back to watch Jimmy Werntz copy a long compound fraction from a book of past examinations. "Every year they give one or two of these to be simplified," Jimmy said with his chalk poised. "You'll be working against time, so you can't fool around." He began cancelling terms as fast as his chalk would fly and scribbled the answer while he was still saying, "With enough practice you can learn to see cancellations at a glance this way."

"Ellyson, Virginia" was impressed. "Gosh, do you think we can really get to be that fast?" he asked "Caldwell, Tennessee" in the next seat.

Caldwell missed the bucket with a squirt of tobacco juice. "Hell," he said. "I hear Jimmy's been using that same prob for years. Got the answer memorized."

The school did not billet students. "Ellyson, Virginia" roomed with "Spears, Tennessee" in a boardinghouse run by two motherly sisters, "Aunt Alice" and "Aunt Em." He liked their food, especially the potatoes, asking for more so often that his roommate Oscar began calling him "Spuds." Soon everyone in the house took up the name. Ellyson laughed at them until the weekend his mother and sister May visited Annapolis. Both disliked the nickname, and said so. "Make them call you 'Gordon,'" Lizzie ordered. "It's a good name, and it's yours." Ellyson immediately adopted Spuds. He used the name for the rest of his life.

Spuds had expected to breeze through Werntz's school; he had done well at McGuire's with less work than the old man suspected. Instead, he was shaken by each Saturday examination. The errors he remembered afterward always discouraged him. Each Monday he was relieved, and a bit surprised, when Bobby did not warn him to do better, or else. He had survived several Saturdays when two boys who liked horseplay better than books were sent home. By Christmas, others were buying extra instruction. Spuds was running scared.

On the first of February, Congressman John Lamb named Spuds an alternate for his principal appointee, Robert Whitehurst. Two months later, on the April Sunday when Bobby took his candidates to a Baltimore hotel for the exam, Spuds thought he knew all the answers. Next morning, in a big loft of the post office, he was one of some fifty boys who began writing under the eye of a sour-faced, civil service examiner. During that week, each morning and afternoon was like a Saturday at Bobby's, except this test was the real one, and Spuds could not laugh off careless mistakes. His nerves tensed. He fumbled answers he had known well. Several times the sour examiner called time before he was finished. Friday night, worried and exhausted, he went back to "Crabtown," as he had learned to call Annapolis.

He bounced back after a night's sleep. "I knocked it for a loop," he told Oscar confidently. "Wish I knew what my principal, Whitehurst, did. Don't even know the guy. Wonder where he took the exams?"

As they waited for results, with no classes and no studying, the candidates knew sudden freedom. Spuds began dating "crabs," as the local girls were labeled, when no cadets were on liberty. He joined alcoholic experiments in the candidates' boardinghouses or took postgraduate work in poker and bridge. The cards soaked up his allowance, but he considered himself an expert before the hot May afternoon when the cry "The marks are up!" broke up a game.

Ignoring the stink of Crabtown's overripe fish, candidates swarmed down Maryland Avenue and jumped, jostled, and pushed around the bulletin board beside the Academy's main gate. Front-rankers finding passing marks clung to their positions, comparing their scores with those of others. While they whooped their pleasure, failures slunk away, choking on their disappointment. Spuds, too excited to notice these silent failures, hurried past Bobby's, elbowed himself into the front rank, and read marks that justified his confidence. He felt ten feet high, until he noticed a blank where a reporting date should have been noted beside his name. Fear gripped his stomach. He skimmed down the alphabet. Spears would report on May 21. So would his principal, Whitehurst.

Spuds flattened like a pricked balloon. Whitehurst was in. Ellyson was out. He struggled free of the crowd as glum as any other reject. Oscar caught his arm. "Come on. Let's celebrate. We passed," he said.

"Nuts. So did my principal. What'll I celebrate?" Spuds retorted.

"You can get another appointment next year and get in without any more exams. That's a lot," Oscar said.

"Maybe so," Spuds admitted grudgingly. "But I don't feel like celebrating. I think I'd better head for Richmond to start hunting that appointment."

In Richmond the three Ellyson sisters stuffed their brother with his favorite chocolates, but only Papa understood that Spuds disliked the city even more than Gordon had. "I want to go to Washington, Papa, and get an appointment for next year," Spuds said. "I can start with Mr. Lamb."

"Will he have a vacancy, son?"

"I don't know, but I can ask him."

"No sense in bothering a man for something he doesn't have," Papa said. "I knew you wouldn't quit. So I asked your uncle Taylor to find out who would have a vacancy. He knows Representative Lamb and the senators."

Spuds recognized a smart approach, but he wanted action. Even the few days of waiting for Uncle Taylor's research got him down. Spuds was lonesome and bored with his local chums and older brothers away at college. At thirteen, his favorite brother Donald was much too young to be company for an experienced man of the world. Fed up with books, Spuds could not sit still long enough to fish. Wishing for his Crabtown companions, he pushed through the swinging half-doors of the saloon under McGuire's school. Chacy Trefini, its curly-haired owner, yelled, "Hey! You know McGuire boys can't come in here."

"I'm not a McGuire boy anymore," Spuds protested.

"Well, you can't come in anyway. I know how old you are. Want I should lose my license?" So the saloon offered no solace.

Lizzie Ellyson was glad to have her Gordon home again. The Park Avenue house had been uncomfortably quiet with three of her boys away. She watched his restless rambles, waited for him to simmer down. He had moped for a couple of weeks before she said, "Let's put in your application for Virginia Military Institute, Gordon. I'm sure you'll love it. I have some forms in my desk."

Gordon choked back a goddammit. He did not swear before ladies.

"Darn it, Mamma, I'm not interested in VMI. You know I'm going into the Navy somehow."

"A year at VMI first might help you."

"I don't want to talk about it now, please," he said and went out of the house. It's a trap of hers, he told himself as he walked rapidly down the street. She thinks I'll stay there if she once gets me in. She might be right. Dammit, I'll go nuts if this keeps up. Damn Whitehurst. Why wasn't he dumb?

CHAPTER TWO

Annapolis:

Academy and Sea

*L*ate in May, a wire from the Academy flipped Gordon's world right-side-up again.

REPORT FOR PHYSICAL EXAMINATION AT TEN AM JUNE FOURTH

Gordon read the wire twice, let out a rebel yell, and raced to his room. Spuds Ellyson was in business again.

He packed the few things he expected to use before getting into uniform, then carefully stowed his boyish treasures, as though he were leaving for only a short visit. He intended to make the grade at Annapolis, but he had not thought ahead far enough to realize that he would never live in his Richmond room again. His mind never worked that way. Nor did he ever ask what happened to his principal; that he was out of the way was sufficient. Soon, Spuds forgot even Whitehurst's name.

On June Week Tuesday, the naval cadet battalion paraded on Worden Field. Band music drifted into the old brick dispensary where Spuds stood naked and perspiring near an open window. A doctor poked, thumped, measured, and tested him and the

9

other four candidates who checked in that day. At last the man said, "OK. You'll do. Dress, and go see the paymaster."

Spuds walked out, feeling himself almost an admiral.

The paymaster took his money for uniforms and equipment. A storekeeper piled a mountain of gear in front of him, with a seabag and canvas hammock topping the heap. "You'll draw the rest of your gear when you get back from the cruise," the storekeeper said. "Sign here."

"The rest?" How was he to handle this much?

"For fifty cents, one of the janitors will help you get your stuff over to the gym," the storekeeper volunteered.

Spuds fished out a coin.

Under the Academy's old trees, proud parents rested on the class benches. Young women in white, ground-sweeping skirts held floppy hats atop high-piled hair and twirled two-foot parasols at the end of five-foot handles. Even those on their first Annapolis dates had been briefed on uniforms and ranks. None had a glance for a fifth classman, a mere "function," still in civilian clothes. Ellyson never suspected such an attitude possible. He felt so important as he strutted across the yard behind his porter that he was sure all were admiring him. Beyond the pile drivers banging foundations for Bancroft Hall, the man led him to a circular building near the sea wall where the "functions" who had reported two weeks earlier were sleeping on cots.

Oscar Spears pumped his hand. "Sure glad to see you made it. Heard you were coming." Others who had prepped at Bobby's joined in the welcome.

"What's this about a cruise?" Spuds asked.

"We're going," Oscar said. "The contractor's behind on the new buildings. They're shipping us all out of his way, I suppose."

"Lucky, huh? Go places right off?" Spuds asked.

Oscar hesitated. "I don't know," he said. "We'll get the hell run out of us. There wouldn't be any upperclassmen around here for a regular plebe summer."

"Are they that bad?"

"You'll see at mess, if not before," Oscar said.

Traditionally, the functions entered in weekly increments throughout the month of June, then had the school almost to themselves until October. Their plebe summer was pleasantly filled with new uniforms and routine drills. Life changed drastically when the upperclassmen returned to supervise every moment of the plebes' days. Each plebe was then required to march like a mechanical man, ramrod stiff, down the center of any corridor or path. He looked neither to the right nor left and had to pivot corners as though doing close order drill. He dined erect on the front inch of his chair, with his eyes strictly directed toward his plate. Plebes spoke only to answer questions. Woe to the unfortunate who answered incorrectly when he was asked, "How many days, Mister?" "What's the dessert, Mister?" "How do you get a rat out of the lee scupper, Mister?" or the other questions put to him by his superiors.

Growing pains afflicted the Navy and its Academy in 1901. New boys entering before graduation as "functions" were far more humble than the plebes who had nearly completed their ordeal. That first day, Spuds received corrective orders every time he moved. "Square your shoulders, Mister!" "Suck up that gut, Mister!" "Shoulders back, Mister. Farther! Show some wrinkles in that jumper!" "Get your greasy eyes off me, Mister!" Before evening he understood Oscar's reservations about the cruise; he no longer felt himself almost an admiral.

On Friday, Ernest Joseph King, the lanky, future fleet admiral of World War II, graduated with sixty-six others in the class of 1901. All other classes moved up a grade.

Spuds's white work uniform was still scratchily unlaundered, and his blue-rimmed white hat dropped unnautically to his ears, but he spoke like an old-timer to the twenty-two classmates who checked in the day after the class of 1901's graduation. "You guys got here too late," he told them. "Can't ever say you started at the bottom like us. We got promoted to plebe; you started that way. It was really tough here when ought-one was running the show."

Next day a senior officer gave the new cadets a few facts of naval life. "You're in the Navy now," he began. "You can be useful and enjoy it, if you learn to live by the rules of the sea. Your country wants you to become competent, professional officers. If you do, and keep your noses clean, the country will take care of you. You'll never get rich, but you can have a satisfying life of patriotic service and will always be able to live as respected gentlemen. On the other hand, if you fail to live up to service standards of character and skill, you will be discarded.

"Navies are not democracies," he explained. "They can't be. Survival at sea demands sound decision, unquestioning obedience, teamwork. To assure those qualities, the Navy is an autocracy, organized by rank. You must remember that 'R.H.I.P.'—Rank Has Its Privileges—and its responsibilities. An admiral rates doing

things I do not. He also has more worries. I rate doing things a
cadet doesn't. A first classman rates doing things you plebes don't.
Some rates are regulations, some are custom. Observe both sorts,"
he advised, "or you will be known as 'ratey,' and that will com-
plicate your lives here.

"Rates are neither snobbery, discrimination, nor silly customs,"
he explained, "but practical working rules to help men live in
crowded ships. Passing the entrance examinations may have set
you apart and made you feel big in your home towns. Forget it.
Everyone here has done as much, or more." He ended by telling
the cadets they were at the bottom of a long ladder and wished
them luck in their climb.

"Sounds like Plato's guardians," muttered one of the older plebes
as they filed out. The crack meant nothing to Spuds; he had never
read Plato's *Republic*. He walked out with stars in his eyes, determined to excel the highest service standards.

"Wipe that silly smile off your foolish face, Mister," ordered a
new youngster. "Now put it where it belongs." Spuds did.

Next day the cadets crowded into two ships for the summer
practice cruise. The *Indiana,* the Navy's first battleship, took half
the upperclassmen and most of the new plebes. The rest of the
cadets went into the "Cheesebox," as they called the three-masted
training ship *Chesapeake.* She had no engines and the tonnage of a
World War I destroyer. Spuds, Oscar, and the other fourteen
Cheesebox plebes were billeted beside the galley in her starboard
passage, which was furnished with hooks on the overhead for sixteen hammocks and had a jackstay, or pipe, along one side.

"Kinda small, isn't it?" Spuds asked after their bags were hung
on the jackstay.

Oscar slowly turned all the way round before answering, "Lux-
urious white paint. Otherwise unlike my idea of Mr. Morgan's
yacht."

That first night the plebes dozed fitfully. Because their hammocks were jammed so closely together in the tiny compartment,
only one of the plebes fell out during the night. At 2:30 A.M., they
all heard the cooks dump coal into the range and begin rattling
galley gear. Two hours later, all were still awake when the "Jimmy
legs"—the master-at-arms—shouted, "Hit the deck! Heave out
and lash up!"

By 5 o'clock, first classmen had Spuds heaving round the anchor capstan. They drove him aloft to make sail, down again to

scrub decks and shine brightwork. He thought he had done a day's work by the time breakfast was piped down. But the work had only begun. All day he heaved on lines while the ship tacked and tacked again, going slowly south in light airs. Whenever he tried to sit a moment, the boatswain's pipe shrilled him to drill, or someone shouted an unintelligible order such as, "Look alive, Mister! Lay onto the mizzen brace!" After sunset, they anchored. Spuds's hands were raw. His feet hurt all the way up to his neck. Sleep in a hammock? Sure, sleep anywhere. But at midnight he was hauled out for his two hours of anchor watch. After the first night, Spuds never again heard the cooks fire up the galley. At each reveille the Jimmy legs beat Spuds's hammock with a club until he began to move.

Before he finished the Academy, Spuds began four cruises in the Cheesebox. Each followed an established pattern. Ten or twelve days of slow sailing to the Virginia Capes were followed by a steady run to Long Island Sound, with summer weeks of drills underway and weekends anchored off summer colonies from New London on the Fourth of July to Bar Harbor in mid-August.

On the first cruises Commander Hugo Osterhouse, head of the seamanship department of the Academy, skippered the Cheesebox. "Liberty," professed the commander, "is a privilege, not a right." He believed liberty degraded innocent young cadets and granted it only in driblets. Spuds saw New England through a porthole that first summer and spent part of each Sunday writing long letters home. His seagoing adventures grew in the telling, with old Hugo as the supervillain.

Upperclassmen swapped ships in midsummer, but the same sixteen plebes were still living beside the galley when the Cheesebox docked at the Academy on 27 August. Spuds, with a red, peeling face, was heavier muscled without his Richmond fat. His calloused hands had scrubbed his uniforms to comfortable softness; he had spiked a white hat atop the mainmast. Upperclassmen permitting, he wore this ragged trophy with a don't-give-a-damn list to starboard like that of bilger Kenneth ("Ken") Whiting, who rated as a youngster because of his previous entry.

From that first cruise on, throughout Spuds's life, Whiting consistently influenced his career. Few Navy men knew all of Ken's background; few suspected that he wanted to be an artist instead of a naval officer. As in Ellyson's family, a determined, intelligent, redheaded mother ruled Whiting's home. A successful businesswoman with political influence, she vetoed art studies,

deciding instead upon the Navy as a sure home for a son who
might turn out to be as improvident and impractical as his father.

She obtained an Academy appointment for Ken in 1899. He
flunked the entrance examinations. She tied him to books for a
year and arranged another appointment. This time Ken passed.
He so enjoyed the unbookish parts of a cadet's life that he "bilged"—
flunked out of the Academy at the February semiannual examinations. His persistent mother scared up a third appointment; Ken
was sworn in again a couple weeks before Ellyson.

That summer, without apparent effort or desire, he became the
unofficial leader of the Cheesebox plebes. His suggestions were
usually followed without discussion, possibly because the plebes
found them good, perhaps because Ken seemed never to give a
damn whether they were followed or not. At something under
150 pounds, he was a smallish chap who wanted to try everything
at least once. Since he blended into any crowd and talked little,
strangers mistook his modesty for shyness.

Born in Massachusetts, raised beside Long Island Sound, Whiting
had a feeling for sails and the sea. He had unusually fine muscle
coordination; he could stand spraddle-legged, wearing a deceptively
sleepy, relaxed smile, then explode into action like a grenade.

The sun that blistered Spuds tanned Ken like Cordovan leather.
In many others ways, the two men seemed opposites. The books
that defeated Ken were easy for Spuds. Ken thought in essentials,
grandly ignoring the details that often entangled Spuds. A touch
of flattery made Ellyson work like a slave. Without praise, his efforts quickly flagged. He boasted freely of his winnings, spoke
often of his ambitions. When opposed, he fought hard but angrily,
blindly.

In contrast, praise or acclaim embarrassed Whiting. He refused
to talk of his accomplishments or ambitions. He appeared indolent
while working persistently, often invisibly, for the few things he
thought worthwhile. When opposed in these, he could be cagey,
sharp, and tough. Everyone in the Cheesebox liked him. His classmates hoped he would win with the books, for they knew he was
too old to make another start.

When the cruise ended in late August, the upperclassmen went
on leave. The plebes moved into Main Quarters, the sagging old
brick building a block inside the Maryland Avenue Gate. "Now we
have plebe September, instead of plebe summer," said Oscar, as he
and Spuds stowed their gear in a second-floor room. Drills filled

their days and tired their muscles, but no upperclassmen yelled, "Heads up!" "Chin in, Mister!" "Feather your tail!" and the other orders plebes might expect. On the first Saturday Spuds felt quite superior when four new members of his class arrived. A week later, fifty more, including Chester Nimitz, a future fleet admiral of World War II, straggled through the Main Gate in civilian clothes. Spuds summed them up as he marched past to drill: "ignorant-looking lubbers." Next morning he wrote:

Dear Sister May:
    Mamma reached here yesterday morning on the early train, but I could not get liberty until after dinner formation, as we had drills in the morning. Spears saw Mamma go into the building a little before twelve o'clock, and as we had finished all of our drills by that time, I could walk around the yard with her until dinner formation. We have to come back to quarters at six o'clock, but I put in a "rec" for 9:30 liberty and it was granted. I also obtained permission to fall out after dinner formation so I could take dinner with Mamma....I have 9:30 liberty again tonight. I will take dinner with Mamma today, and I expect Spears will also. I will also take supper with Mamma. I certainly am *very* much obliged for the cake, candy, crackers, work basket, and blotter. The cake is the finest I have had since I was home. I had no room to stow anything in my locker, except one box of candy and two boxes of crackers, so I had what may be called a "spread." That is, about ten of my classmates in to help me eat it, and you have no idea how everybody enjoyed it, and all of them that had seen you at Aunt Alice's told me to send you their regards and tell you how they enjoyed it, especially the chocolate cake. Among those who wished to be remembered are Caldwell, Smith, Spears, Atkins, Stanton, and others I can't remember....
    With much love I am your affect. Bro.,

                                                                Gordon

    Gordon's cruise letters had alarmed Lizzie Ellyson. She arrived in Annapolis prepared to rescue an undernourished, overworked victim of salty brutality. Finding instead a healthier, huskier, happier Gordon than ever before, she treated him and his friends to hotel meals, marveled at their appetites, and went back to Richmond pleased with what she had found. Hardships and perils detailed in Gordon's long letters never worried her again.
    The academic year began in October. As the upperclassmen returned to Main Quarters, the plebes became subject to constant

hazing. They moved into the annex where Ellyson and Whiting began four years as roommates. The ratey pair feuded, for kicks, with upperclassmen and all other law enforcers. The two got away with plenty, but not all that they tried. They "hit the pap" — they were reported for being out after taps — when authorities suspected but could not prove the more serious offense of "Frenching" — going AWOL over the wall for an evening in Annapolis and getting back without getting caught. Spuds hit the pap again after a crab dared him to crash a dance — out of bounds for plebes.

Both men enjoyed athletics. Spuds was a dilettante in several sports, while Ken participated in more athletic activities and starred in them all. He was the only plebe on the varsity football team, playing left end. When the football season was over, he won the Academy swimming championship.

When June arrived, they found themselves no longer plebes, but they were once more the juniors aboard as they sailed together in the Cheesebox. A month later, after a new law had transformed all naval cadets into midshipmen, they moved into the *Indiana*. She broke with established routine and carried them to Halifax, Spuds's first foreign port. He shopped for hat pins for Mamma, bought belt buckles for his sisters, and drank the hospitality of the city's clubs.

The *Lucky Bag,* the Academy's annual, recorded the visit: "The city was holding a great celebration in honor of the new King Edward and us. So we did as the Halifaxians did and also celebrated." When the officers and midshipmen hosted a dance in the *Indiana,* the "mids" held a reception in the sick bay. "We coronated the King...drank toasts to the King, to each member of the Royal Family, to the President, to England, to the United States, to both navies, to our hosts, to ourselves. Then we started all over again." They all survived. After that cruise, their later ones seemed like dull routines.

The *Indiana* reached Annapolis a week early, so Spuds had an extra week of leave. He spent all, or most, of his first leave in Richmond. Perhaps his Baptist family was too tame for an old salt or perhaps they belittled his adventures, for he never again spent that much time at home. On most subsequent leaves, he was to be found at some other address.

Spuds returned happily to Crabtown to pals, familiar routine, and a third-floor room in Main Quarters, shared with Ken Whiting. The roommates recommenced their vendetta with authority. Spuds hit the pap for disrespect when, red-faced, he yelled at one of his profs and again when he skipped drill for a tennis game. The two were never "ragged"—never caught—going over the wall for a late drink and a little gambling in Madam Bond's back room. But too many smoking paps sent them to the *Santee* together.

She was an eighty-year-old ship-of-the-line which had carried the Academy—cadets, instructors, equipment, and records—back to Crabtown from Newport after the Civil War. The *Santee* then stayed on as sailors' quarters and cadets' prison. Offenders berthed and messed aboard, marched to classes, and were forbidden athletics and other recreation during the term of their sentences. For something to do, Ken had Spuds lower him from the poop to snitch a fresh-baked apple pie whose fragrance had drifted up from the skipper's pantry. Ken had to apply most of his athletic skill to squirm through the port. When he stood inside, he saw, instead of pie in a galley, only the captain's toilet. The two had miscounted ports.

Once out of the *Santee,* Ken applied his strength once more to athletics. Swimming and boxing championships were at that time decided in straight elimination tournaments without class, age, or weight divisions. The 150-pound fighters must have been too fast for the big fellows; in his plebe year, little Aubry Wray ("Jakey") Fitch, who entered aviation after Spuds's death and became a flying vice admiral during World War II, defeated Ken in the semifinals, then later the same evening lost the final bout. After that match, the rivalry of the two became verbal when doctors diagnosed Jakey's "athletic heart" and forbade all athletics during the rest of his school years. The year after Jakey eliminated him, Ken won the boxing crown.

Even the best athlete had to stay "sat" to remain in the Academy. Every midshipman had to have a satisfactory average in each subject each semester, or resign. The coaching Spuds and other classmates gave Ken undoubtedly raised their own marks, and it may have saved Ken. But until he had completed his final examination, he was never out of danger. He could always think of several things more interesting than the book under his nose. The *Lucky Bag* noted, "He can study for hours and never know what he has been reading."

Every new subject or extra requirement added to his peril. The Engineer Corps had been abolished, so all midshipmen were required to study engineering. When the Navy put wireless telegraphy into ships, study of it crept into the Academy curriculum. Commander William Snowden Sims convinced President Theodore

Roosevelt that Navy guns should hit consistently at long ranges and that he had developed a method to assure that they did. The president ordered the Navy to use Sims's system, and the midshipmen's gunnery course got tougher. In Spuds's time, however, they were spared any study of aeronautics by the spectacular failure, in December, 1903, of Professor Samuel Pierpont Langley's flying machine. The ridicule that followed drowned the Wright brothers' claims of flight at Kitty Hawk and for five years prevented American belief in the possiblity of human flight.

As far back as tradition ran, "gouging"—cheating on examinations—had occurred at the Academy. The night before most examinations, copies of stolen questions were sold in Main Quarters at $5.00 a copy. On the eve of an examination partway through youngster year, Ken Whiting was "unset"—he had less than a 2.5, or passing, average to date and had to bring his grades up to average. Some classmates offered him the next day's questions for free. "We know you need help," they said. "We want to keep you in the Navy, so we want you to have these."

Ken was embarrassed. He knew the offer, made by men who liked him immensely, was kindly intended. He was aware that question stealing was an ancient practice, but neither he nor Spuds had ever used such aid. "Thanks," he said, "but I can't use them. I'll make out without them."

"You like to hang one on the authorities with your smoking and Frenching," they argued. "This is the same game, only more practical."

Ken's refusal was adamant. He struggled to explain what he felt to be the differences, without hurting well-meaning friends. He thought gouging akin to cheating at cards or welching on a bet. It was not revolt but complete dishonesty. But he could not say so bluntly. He never wanted credit for any work not entirely his own. Besides, classes were not a game with authority, they were a man's chance to learn a profession. Gouging therefore cheated only the cheater. His friends carried the questions away, and Ken skinned by another examination without their help. His refusal must have been diplomatic, for later that year the battalion adopted a similar attitude. From then on, gouging was the one offense for which a midshipman was always expected to report a classmate.

Two battleships, seven of the Navy's first eight submarines, and its first sixteen destroyers were commissioned in 1902 and 1903. An expanding Navy needed an expanded officer corps. Each class entering the Academy was larger than previous ones. By reducing review periods and eliminating some leave, instruction was compressed so that classes were graduated in February instead of June. Shipyards were riveting other battleships and big cruisers as Spuds's graduation approached.

Near Thanksgiving, 1904, when desirable duty was discussed, Spuds held to the party line. Battleships were the backbone of the Navy. Their big guns and Sims's new gunnery would win future battles. It was smart to have battleship duty on one's record.

"Don't be so serious about it," Oscar Spears remonstrated. "China's the place to go. Let's have mystery, adventure, strong drink, and willing women. Plenty of time later for a gun-club career."

Chester Nimitz thought they might have both battleship duty and Asiatic adventure. The newest battleship, the *Ohio*, had just been commissioned at San Francisco and was going to the China Station.

Spuds liked that idea, but Ken objected. "She's to be a fat, tubby sister of the *Missouri* that we saw at Newport News on our way back from Halifax. She was almost as dumpy as the *Indiana*— probably crabs through the water the same way."

"What do you like, then?"

"Remember the armored cruiser hull they had on the ways? Beside the *Missouri,* she looked like a racing shell alongside a coal barge."

"But her biggest guns will only be eight-inch," Spuds said.

"Nobody's ever seen one at sea yet. It's an untried type," someone else objected. "They may be lemons."

Ken smiled his sleepy smile and said, "I don't think they will be, not with lines like they have. Anyway, they'll carry more coal, go farther and faster than any battleship. That's my way to see the world."

Spuds was not convinced. On 4 December, he signed his request for assignment to the *Ohio,* with duty in the Asiatic Station listed as his second choice. Ken looked at Spuds's paper, rolled a Bull Durham cigarette, and wrote out his request for duty aboard the armored cruiser *West Virginia*.

Although Ken was near the bottom of the class scholastically, by graduation on 30 January 1905, he had served high in the midshipman officer pyramid, won the presentation sword, and left a record of phenomenal athletic accomplishments. Ellyson, near the middle of the class, was popular and sociable but was distinguished primarily because he had been Ken's roommate.

Snow fell during most of graduation day, with Crabtown's temperature hovering near 20° F. On the steaming June day when he was sworn into the Academy, Spuds had little expected this sort of graduation day. He snuggled his chin into his bridge coat, like a turtle withdrawing into its shell, and mushed to the train. Everyone had the same orders—"to home to await orders"—which was one way to grant leave without calling it that. Instead of going to Richmond, Spuds asked for ten days' delay at a Buffalo address and rode the New York train with Ken. He was nineteen years old and eager to begin his career.

CHAPTER THREE

Passed Midshipman:

Final Exams

*D*espite the charms of a Buffalo girl friend, his leave soured when Spuds read orders for his class in the *New York Times*. He and Bob Jackson were ordered to Guantanamo for duty in the ancient, second-class battleship *Texas*. The list showed that his particular pals had gotten the orders they wanted: Ken to the *West Virginia*, Oscar to the China Station for assignment, and Chester to the *Ohio*.

His mood was as dark as the sky burdened with unshed snow on the day a little mail steamer crunched the skim ice as it carried him out of Baltimore harbor. But Spuds was a hard man to keep down. Long before the packet stuck her nose into the Windward Passage, the sun flashing on the deep blue waters of the Gulf Stream had restored his spirits to normal. He sat in a deck chair and regaled Bob Jackson with the charms of *the* girl in Buffalo. She was special; nobody could match her. Bob, a fellow Virginian, listened with reservations. Spuds had always found *the* girl. She was always special. She was unique. And she was always superceded by another specially unique girl. It had been that way at McGuire's, at Bobby's War College, and at the Academy. His friends thought Spuds was enthusiastically susceptible, rather than fickle.

On Washington's Birthday, the packet anchored in Guantanamo. Around the crystal-clear bay, the tropical sun burned nearly straight down on dusty rocks and cactuses. Spuds had hoped for señoritas in lush gardens. Instead, he got arid desert. The *Texas,* looking even smaller than he had feared, lay near the coal pile on Hospital Quay.

Her officer-of-the-deck, a midshipman who had known Ellyson in the Cheesebox, called Spuds lucky. "Your orders to the *Missouri* are here," he said. "She's due in tomorrow."

"That's good?" Spuds asked, trying to appear indifferent to a change from the oldest to the newest battleship in the Atlantic.

"She's newer. Her bedbugs are less experienced," the officer-of-the-deck replied.

The *Missouri* left Guantanamo a few days after Spuds joined her. She logged a visit to Havana, a month at Pensacola, a summer off New England and in the New England harbors, Thanksgiving and Christmas at Boston, and a return to Guantanamo for four more monotonous months of drill. Mess bills, wine mess chits, cards in the steerage mess, and liberties in New England quickly swallowed Spuds's monthly pay of $77.50 to keep him in debt for the sixteen dull months. After twelve months, he asked for a transfer to a torpedo boat leaving for China, but his request was turned down.

He was bored and broke in May when he saw Ken and the *West Virginia* in New York. As Ken had foreseen, the cruiser was prettier, faster, longer, and larger than the *Missouri.* Whiting's quarters were far better than the gun-deck cubbyholes alloted to lieutenants in the battleship. Furthermore, rumor had it that the cruisers were going round the world.

Spuds requested armored cruiser duty.

Late in July, his orders reached the *Missouri* in Maine. Spuds caught a night train. In the Brooklyn yard, he reported aboard the *Pennsylvania* and found Jakey Fitch in her steerage mess. "Heard the new cruiser song?" Jakey asked when the preliminaries were over. "Goes like this," he said:

Away, away, with sword and drum
Here we come, full of rum
Looking for something to put on the bum
In the Armored Cruiser Squadron.

We are the boys who shoot six inch
Or anything else when we're in a pinch
Gee, but the battleships are a cinch
For the Armored Cruiser Squadron.

The USS *Pennsylvania*, armored cruiser number 4 (ACR-4), built by William Cramp and Sons, Philadelphia. She was 503 feet long, 69 feet 7 inch beam, carried a main battery of four eight-inch guns and had a speed of twenty-two knots. The *West Virginia* (ACR-5) and *Colorado* (ACR-7) in which Ellyson also served were similar. The *Pennsylvania* was the first American naval vessel to have an airplane land aboard, and the first to hoist a seaplane aboard. Before World War I her name was changed to the *Pittsburgh* and she continued in service until 1931.

"Where'd you get that?" Spuds asked.

"Your classmates, Wilcox and Strassburger, put it together. I think Ken helped with the chorus."

"Ken? He couldn't carry a tune in a wheelbarrow."

"Maybe not, but when they had the *Alabama* gang aboard for dinner, he got results belting that one."

"Results?"

"Damndest riot you ever saw. Busted everything in the messroom before they quit. Now the song's sort of a squadron anthem, with everyone trying to add verses."

After one weekend in New York, Spuds asked for two weeks' leave. "A bit of time with *the* girl before we sail," he said. A new one he met that weekend?

He came back from leave to find himself transferred across the dock to the *Colorado*. Bill Eberle, a classmate he had left in the *Missouri*, was there to hear all about Spuds's wonderful leave. "Certainly hated to kiss *the* girl goodbye. She's special," the recital ended. "When do we sail?"

"Leave the yard in about ten days."

The four armored cruisers gathered at Newport and on 9 September 1906 sailed together for Gibraltar. His duty, a watch and division officer, changed him from schoolboy to pro. Nearly time, too. Before January, he would be examined for an ensign's commission.

After stops at Gibraltar, Italy, and Greece, the ships followed each other down the Red Sea to the tropics. The gentle northwest monsoon left the Indian Ocean flat and glossy under stagnant, steamy air. Each day and each night seemed hotter and stickier than the one before. Even the best ships were uncomfortable in the tropics, "BAC" (before air conditioning). Officers and men slept on deck, wherever they found room to lay a mattress. Captain Sidney Augustus Staunton cut the fire room watches from four to two hours, sent deckhands to help strike coal from the bunkers. Still, on every watch, boiler room heat knocked men unconscious. Salt pills were still in the future.

At Bombay, Columbo, and Singapore, all hands rested briefly, while contractors' coolies filled the bunkers. Each port was hotter than the one they'd left behind, but the ships were always hotter still. Each port offered the men from the sea its own variety of vice.

The *Colorado*'s crew needed more muscular skill than intellect

to feed coal to her thirty-two boilers and ammunition to her six-
and eight-inch guns. Many of her men could not write even their
names, but they worked well for officers such as Spuds, who made
the most of their abilities and allowed for their limitations. Their
payday fun was to "get stewed, screwed, tattooed"; they were
often rolled in the dives they frequented, such as those along
Brooklyn's Sand Street. Incurious, they feared a foreign cruise
would keep them from such familiar haunts, without adequate
compensation. Many deserted before the ship left New York
harbor; twenty-five left at Newport.

Once at sea, others vented their feelings in offenses ranging
from spitting on the deck, washing hands in the drinking water,
and stowing dirty clothes on the breakfast meat to refusal to obey
orders. Each port added shore offenses such as assault, robbery,
and liberty breaking. The day after leaving Gibraltar eighty-one
sailors were at mast, and the number increased as the temperature
rose. The captain's legal punishments failed as deterrents, and he
more and more frequently awarded courts-martial at mast. The
ship's log recorded the court's usual sentence: "ten days, solitary,
on bread and water, in double irons." That sentence translated to
ten days and nights alone in a hot, stuffy, dark hole with heavy
chains on wrists and ankles and nothing to eat but dry bread. The
daily parade of offenders grew longer, with many repeaters.

A culprit's division officer was his character witness at the captain's hearing. As such, Spuds felt sorry for most offenders. Both
their acts and their excuses for them seemed unbelievably stupid.
He knew Captain Staunton to be a pleasant man who would never
mistreat a horse; why was he so tough on these other dumb animals?
Spuds sympathized with his men; not for many years did he understand the captain's problem.

Two months of tropical steaming in poorly ventilated old ships
wore everybody down, including those who never pitched coal
into hungry boilers. Before Wednesday, 18 November 1907, when
the cruisers' anchors first splashed into Manila Bay, Spuds had
sweated off twenty pounds and was always tired. Trans-Pacific
mail came aboard. Among other things, it included months-old
letters from home and Spuds's final examination papers for promotion to ensign.

Promotion examinations began with a physical examination,
much more rigid than later ones would be. The Navy wanted to
commission only perfect physical specimens. After he passed the
physical, a midshipman faced nearly a week of written tests on

technical subjects. Spuds was confident that a few days in port would rest him, and he was impatient to get the examinations behind him.

The next day, Thursday, he climbed the gangway of the cruiser *Maryland*, saluted her colors and the officer-of-the-deck, and asked, "Permission to come aboard for physical examination." Anticipation of promotion made him chipper in spite of his weariness. He had worked a long time for a commission in the Navy. The physical was just a routine hurdle; he expected it would give him no trouble. He had never had trouble with either doctors or with technical books. The papers had to go to Washington and back. That would take three months, at least. But when they came back, he could replace the anchor on his cap with a commissioned officer's cap device, which he referred to as a "scrambled egg." He felt good about starting this last routine step.

A couple of hours later, he again saluted the *Maryland*'s officer-of-the-deck and muttered, "Permission to leave the ship," then slowly descended the accommodation ladder. The doctor's report had knocked his wind out. "Unfit for the naval service." It sounded so horribly final. He rubbed his eyes with his fist as he went down the ladder, realizing for the first time how much he really loved the Navy, how much he wanted to remain a part of it. Leaving it would break his heart, toss him into limbo. He could imagine no future out of the service.

Two weeks later, the three doctors at the Sangley Point Hospital organized themselves as a Board of Medical Survey and went over Ellyson. He was not happy that night, but he saw a glimmer of hope. He told his shipmate, Bill Eberle, that the board had called him anemic and busted him again, but, instead of the boot, they had recommended a re-exam after treatment in a cooler climate. The papers would have to go to Washington for a decision. Spuds would not know for months whether the re-exam would be allowed, but in the meantime he would go for treatment.

Captain Staunton's detachment report called Spuds efficient, with mature good judgment and an equable temperament. The captain noted that he particularly wanted Ellyson back on his ship after treatment.

Halfway around the world, Papa Ellyson put down his Richmond paper and wrote the Secretary of the Navy. He had read, "Orders to officers, by cable from Admiral Brownson, Manila, 12 December...Midshipman T.G. Ellyson, detached *Colorado* to report to

The USS *Rainbow*, built in England in 1890 as a merchant ship. In 1898 she was purchased by the American Navy for the Spanish-American War. She arrived in the Philippines in 1902 and served in various capacities on the Asiatic Station until July 1914. In 1907 while Ellyson was her navigator she carried Secretary of War William Howard Taft to Vladivostok. She later became a submarine tender.

the U.S. Naval Hospital, Yokohama, Japan, for treatment." Papa
wanted to know what was wrong with his boy, and what his address was. In those days before air mail, months passed before
Washington could tell him more than the address.

With his tropic-thinned blood, Spuds shivered through a sorry
Christmas aboard a smelly little steamer which staggered through
smashing seas. Later, stepping ashore into ankle-deep snow on
Yokohama's windswept pier, he knew that if cooling was what he
needed he had found it. For the first month, he huddled over a
hibachi wearing everything he owned.

The two doctors who ran the little hospital where he stayed built
him up with rest, tonics, and food. The dreary, chill weather hardened him. His energy slowly returned until playing bridge with the
doctors was fun again. But on 26 March, when the hospital dis-
charged him, he was still wondering about Washington's decision
about a re-exam. Orders sent him to Kobe in charge of a draft of
men for the Philippines.

Broken clouds boiled around Fuji as their train clicked south.
Near Honshu's south coast, blossoming plum and cherry trees bor-
dered the tracks. Late in the day Spuds delivered the draft aboard
the cruiser *West Virginia*, then found Ken Whiting in the steerage
messroom and went ashore to see Kobe.

Three days later, the *West Virginia*'s crew paraded on her quar-
terdeck. Rear Admiral Willard Herbert Brownson read orders that
ended both his tour as commander-in-chief of the Asiatic Fleet
and his active career. The band played while the admiral's blue flag
fluttered down, and the old man went down the ladder to the boat
manned by officer-oarsmen. He had been an admiral for only eighteen months before he reached retirement age. Spuds and Ken knew
him well. He had been superintendent of the Academy during their
last three years there. Spuds thought of his own uncertain status.
"Wouldn't it be great to be an admiral?" he said.

"I could take it or leave it," Ken answered. "Maybe Browny
didn't miss anything as he went along, but I'll bet he'd like to swap
seats with you right now. Can't be any fun to be finished."

In the Philippines, Spuds moved into the second-class cruiser
Rainbow. "Done any navigating?" Commander Ben Ward Hodges,
her skipper, asked. "No? Well, brush up. You'll be the navigator's
assistant for about a month. Then you'll be the navigator."

The ship spent that month under Manila's cloudless sky. Each
morning a blazing sun cooked her paint and made griddles of her

decks and ovens of her cabins. After work, all but the watch took the first boat ashore, hoping the ship's metal would be cool enough to handle when they returned.

The *Rainbow* was no hotter than other ships in that season. Young officers looking for cool drinks and interesting trouble got together at the Army and Navy Club inside the old, walled city. Often as not, Spuds teamed up with Jakey Fitch and Oscar Spears, skipper of the *Pampanga*. Oscar had achieved a certain fame by teaching the club barmen to pour a "Spears Special"—six ounces of gin and one ounce of vermouth over ice in a highball glass. "Efficient," Oscar called it. The boy wouldn't have to run back and forth for so many little martinis.

In June, the *Rainbow* steamed to Hong Kong where Rear Admiral Joseph Newton Hemphill hoisted his flag in her as commander of the Philippine Squadron. The *Rainbow*'s old navigator went home, and Spuds became the new one. Navigating a flagship was a top gamble for a busted midshipman. A good job of it couldn't help much, but if he muffed it—if he put the admiral on a reef—he was really finished. Spuds preferred gambles with quick action, not long tension. Each time a mail steamer arrived, he wondered if she brought the decision about his future. Nearly seven months had slipped away since he had failed the physical examination on the *Maryland.*

The *Rainbow* passed Corregidor, inbound, on 17 June. Overlooking his past navigational errors, Spuds paced her bridge, convinced he was the world's best navigator. After the anchor splashed into its old hole in front of Manila, mail came aboard. The Secretary of the Navy had granted Ellyson a delayed re-examination, and the Sangley Point doctors were waiting to give it to him.

Spuds was gun-shy around doctors, but he wanted to end his suspense. Feeling as though he were diving into cold water, he grabbed his orders, and, forgetting to take along his health record, rode the steamer *Mindoro* across Manila Bay. The doctors had other things to do; they wanted to finish this job. Rather than convene again next day, when Spuds could return with his medical record, they looked him over, asked him to sign a statement that he felt well, called him "passed," and sent him back to the *Rainbow* to face his written examinations. The medical exam had, in the end, been simple, but the tension of waiting left its mark. For the rest of his life, Spuds Ellyson distrusted medical examiners.

Manila's wet season began. Temperatures climbed even higher than they had in the hot season. Rain fell, sometimes as much as an inch an hour, sometimes a drizzle, but the gray sky dripped endlessly. Sweaty clothes never dried. Leather grew green mold whiskers overnight.

The *Rainbow* divided four saturated months between Manila and Cavite, ten miles across the bay. "Can't you get the admiral to leave this mildewed dump?" Spuds asked Lieutenant Daniel Pratt Mannix, the senior half of the admiral's staff.

"He's waiting for Admiral Dayton to leave for San Francisco on the *West Virginia*," Mannix said. "Then Hemphill'll be boss of the Asiatic, and we'll get around." They were still waiting late in October.

The rain stopped, and Manila dried out. Spuds's commission, dated the previous January, arrived. He took the oath, changed his cap device, and drew a wad of back pay. He still had money in his pocket on 7 November when the *Rainbow* led the gunboats *Chattanooga* and *Galveston* out past Corregidor, and Spuds laid a course for Vladivostok.

CHAPTER FOUR

High Seas:

Pranks and Courts-martial

*Y*ears later, the *New York Sun* added its version of this cruise to the Ellyson legend. It quoted "world rover Bob Murray," who prized "a regulation service cap bearing the insignia of a lieutenant in the Navy" he had gotten from Ellyson on Admiral Hemphill's flagship in a poker game.

> I must go back twenty years, October 1907, to the junior officer's wardroom of the flagship *Sunbeam,* converted Spanish merchantman taken prize by Dewey after the battle of Manila Bay, 1898. Her lines were those of a table knife, long and narrow. How she could roll! We were bound from Manila to Vladivostok. Five days with fierce gales all the way. Nursing a smashed arm I was lashed to my bunk by night, or a chair by day.
> Returning to the wardroom. Poker is the business of the meeting. Outside a howling gale and the vexed waters of the Strait of Tsushima, and under us, for we had worked out the position at the dinner table, that evening, the salt cankered and riddled wrecks of the great fleet of Russian war ships led by Admiral Rojestvenski, annihilated by the Japanese navy toward the end of the Russo-Japanese war. This night our seven-handed tournament led to frequent horn lockings between a young lieutenant and me. We found ourselves wrangling as survivors in at least three pots out of five. He knew his poker better than I, but I held the cards. Finally, after I had tapped him for his pile, he gave a

half turn of his revolving chair, threw up his hands and said, "Nuff. I'm broke."

Then I made him a sporting proposition. "Look here," I said, being a soft-hearted fool and hating like the devil to see an officer and a gentleman slinking around his frisky ship without a cent in his pockets. "I like that cap you're wearing. Ten dollars against it. Cold hands. Three of 'em. Are you on?" "I be. Cut," plugged back the lieutenant laconically. Two hands. That was enough; both were mine and I took the covering.

Then a rather dramatic thing happened. We were still sitting at the table when the siren of the *Sunbeam* moaned three times. Unusual; right in the middle of the ocean, a pitch-black night, and close to eight bells—which landsmen call 12 o'clock. The wardroom emptied in a jiffy, of all save me, as the young officers tumbled out on deck. I hitched along after them. The *Sunbeam* had her searchlight going. It bored a bright tunnel through the dark. At the end of the tunnel, perhaps a brace of miles to leeward, three cruising Japanese destroyers leaped and bounded in the rough sea like frolicsome marine mastiffs. And, as I said before, right about in the position where the Russian ships and sailors had gone down two years before. As I looked at the ramping destroyers I thought of lions guarding their kill.

Seven years later....

The story went on, but just this much of it is enough to illustrate how newspapers helped build an Ellyson legend.

Ellyson's only visit to Vladivostok was as an ensign (not a lieutenant) aboard Rear Admiral Hemphill's flagship in November (not October) 1907. Quite likely he played poker on board; he may have gone broke at it. The rest of the story is pure invention.

Officers took off their caps when they entered a mess room. Ships did not blow sirens and illuminate when they met one another at sea. Flagship *Rainbow* (alias *Sunbeam*) had no "junior officers' wardroom," was no knifelike, rolling greyhound, but a tubby, broad-beamed, ex-tramp. She was purchased in the Atlantic in 1898, not captured by Dewey, who took no merchant prizes at Manila. Her log for the Vladivostok cruise shows eight routine days of smooth weather. No storms, no smashed arms, no Japanese destroyers, no sightings in Tsushima Strait, and no one aboard named Bob Murray.

Her log also shows that during her visit, Vladivostok's temperature never got higher than a dozen degrees below freezing. Her thin-blooded crew must have been glad to leave. Shortly before Christmas, they anchored again in front of Manila and went ashore in Luzon's best season. As a navigator, Spuds had pleased four skippers.

Commander Edward Everett Wright, the fifth captain of the *Rainbow* under whom Ellyson served, took over after New Year's; then the ship steamed south to show Admiral Hemphill the southern islands. Spuds navigated to ports scattered from Samar to Jolo.

After that cruise, the *Rainbow* berthed in Cavite Navy Yard, near Fitch's destroyer. The *Concord* arrived from China soon afterwards. The 1890-model, three-masted schooner, a gunboat with a cigarettelike smokestack, had been Whiting's billet for some time.

When the work was done, Spuds and Ken, in crisp white uniforms, relaxed in canvas chairs for the hour it took the little steamer *Mindoro* to snuffle them over to Manila. The sun flashed from the glassy water, but the ferry's motion pushed a pleasant breeze across her open, awning-shaded deck.

Ken sighted Jakey Fitch as they entered the bar. He pointed with a stiff arm and yelled, "I can lick you!"

Jakey spun around. "Licked you once, can do it again," he retorted and led with his left. Before any peacemakers could intervene, they swapped a few healthy punches, then linked arms, bellied the bar, and called for drinks. They regularly put on this act after Ken took Crabtown's boxing crown. Barflies halfway around the world had been disappointed in the sudden ending of what started like a good grudge fight. The act was only a curtain raiser that night in Manila. Their fun grew bigger, lasted longer than usual. Spuds squinted at a clock while the last bar was trying to sweep them out. "We'll never wake up for the morning ferry if we turn in at the club now," he said.

"Everything's closed," Jakey said. "No place to stay up."

"Sleep on the boat," Ken proposed. "Can't miss it then." He led the way to the *Mindoro,* snugged down at the seawall. Her Filipino crew awakened as the three stumbled through her side curtains and fell over a bucket. They were unfolding stacked deck chairs when the patron, or skipper, rubbing sleep from his eyes, "objected very vigorously to our using his ferry as a hotel," as Jakey put it. "And, when he continued to object to our sleeping on his boat, without any words we three picked him up and threw him overboard into the Passig River. His crew pulled him out. We slumbered without interruption the rest of the night."

When other passengers boarded the ferry for its first trip of the day to Cavite, they found the rumpled, unshaven trio already aboard.

Spuds drank from the uniced water cooler amidships; its tepid, brackish water, tasting of tin and chlorine, made him vomit before he got aft to his seat beside Ken. An old gentleman in civilian clothes sitting nearby looked at their stubbly chins, red eyes, and dirty suits. His nose wrinkled, his mouth drew down.

Ken glared. "So we slept in these clothes," he said. "We wouldn't have if the damned commandant's lousy ferry schedule let a man get back to his ship at night, instead of waiting for this market boat. Blame him for our looks. His boat schedule stinks, like most things in Cavite."

One of the old gentleman's eyebrows went up. "What else stinks in Cavite?" he asked.

Ken, ignoring the old gentleman's menacing tone, looked him in the eye and told him in considerable detail.

By evening the three midshipmen knew they were in trouble and wondered when it would catch up with them. Surely the patron complained of his ducking, but for a couple of weeks nothing happened. The *Concord* took Ken back to China. Jakey Fitch transferred to the *Rainbow*. Then Spuds saw the old gentleman of the ferry, in uniform. He was Captain Uria Rose Harris, the commandant of Cavite.

"How did we ever get away with it?" Spuds asked Jakey. "Especially after Ken sounded off to the old coot." The two kept out of the captain's sight till the *Rainbow* sailed. Not until she moored to the flagship buoys off Shanghai's Bund did they feel safe. Spuds took Jakey ashore, promising a tour of the best spots, including the very British Shanghai Club, which treasured its highly polished mahogany bar. Officers had been court-martialed for scratching it with broken glasses. Members called it the world's longest bar. Thirsty customers crowded its length when Spuds and Jakey found places near one end of the famous woodwork.

They ordered whisky, hoisted their first sips. Then a sudden, protesting clamor made them look right. A voice above the hubbub yelled, "I can lick you!" Ken Whiting pranced toward them atop the sacred mahogany.

Jakey, chin-high to the tall bar, slammed down his glass, jumped, fell back. "Boost me up! Boost me up!" he ordered Spuds. In a split second, he was up and running. Both swung round-house rights. Both connected. Ken landed on a barman, Jakey on a member of the house committee.

For seconds a scandalized hush stilled the room. Then some ir-

The USS *Porpoise* and USS *Shark* (later renamed A-6 and A-7). They were decommissioned at Annapolis and then shipped, via Suez, propped up on the well deck of the collier *Caesar*. At Manila they were launched by sliding them over the *Caesar's* side to splash into the bay. Each submarine torpedo boat was 63 feet 10 inches long, 11 feet 11 inches in diameter, and rated a crew of one ensign and six men. Powered by a German-built gasoline engine, an A-type submarine was rated at eight knots on the surface and at seven knots submerged, running on its electric motor. The masts (shown above) were removed before diving. On the surface, the skipper conned while standing half out of the hatch (see man in the right-hand vessel). Submerged, he could stand on the ladder and peer through the glass deadeyes just below the hatch cover. A-type boats had no periscopes. A man leans out of the eighteen-inch torpedo tube of the left-hand boat.

reverent drinker yelled into the void, "H'ray!" Another laughed alone. Then the room laughed with him. By the time Ken vaulted the bar and grabbed Jakey's arm, the committeeman was laughing so hard he forgot to look for heel marks on the bar.

This little skirmish, on top of the *Mindoro* caper, made the three sure they were untouchable. They could get away with anything.

The *Rainbow* carried Hemphill to Japan, where Yokohama was decked with blossoms instead of snow, then back across the China Sea and up the river to Hankow. Spuds heard that Ken was being transferred to the U.S.S. *Supply,* the station ship at Guam—then the Navy's private Siberia. Mail reached Guam at least twice in normal years, and out-of-favor officers might be forgotten there indefinitely. How long could the place hold Ken?

At Wusung, a new admiral, on the *Charleston,* relieved Hemphill, who caught a liner for home and retirement. Old *Rainbow,* with no admiral in her cabin, reached Manila in the season of hot rain and short tempers.

On 4 August, the semiannual transport landed Whiting in Cavite, where he was placed under arrest and handed charges and specifications for a general court-martial. On the *Rainbow,* the same thing happened to Ellyson. He read through three long charges that began, "...at midnight March 17, 1908, went aboard the naval ferry *Mindoro,* at Manila, P.I., in an intoxicated condition...."

"K-riste! They threw the book at me," he said at the end. "They can kick me out and put me in Portsmouth for that."

A general court-martial aboard the *Cleveland* acquitted Ken, then Spuds, of everything except drunkenness, a charge which could have held against anyone on the Asiatic Station. Both were sentenced to reprimands and to lose five numbers on the promotion list; then clemency was recommended. The commandant fumed that the sentences were entirely inadequate, but he approved them to keep the ensigns from going unpunished.

While the court was in session, the *Rainbow* got another skipper. The departing one gave Ellyson a good report, denying any knowledge of the charges for which he was being tried. A month later skipper number six also gave a good report as he turned his duties over to number seven. He merely recorded the trial and the sentence. The conviction must have shown Spuds that he could not get away with some things. It seems to have made him a bit more discreet, but he never outgrew a love of rough fun.

"We got away with murder," Ken summed it up. "But I'll bet we would never have been tried if I hadn't told old Harris some

unpleasant truths that morning." Jakey Fitch was never quite sure
how he escaped trial with his pals.

In mid-September, the three chums rode the *Rainbow* to
Shanghai, where she moored to the French Bund. Ken went back
to duty in his old gunboat, the three-masted *Concord*. Fitch got
ordered to the States in the U.S.S. *Supply*. Before Spuds sailed
for a swing around North China in the *Rainbow,* he heard that the
Concord was to replace the *Supply* at Guam.

Whiting had seen enough of Guam before his court-martial.
Searching for an out, he remembered the two little submarines
that had reached Manila about the time he was tried. They might
offer a new adventure and keep him off Guam. He asked for duty
with them.

Spuds and the *Rainbow* had been back in Cavite's rain for two
weeks when Ken arrived. On 8 October 1908, he reported for duty
in the submarine *Shark*. Bored by routine, Whiting always resented
supervision and regularly flaunted protocol. Duty in an A-class
sub on the Asiatic Station fitted him perfectly. The five-year-old
boat challenged his ingenuity. Lieutenant Guy Wilkinson Stuart
Castle, who had been assigned to commission and operate the subs,
was too busy, and too smart, to heckle him. Ken worked harder
than ever before and loved it. He soon believed bigger and better
submarines would be built and wondered how they should be
used. He never boasted, but, at the club with Spuds and other
cronies, his enthusiasm showed. When pals kidded him about his
coast-defense toy, Ken merely took a long swallow of his rye and
told them to have fun. "Someday you children'll know better,"
he said.

Six weeks after he reported to Castle in the *Shark,* Whiting
moved over to command the *Porpoise,* the other submarine in the
Asiatic fleet's flotilla. Three weeks after that, Ellyson was ordered
to the *Shark* as Castle's executive. Spuds had spent most of those
three weeks on a trip to Hong Kong where he filled in as a relief
captain aboard the gunboat *Villalobos*. He returned to the *Rainbow*
for only a few days before beginning his submarine career. He had
followed Whiting into subs, as he had followed him to armored
cruisers, and thus to Manila. Complying with orders dated 9 December 1908, Ellyson reported to Castle on the fourteenth.

[CHAPTER FIVE]

Experimental Submarine Duty:

Escape Attempts

*S*ince the A-boats had no living accommodations, the officers and the dozen men who manned them lived aboard the slightly larger gunboat, *Elcano*. From her, Ken led Spuds out on the pier on his first morning as a submariner. The *Shark*, stripped of portable deck and masts, showed only the little round hatch on the humped center of her hull above water. Spuds followed Ken into her for his first peek at a submarine's cramped interior, crowded with tanks, machinery, and men.

Castle stood on the ladder, head and shoulders above the hatch coaming, conning the boat into the bay. Sweat ran down Spuds's back, plastering his shirt to his hide. The chugging gas engine drowned the questions he wanted to ask. He alone had nothing to do. He wished he could see out, tried to stand erect, then damned the valve wheel that cracked his head. When the engine coughed to a stop, he could hear the bay swishing by the hull plating. One man unclutched the engine. Others twisted valves, pushed or pulled various levers. Castle slammed the hatch cover and spun the wheel that made it tight. As air hissed from the vents and the electric motor whirred softly, Spuds watched a needle move up a scale marked in feet.

39

"We're right beside the *Rainbow,*" Castle told Ellyson. Castle stood lower on the ladder, peering through a little, round, glass deadeye below the hatch lid. "We dive near a surface ship, every day, just to show the rest of the Navy we can. Wish we had a periscope, like the newest boats. Can't see much beyond our bow through this."

During the following months, at least one boat dove nearly every working day. On paper, Whiting commanded the *Porpoise* and Castle the *Shark,* with Spuds as number two. Until Castle went home, however, the boats were operated more like cars in a pool than as separate commands. Usually only one of the officers dove a boat, sometimes two; occasionally, all three went together on the daily dive. After each dive they repaired, improved if they could, then dove another day. The fix-improve-try again routine became a habit that Ellyson carried to his later assignments.

While their luck held, the officers wondered how they could help a boat stuck on the bottom by an unfixable casualty. How could they find it before her men breathed all her oxygen? For diving practice, they used a big area of the bay. Its thirty-foot depth completely hid the twelve-foot-high boats.

Whiting suggested a man might go out through the torpedo tube, swim to the surface, and get help. The tube, somewhat longer than a man, was no smaller than some of the boats' manholes. Its domed door, or cap, had been the parrot beak when the red subs sat on *Sirius*'s deck.

Someone pointed out that time was required to wriggle through an eighteen-inch manhole. An eighteen-inch tube would take longer. Who could hold their breath long enough to do it under water? Could anyone hold it even long enough for the slow cap engine to raise the outer door?

When a torpedo was fired, a burp of high-pressure air blasted it from the tube after the cap was open. The air bubble boiled to the surface. Could a man be pushed out that way? Could he ride up with the bubble?

"Not a chance," said Castle. The air would crush and kill a man, as it had the dog someone tried to put out that way. Calling the tube exit too dangerous to try, he insisted that route gave a man no chance of getting to the surface. He would either drown in the tube or be broken by the air charge.

Unconvinced, Whiting looked for a safe way out of the tube. He had often tried dangerous stunts and gotten away with them. Friends were sure he always made an adequate, if unusual, plan before he began. He never told them how he worked out his plans; he seldom spoke at all of his exploits. Could he plan a quick way out, avoiding that crushing high-pressure air?

Ken peered into the tube with a flashlight and saw the crossbar that stiffened the domed cap. He timed the cap engine when it was run for a daily test, tried holding his breath for the time it took to open the cap. Then, imagining how the water would rise in the tube, he decided his plan was worth a try.

He told no one of his intention, asked no permission. He wanted never to embarrass a friend. If Castle did not know of the event beforehand, he would not have to answer embarrassing questions in case Whiting died.

At a depth of twenty feet he adjusted ballast until the boat was slightly heavy. Then he stopped the motor and let the sub sink to the bottom of the bay. He explained his plan to his six-man crew in a way that infected them with his confidence. None of them even considered the possibility that their captain might not succeed or that they might be accused of murdering him if he died in the tube. Like most people, they just naturally followed Ken's lead.

No one ever saw Ken show any indecision. In every situation he ever faced, he appeared completely confident that he could handle it. If he felt any qualms as he stripped off his clothes in front of the open torpedo tube, they did not show. He gave his men their individual instructions.

The inside of the tube was lightly greased when Ken lay on his back, put his arms over his head, and pushed with his heels on the torpedo loading rack. After his knees were inside, his men pushed his feet until he grasped the crossbar on the outer cap. Then he pulled himself as far forward as he could and called to the men to do their stuff. They dogged the rear door and started the cap engine.

Ken heard the door clang behind his feet. He was on his own. In the dark he felt warm sea water flow down his spine, heard the grinding cap engine, and felt the bar he grasped move ahead and up. Warm sea water wrapped around his body, and he took a deep breath just before it covered his face. The door swung up until it dragged Ken's elbows clear of the tube, then he easily pushed himself clear and swam to the surface. The test took seventy-seven seconds.

A man on the ladder pressing close to the forward deadeye saw his captain get clear and swim up out of sight. He passed the word, and men below blew the ballast tanks. As the submarine broke the surface, the man on the ladder opened the hatch and popped out of it with a heaving line in his hand. Whiting was floating easily nearby. A few lazy strokes took him to the submarine where the man who had opened the hatch pulled him aboard.

Ken used only fifteen words to describe the event when he covered the week's activity with forty-nine words in the log on 17 April 1909:

> Whiting went through the torpedo tube, boat lying in water in normal condition, as an experiment.

Guy Castle reported the experiment, including Ken's method, in a letter to the Navy Department dated 21 April.

The letter was later published and sent to the Atlantic Fleet for information, called to the special attention of submarine commanders.

Today, only a few persons remember Ken's "experiment." Fewer recognize it as the original forerunner of one of the escape methods successfully tested for American deep-diving nuclear submarines.

Before Castle's report of the "experiment" was in a mailbag, legends were being forged. As usual, Ken said little or nothing. Spuds's and Guy's versions table-hopped the club, then blended with the stories the men told in the Nutshell Bar and the Santa Anna Dance Hall. Reporters picked and chose, combining details into versions of their own for transmission to the States. Eight years later, during World War I, editors reprinted impossibly imaginative accounts as inaccurate as Bob Murray's yarn of Spuds's Vladivostok voyage. One had Whiting coming up right beside Castle, on the deck of the *Shark,* whereupon "he threw up his hand in a snappy salute."

Amidst all of this garbling, Whiting's experiment became a part of the Ellyson legend. The mix-up may have begun in Manila where men who knew the submariners only slightly knew that Ken and Spuds often operated together both ashore and afloat. As such people relayed the story, they assumed both men were involved.

But by 1925, young officers awed by the number one aviator were telling each other that Spuds was also the first man "who had himself shot out of a torpedo tube." After Ellyson's death, Richmond chums who had seen nothing of him for over twenty years but had followed his career in the newspapers were certain they had read that he was the first to demonstrate this escape method. By 1961 even Fleet Admiral Nimitz could not remember which of his pals was the innovator.

No reliable record has been found to show that Ellyson had anything to do with the experiment, or that he ever claimed participation. The original torpedo tube escape test was Ken Whiting's solo show.

While navigating the *Rainbow,* Spuds had explored the southern islands, with rice paddies and jungles to match Luzon's and cities smaller than Manila, with more insects, fewer Americans, and the stink of sun-drying fish. He was drawn south again for three weeks' leave in June 1909—a long trip just to go fishing. If a lady, another *the* girl, was the magnet, she remains unknown.

[CHAPTER SIX]

First Commands:

Shark and *Tarantula*

Castle sailed for home, leaving the command of the *Shark* and of the submarine flotilla for Ellyson to assume when he returned to Cavite in his third typhoon season. Between showers, it drizzled. Even in rare moments between drizzles, the air was as hot and damp as the inside of an A-boat on a long dive in the bay's warm water. Life on the boats may have accustomed Ken and Spuds to damp clothes, mildewed shoes, and prickly heat, for they took the dank, muggy weather in their strides. They carried on the established routine of dive-repair-improve-dive-repeat.

A dozen times in four months, a typhoon sideswiped Cavite. The showers closed up on each other, merging into constant heavy rain. The barometer would ease down slightly, then dive like a loon as another typhoon approached. An aerologist once said that Manila has no rainy season. It rains there only when a typhoon is near—it just so happens that between June and November, a typhoon is almost always found within two hundred miles. Wind churned the bay into creamy froth, driving the ferry *Mindoro* from her scheduled run. Rain and spray beat through the submariners' thin clothing as they put their boats into sheltered berths. Securing the boats with heavy chains, they closed the hatches and went ashore to relax, logging such days as "Typhoon, usual holiday routine."

Rain fell an inch an hour. Then it rained harder. No one could stand against the roaring wind which destroyed the boundary between air and sea; it drove rain, sea foam, roof tiles, and tree limbs in a horizontal torrent. Tall seas battered old Spanish sea walls, ripped over docks, thudded down on the moored submarines. The little boats took the beating better than any of the objects on land.

After a day or two each storm moved slowly into the China Sea. Wind and sea went down, the barometer went up. The rain broke into squalls, with longer and longer drizzle spots between. Submariners unshackled the *Shark* and *Porpoise* and returned to their daily dives. Typhoons, dives, repairs—all were part of Spuds's and Ken's routine.

Between October's typhoons, the collier *Caesar* joined the flotilla. That event made news on the Asiatic Station. The small newspapers, which could afford only limited cable service, concentrated on local events, spiced with small stale items condensed from papers that had been at least a month in transit from San Francisco or London.

During Ellyson's years in this news vacuum, President Theodore Roosevelt's Great White Fleet circled the globe. Admiral R.E. Perry reached the North Pole. The financial panic of 1907 brought hunger and trust-busting to America. Simon Lake designed a new type of submarine. The Wright brothers thrilled Europe, then the United States, with their flying. Louis Blériot flew across the English channel. The United States Army bought its first airplane and its first dirigible; and an American, Army Lieutenant Thomas E. Selfridge, became the first to die in an airplane crash. Of these events, only the movements of Roosevelt's fleet made headlines in Manila.

Few in the Far East believed men had really flown. If they discussed them at all, they agreed that the meagerly reported flights were either lies to build yellow-press circulation or tricks, like legerdemain or hypnotism.

In December 1909, the Navy Department ignored the Asiatic Fleet commander's requests for qualified submarine commanders. Perhaps no commanders were available to be sent; perhaps no one in Washington thought subs important. In January, when Ellyson and Whiting were three months overdue for relief, the admiral ordered Ellyson home and kept Whiting on to turn gunboat ensigns into sub skippers.

After giving the flotilla to Ken on the last day of the month, Spuds moved into the club. For the two weeks it took an Army transport to arrive, discharge, and get ready for the return voyage, the cards went against him. He sailed broke, leaving Manila gamblers holding IOUs that haunted him for several years.

Ellyson discovered a new world in mid-March when he stepped ashore at San Francisco. In front of the Ferry Building, streetcars rattled over a maze of switch-points, hesitating to dump ferry-bound passengers and scoop up a new load. Then, with clanging bells and screeching wheels, they clattered around the rest of the circle and were gone. Beyond the cars, he saw taxicabs for the first time but passed them up for a row of hotel omnibusses. They looked odd without their horses, but stood tail-to-curb, with rear steps hanging over the sidewalk in the old familiar way. Beside each open door, a top-hatted driver hawked the advantages of his hotel like a side-show barker.

Ellyson's porter tossed his bags to a man standing atop the bus marked "St. Francis," and Spuds climbed inside for a free ride. The engine smelled like a submarine's as it chugged up Market Street. Clanging streecars, on four lines of track, roared past unchecked by traffic lights or crosswalks. Swearing teamsters of horse-drawn drays competed for the side lanes with honking chauffeurs of assorted, snorting, popping motorcars. Veteran pedestrians jumped, dodged, and sprinted in daring crossings. The timid never crossed. New-looking buildings alternated with those under construction as the city obliterated the last scars of the 1906 earthquake and fire.

From his hotel window, Spuds looked down on Union Square and its monument commemorating Commodore George Dewey's victory at Manila Bay, then turned to the desk and penned the required letter to the Secretary of the Navy:

> Sir:
>   I have the honor to report my arrival in the United States.
>   Enclosed is a copy of my orders.
>   My address (while awaiting orders) will be 814 Park Avenue, Richmond, Virginia...

Next morning the omnibus chugged him to the Southern Pacific ferry. Before his train was fifty miles beyond the Oakland Mole, where trains and ferries met, he asked the conductor to change his ticket and send off a wire to the Navy Department. His night letter asked for twenty days' delay in reporting home, and a reply to be sent to the Hotel Bartin, San Diego. He had been drawn to San

Diego, perhaps by someone he had met in San Francisco or on the train, perhaps to write the last chapter of a shipboard romance.

Years later, a reminiscing Ellyson told a younger officer how the party ended. He had boarded another train for the East with a terrific hangover, his ticket, and no money whatever. After a few hours, he was hungry enough to confide his problem to an older man who had been friendly. The chap stiffened and chilled, but he stood Spuds to meals during their six-day ride.

When they parted near the end of the trip, the man shook his finger under Ellyson's nose. "Listen, you young punk," he said. "I've staked you because I'm from Richmond. I know your family. You're a disgrace to fine people. Straighten yourself out."

Lizzie Ellyson was disappointed because her Gordon had to leave Richmond almost as soon as he arrived, to carry out the orders he found waiting. On 16 April at Charleston, South Carolina, he took command of the B-class submarine *Tarantula*. She carried more torpedoes, was four years younger, one-third longer, and rated two more men than the *Shark*. Spuds considered her command a deserved promotion, until he tried her in the Cooper River. He soon knew her American engine needed more fixing than the *Shark*'s older German one. Thirteen days after he took command, he sailed the *Tarantula,* with the rest of the flotilla, for Annapolis.

Three hours out, the *Tarantula* cracked a cylinder and wallowed with her deck awash. Ellyson and all his men were soaked before they secured the towline of the tender *Prairie*. Then, while their boat bucked and jerked astern of the tender, they skinned knuckles and mashed fingers as they changed the cylinder.

Some hours later, the engine thumped into life again. They threw off the towline. The boat plowed steadily through the ocean for almost four hours before the engine quit again. Seas washed over the deck as they again wrestled the towline on board. When it was secured, all but the helmsman went below, wrung seawater from their clothes, poured it from their shoes, and went to work on the engine.

For seven days they lived that way. Run-tow-fix-repeat. The sea was too rough to allow them to cook on their little hot plate. When they got into the quieter waters of Chesapeake Bay, they were too tired to cook. They opened cans and spooned the cold contents from can to mouth.

No one could sleep. Later they had trouble staying awake. Spuds dozed on the cold floor plates, dreaming of the hot, stuffy *Shark,* awoke shivering, with condensate dripping onto his head. When they reached the Academy dock, he and his men charged the air banks and battery, then rested for a week.

Operating from Annapolis, Ellyson's life fell back into the run-fix-run routine. No matter how he worked at it, he was never able to make *Tarantula*'s engine dependable. She logged far more repair than operating time under his command. Once he kept her running long enough to lose a torpedo, another time long enough to run aground in the Patuxent River.

A month after he was promoted to lieutenant junior grade, Ellyson took his boat to Norfolk. Although it was a go-fix-go trip, he enjoyed operating independently again. The Navy Yard tinkered with the *Tarantula*'s engine for a day, declared it perfect, and sent him out again.

"Drop me off at Fort Monroe, as you go by," said Lieutenant Commander Williams, Commander of the Atlantic Torpedo Flotilla.

Spuds charged toward the dock at full throttle, bucking a strong tide. He promised himself a snappy landing to impress his boss. Twenty feet from the wooden dock, he called down the hatch, "Full astern." The throbbing engine cut off at once. Tide and momentum angled the boat silently and swiftly toward the pier. Spuds listened anxiously for the motor's whirr, heard instead the bang! bang! of a heavy hammer somewhere below. Inches from the piling, the motor hummed and the propellor churned white water. Too late. The bow glanced off a pile, went inside of the next one, and crunched under the dock. Splinters flew as diagonal braces snapped. Big spikes squealed and bolts grunted as a foot-square beam wrenched up from the pile tops. The *Tarantula* rolled to port, slowly righted herself, and stopped with the big beam jammed between the dock planking and some deck projection ten feet aft of the stem.

The sound of water, splashed alongside by the spinning propellor, was all that could be heard when the timbers finished protesting. The boat did not move. Boss Williams spoke in the quiet. "You shouldn't have held onto your gas engine so long," he said. "Send your report of the accident through me for endorsement." He climbed onto the splintered dock. "Thanks for the ride," he called back, then moved out of sight.

On the edge of the dock, a few idle soldiers gawked. Obviously the boat wasn't going to move with the whole Army pier locked to her foredeck. Spuds, blushing under his sunburn, stopped the motor. The tide gurgled alongside as he wondered how to free his boat.

"Flood the forward ballast tank!" he called down to the chief of the boat. Air hissed from the vent, then died to a whisper. For a moment nothing happened; then, sounding like a giant file, the hull dropped, stripping barnacles from the pilings. "Back full," Spuds ordered. Again the propellor churned. Water swished forward along the hull. The soldiers gawked and snickered. Spuds's ears burned. Then, as suddenly as it had dropped, the bow wrenched free. Spuds swung his vessel around, started the engine, and headed out the channel.

Before he rounded the Tail-of-the-Horseshoe light, the engine began misbehaving again. He had planned to make a Saturday night party in Crabtown, but the stop-fix-go routine let him arrive only at breakfast time on Sunday. Next morning his division commander agreed that nobody should have to change a cylinder every watch.

On Wednesday, Ellyson headed back for the Navy Yard. The engine resisted, but he made it. While mechanics reworked the engine, Spuds spent two weeks in the hospital with flu. The disease laid him low at intervals for the rest of his life, though he was somehow spared when it was epidemic among American forces during World War I.

When the *Tarantula* and her skipper were in commission again, Commander Williams sent them back to Annapolis. "On your way," he said, "stop at the Newport News Shipyard, and inspect the experimental sub, *Seal*. She was supposed to be finished last May. The Department wants to know what's holding her up, and what a sub skipper thinks of her design."

Ellyson spent a Friday at Newport News, mailed his report, and, thinking he was finished with the *Seal*, rejoined his division for torpedo practice near Solomons, Maryland.

CHAPTER SEVEN

Seal in the Shipyard:

Request for Flight

Spuds was thinking of promotion when the division berthed in Norfolk in November. Though he had been due for promotion to lieutenant junior grade in January, 1910, his examination papers had missed him in Manila. In July, the Washington examining board had quizzed him and decided to give his court-martial little weight, "because of his subsequent good record." A few weeks after his new commission reached him in August, expansion of the Navy made him due for promotion to lieutenant and swamped the examiners. Before they got around to Ellyson again, somebody read his report on the *Seal*. The somebody told the detail officer to send an officer to the shipyard to get the *Seal* finished.

Such directives pained detail officers. Struggling to keep fleet ships fully manned, they were chronically short of bodies. Each unexpected demand for an officer forced the detail officer to re-slate a long, interlocking chain of reliefs. "This Ellyson, who inspected the *Seal,* is due here for examination, isn't he?" the detail officer asked Joe, his clerk. "All right. When the board finishes him, send him to Newport News as inspector of machinery, and prospective commanding officer of the *Seal.* Let him fix what he said was wrong."

Orders to command the *Seal* pleased Spuds. She was twice the size of any other sub and looked far more roomy and comfortable because Mr. Lake had designed her with all of her ballast and fuel tanks outside the pressure hull, instead of filling the lower half as in previous boats of the Holland type. And Spuds didn't think anything could be less reliable than the *Tarantula*. The *Seal* could not be ready for sea for several months, so he would be on shore duty near his Richmond home.

On the first of December, the examiners noted that Ellyson had grounded the *Tarantula*, lost her torpedo, and smashed her through Fort Monroe's dock. But "in view of the fact..." they passed him again. Next day Spuds arrived in Newport News.

The builders of the Ellyson legend ignored his unhappy months in the *Tarantula*, and, brushing aside the "prospective" in his orders, incorrectly called the *Seal* his third submarine command. But the sub was not commissioned until years after Spuds left her.

The *Seal* was the first submarine to be built at Newport News Shipyard. Ellyson was determined to see that she was built correctly—and promptly. As the only man in town who had commanded a submarine, he considered himself the local expert and expected his suggestions to be heeded.

He quickly found that yard officials disagreed. They were building the *Seal* for her designer, Simon Lake, not on a Navy contract. For several years, Lake had argued that his design was far superior to the Navy's Holland types, such as the *Shark*. Conservative naval officials had refused to go out on a limb for him and spend Navy money on his invention. When Lake persisted, the Department agreed to buy his boat, if he built one that performed as well in sea trials as did the Navy's best. The builders wanted instructions from Lake, who was paying the bills, not from some Johnny-come-lately Navy lieutenant.

Impatient to get to sea in his big sub, which was a year behind schedule, Spuds felt slighted. His temper simmered when the yard failed to jump at his every suggestion. Maybe they wanted to make trouble for him? Within a week he was looking for an out. He considered making a request for battleship duty—it would look good on his record.

Then he got Bill Halsey's message from Norfolk, across Hampton Roads.

Before his graduation in 1904, William Frederick Halsey, Jr., had played fullback on the same team on which Ken Whiting was end. A year later, he was in the *Missouri*'s steerage when Midshipman Ellyson joined it. In December, 1910, already known as one of the

Navy's finest ship handlers, Halsey looked much like his later pictures. Slightly overweight, with deep-set, steady eyes, he had a smile which captured everyone. His message to Spuds read, "Ken Whiting is here. Come over and have dinner with us in my new destroyer."

Ken Whiting had landed at Mare Island and had caught a train for his New York home in August, five months behind Ellyson. Air meets were being held across America. Wright and Curtiss exhibition teams, small-time barnstormers, and plain fakes put on air shows, collecting fantastic gates from skeptics who had to see to believe that a man could fly. The skeptics saw, believed, and became evangelists of the air. Sportsmen and society leaders got into the act. Aviation was in. Flying magazines sprouted like spring grass, printing fact, fiction, and crackpot hopes in a medley that few could untangle. Do-it-yourself men across the country built planes. Any of the machines that got off the ground for a few feet and some that never did were headlined; their builders were dubbed aviators.

Ken felt this flying enthusiasm during his seven-day train ride. While on leave, he watched a Curtiss team fly above the race track at Sheepshead Bay, Long Island. As he took command of the submarine *Tarpon* at Brooklyn, the International Air Meet in Chicago was front-page news. A newspaper offered $25,000 in prize money for an "aeroplane" race from Chicago to New York's Belmont Park Air Meet. Whiting knew that the machines he watched could no more fight at sea than his old *Porpoise* could, but, unlike most Navy professionals, he believed these embryos could be developed into fighting machines. In Norfolk, facing his old roommate across Halsey's dinner table, he asked, "Have you thought anything about this flying game?"

The question caught Spuds flat-footed. "No. Not especially," he answered. He had never seen a plane fly. Airshows, in hibernation as he crossed the continent in March, had missed the *Tarantula*'s summer operating areas.

Ken's interest and belief came across the table with his words. "The Navy's sure to find planes useful in the future. I've been watching the Wright brothers and Curtiss. They've got something. I've put in an official request for a course of training in flying," he concluded.

Without much debate, Spuds had followed many of Ken's leads in the years since they first met at Crabtown. The habit had gotten him to China aboard an armored cruiser and into submarines, some trouble, and a lot of fun. He knew most senior officers were unimpressed by flying machines. He suspected airplanes might be only carnival toys. But working with Ken was seldom dull, and if an airplane could lift Spuds out of the Newport News Shipyard, whether they flew or not was immaterial. "Sounds good to me," he said. "Send me a copy of your letter, and I'll put in one like it."

On 16 December 1910, Ellyson sent his request.

> From: Lieutenant T.G. Ellyson
> To: The Secretary of the Navy
> Subject: Requests duty in connection with aeroplanes.
>
> I request that I be assigned duty in connection with aeroplanes as soon as such duty becomes available.
>
> T.G. Ellyson

Whiting was not the only young officer who believed aviation had a naval future. John Henry ("Jack") Towers, Charles Felton Pousland, and others had asked to fly before him. The detail officer gave them all the same brush-off. "Same as before, Joe. The aeroplane letter," he said as he tossed Ellyson's request to his clerk. Like the others, Spuds's answer, dated 22 December, read:

> ...You are informed that this application has been noted and placed on file for consideration at an appropriate time.

An appointment of the previous summer was about to make the "appropriate time" arrive long before the detail officer expected it. Secretary of the Navy George von L. Meyer, believing the Navy no place for airplanes, was bothered by letters from aviation enthusiasts. He told fifty-four-year-old Captain Washington Irving Chambers to answer them. Chambers was a pleasant, earnest officer who liked to know what he was talking about. He read everything he could find about flying with results Meyer had never expected. Chambers became an advocate of naval aviation.

At the end of November, Chambers picked up a letter from Glenn Curtiss prophesying that the Navy would soon want airplanes and offering to train an officer

> ...in the operation and construction of the Curtiss aeroplane. As I am fully aware that the Navy Department has no funds availabe for aviation

purposes, I am making this offer with the understanding that it involves no expense to the Navy Department other than the cost of detailing an officer to the aviation grounds in southern California.

Chambers waited till Meyer was out of town. Then, on 13 December, Acting Secretary Beekman Winthrop, who was more air-minded than Meyer, signed a letter of acceptance.

Chambers spent several days pondering the type of officer to send. He reduced his thoughts to a memo: "A mature man who would make a good instructor later, an athlete with cool nerves, experience with gasoline engines would be helpful, a well balanced, conservative man who would not be a showman, an adaptable man and a seaman." When Chambers received Curtiss's schedule from Jerome Fanciulli of the Curtiss Exhibition Company, he took his memo to Winthrop.

About the time the detail officer tossed Ellyson's aviation request into his file basket, Winthrop signed a note ordering the detail officer to carefully select an officer meeting Chambers's specifications and get him to Los Angeles before the end of the air meet there "to confer (with Curtiss) about aviation instruction." He must also be sent to San Francisco to confer "on 6 January... with the committee in charge of the aviation meet."

That order reached the detail office on Friday, 23 December, while everyone was trying to clear his desk and knock off for Christmas. "A hell of a time to tell me to find a superman like that," the detail officer grumbled as he read. "Wants his orders in the mail today, too. Joe, where's that request for aeroplane duty we had yesterday? Was that bird in the fleet?"

"Ellyson? No, sir," Joe said, fishing through a basket. "We just sent him to Newport News a couple of weeks ago. Here's his request. His aeroplane letter's gone."

"We won't worry about that," said the detail officer, handing the request and Winthrop's note to Joe. "Write him orders like this, then hand-carry them to the Secretary's office for signature and see them mailed."

"Who's to relieve him at Newport News?"

"Nobody today. We'll have to refigure the slate after New Year's to get someone."

And so it happened. Bill Halsey's dinner party, Ken Whiting's faith in aviation's naval future, a harried detail officer, and a coincidence of timing made Ellyson the first naval flier—though legend has it that he was selected only for his very special qualifications.

The day before Christmas, the postman handed Ellyson his lieutenant's commission, good for $100 back pay. A messenger gave
him a night wire from the Department:

YOUR ORDERS TO LOS ANGELES MAILED TODAY

Christmas Eve of 1910 was a very merry one for Spuds Ellyson.

Spuds's orders reached him on 27 December, and he caught the
next train west, well pleased to leave the *Seal* to Simon Lake and
the builders. During his long ride, he studied aviation magazines.
They pictured aviators wearing cloth caps with visors over the
backs of their necks and clothes generally termed "snappy"—the
sort Spuds associated with vaudeville characters or race-track touts.
Glenn Curtiss was mentioned more often than any other name—
as "motorcycle speed king," "airplane racer," and "inventor"—but
Spuds found no close-up pictures of him.

On 2 January 1911, Ellyson reached Dominguez Field south of
Los Angeles on the Dominguez farm. The field, a plateau with
gullies on two sides and a temporary grandstand for 14,000 persons,
was rimmed by lunch counters and side shows. Spuds looked for
a flashy, spectacular, handsome daredevil, head and shoulders above
the milling crowd.

A derby-hatted barker pointed out a small man with unremark-
able brown hair and a bushy mustache who wore a shabby business suit sagging from his skinny frame. "That's Mr. Curtiss," the
barker said.

CHAPTER EIGHT

North Island:

On the Ground with Curtiss

*G*lenn Curtiss, looking like a country man who had strayed onto the field, was hearing all, watching everything, and saying nothing, as he appeared to ignore the meager audience and the fliers in loud dress who stood around him. The other aviators chattered and gestured like ham actors.

Ellyson introduced himself. The inventor came alive with interest. His unusually alert eyes measured his trainee quickly; his sincere welcome, shyly delivered, made Spuds forget the man's modest size and ill-fitting coat.

Spuds had assumed that Curtiss's school was at Dominguez Field, but Curtiss quickly explained that his winter quarters were to be near San Diego. He took Ellyson south with him that evening. Ellyson stuck to Curtiss like a Siamese twin, a practice he was to follow for many months. At San Diego, Curtiss leased a motorboat and showed Spuds North Island, a barren, uninhabited, waterless, jackrabbit heaven. With his foreman, John Cooper, Curtiss paced off a landplane runway to be cleared through the scrubby brush and a ramp to the beach from the old barn that would serve as a shop. Back on the San Diego side, Curtiss arranged for gear to be ferried to the island, talked to a Mr. Baker about using his waterfront machine shop, spoke with a committee arranging an air show to mark the opening of his flying school. "I've quit exhibition flying myself. It's always bored me," he confided to Ellyson after the last conference. "But I have to put machines into air shows to finance my experiments, which are the important things."

Next day they caught the *Lark,* the night train from Los Angeles to San Francisco, where aviators were gathering at the Palace Hotel. The fliers talked aviation to everyone they could buttonhole. Some strutted about the lobby, as did the Frenchman Hubert Latham, who lit one Turkish cigarette after another after placing them in his seven-inch amber holder as he boasted of his Antoinette monoplane. Most preferred the bar where Charles K. Hamilton, a little narrow-faced, hollow-cheeked man with oversized ears, guzzled rye and was said to "have fallen farther than any other man and was getting used to it."

Iowa-born Eugene Ely, the only man who had flown from a ship, was a local boy by adoption. With yellow gloves flopping from a pocket of his new brown suit, he leaned on a cane and ordered champagne for old acquaintances from his pre-flying days on automobile row. He retold the story of his flight from a platform on the bow of the cruiser *Birmingham,* declaring that he would both land on and take off again from the U.S.S. *Pennsylvania* during the San Francisco meet.

"What is your opinion of the ornithopter, Mr. Ely?" a bespectacled hanger-on asked respectfully.

Ely looked at him thoughtfully, carefully removed the long ash from his Havana cigar, then answered, "I wouldn't use one of the machines. The principle is all wrong. But don't condemn them on *my* say-so; that's just one man's opinion."

The hanger-on drifted away, happy with a quote from the lion of the day. Ely turned to a large-eared runt wearing a red-and-white tweed jacket checked in two-inch squares, "Bud, what in hell's an ornithopter?"

"Probably a drink. Ask the bartender," the runt answered while tapping the bar with a monogrammed cigarette. "Doc says I have tobacco heart. Shouldn't smoke," he went on. "So I have these damn things made without nicotine. They cost like hell and taste like crap, but I gotta use them. Gotta match?" Spuds soon learned that aviator "Bud" Mars prefaced every smoke with identical remarks.

After his second evening at the Palace, Spuds wondered if any facts stood behind the boasts he heard. A bunch of hams, he told himself. Each with a corny stunt to attract attention. Except Curtiss.

He's different—never hangs out in the lobby or bar, told me he never learned to smoke or drink.

The machines being set up on Selfridge Field beside the Tanforan race track interested Ellyson more than the flamboyant fliers who were setting themselves up at the Palace. He knew other officers had reported on air meets, but that they could have known as much, or more, about aviation than he did never occurred to him. He had never put his tail on an airplane's seat, but he felt his orders made him *the* Navy aviation expert. As such he checked on both the planes and their loud-mouthed jockeys while trying to talk like a flier. He had occasional humble moments. During one of them, two weeks after meeting Curtiss, he wrote to Chambers:

> ...went to San Francisco on the 5th, inspected the platform on the *Pennsylvania* in company with Mr. Ely. Attended meet at San Francisco on 7th, 8th, 10th, 15th, and 16th. Rain prevented flying on intervening days. I spent most of my time in 'Frisco at the aviation field, studying the standard and the crank machines, made it a point to meet and know all the aviators and talk with them concerning their particular type of machines. My experience is too limited to submit any views, and unless you advise otherwise, my monthly reports will simply cover my movements, as my observations would be of no value...

Spuds always swallowed humble pie quickly. In his next paragraph, he gave this observation:

> I left San Francisco after only five days of the meet were completed [the fliers had contracted for ten flying days] because the flights there were of no practical value, no matter what the newspapers say to the contrary, and I realized that Mr. Curtiss might do work here [at San Diego] which would be of interest. I came down with Mr. Curtiss...

At San Diego a friendly, personal letter from Captain Chambers awaited Spuds. The captain, assuming the detail officer who had selected Spuds had carefully considered all of his prescribed qualifications, had written, in part:

> ...you were selected because you were not regarded as a crank, but as a well-balanced man who should be able to assist in building up a system of aviation training in the Navy. I've no doubt you see the importance of avoiding the hippodrome part of the business and will not do stunts just for the sake of notoriety or to thrill the crowd...

Spuds accepted the "well-balanced man..." remark as evidence that Chambers knew and appreciated his outstanding abilities. He dashed off a ten-page reply which began:

> Your letter received today and it was very much appreciated. If I do not misunderstand your letter, you are looking out for all matters concerning aviation in the Navy, and from the tone of your letter I feel that I can write to you personally, and bring out many small points, as well as receiving advice, which would be impossible to do officially. Having been in the submarine service for some little time, when there was no one in the Department really interested in submarines I can appreciate what your interest and help will mean....

Ellyson then confessed his ignorance of aviation and asked for "advice as to the quickest means of obtaining all standard works on aviation either from the Department or at personal expense." Spuds did not realize how much had been printed on the subject. Fortunately, the captain recommended one volume as a starter. Spuds also asked for all aviation reports, confidential or otherwise, which reached the department. He explained, "I keep a file as well as a diary, and all such information will be availabe for my successor in case anything should happen to me..."

After detailing his movements to date, Ellyson said he

> ...arrived with Curtiss about noon today. We immediately went to North Island where his two planes are, and spent the afternoon there. While here I will work at all times with his mechanics, my idea being to know everything possible about this type of aeroplane from the 'ground up' and I expect to help them in all overhauls because I can gain more by doing a thing myself than by watching others do it....As yet I have done no practical work but hope to start in shortly, though it is possible that I may not receive any instruction until after the meet here as there are only two machines at present, one for water experiments and one for the exhibition flights here. I doubt very much if my work will start before the completion of the San Francisco meet when more planes will be available....

Only ten months before, Spuds had changed his train ticket home in order to visit San Diego, yet he wrote as though he had never been in the city before his arrival with Curtiss. Whatever sparked the earlier trip was no longer important enough to be mentioned.

North Island early in 1911 with Curtiss biplanes and Antoinette monoplanes. The Antoinettes were owned by New York sportsman Harry S. Harkness, who shared the island briefly with Glenn Curtiss. The armored cruisers beyond the island in San Diego Bay are not identified.

The show that Spuds Ellyson missed. On 18 January 1911, Eugene Ely landed aboard the armored cruiser *Pennsylvania* while she was at anchor in San Francisco Bay.

Eugene Ely just after he landed aboard the USS *Pennsylvania.* Ely wore a football helmet and an inflated bicycle tire because he could not swim. Captain C. F. Pond, commanding the *Pennsylvania,* is on the right; others are unidentified.

San Diego papers headlined the opening of Curtiss's flying school when the inventor and Ellyson arrived on 17 January, but Spuds spent his first ten days with Curtiss working as a mechanic. He learned about both the inventor and his machines. Spuds had penetrated Curtiss's shy reserve before they left San Francisco. In the North Island barn, Spuds found him pleasantly interesting to work with.

Though he was largely silent with the stunt men, Curtiss talked fluently when he had a companion who could understand his ideas. The inventor listened to all suggestions, explained his ideas as he worked, and displayed an amazing ingenuity with tools. Spuds soon believed the man could make anything.

The airplane was mechanically simple. Occasionally Curtiss had Ellyson sit in it. "Imagine that a wing drops. What do you do?" Spuds hesitated, then leaned to shift the shoulder yoke. "Your nose jerks up. What then?" Spuds pushed on the wheel. "You want to turn. How? Think of those things and move the controls accordingly," the inventor directed. "Get the feel of the machine before you try to drive it."

While Spuds worked in the barn, the local air show was repeatedly postponed because weather continued to hold the fliers at San Francisco. Late in the month, Lincoln Beachey, Hugh Robinson, Charlie Willard, Harry Harkness, and other Curtiss-trained pilots arrived to put their machines together on Coronado's polo field.

Eugene Ely, now doubly world famous after his landing on and takeoff from the U.S.S. *Pennsylvania* at San Francisco, felt his oats as he flew from North Island to the show. It was one of those crisp, sunny mornings when nothing is impossible and everything is worth trying. Some eight hundred feet above the crowd, he stood his plane on its ear in a vertical bank, cut its engine, and dropped in a tight spiral. The crowd gasped. Spirals in those unstable planes were daring stunts that had ended the lives of several fliers who unknowingly stalled into a spin. Few men understood stalls; the spin had not even been named, let alone comprehended.

Ely made it. Just above the fence he checked the turn and glided to a perfect midfield landing. The spectators cheered. But the fear that had risen up in Curtiss turned to anger. He had thought Ely smarter than the ex-stuntmen and high divers like Bud Mars. He knew the flier had a mechanical bent like his own. He grabbed Ely's lapel. "That stuff is all right for men who live by sensationalism," he said. "But it's not for us. Cut it out."

The next day, crisp sunshine and a purring engine intoxicated Curtiss. He zipped five times around the field at the level of the spectators' belts, lifting his wheels barely clear of each hurdle on the cinder track, dropping a wing within inches of the ground in each steep turn. When he landed, Ely was ready with a crack about sensationalism. Before he got it off, Glenn's usually silent wife, Lena, pushed Ely aside. She scolded her husband, publicly, in mid-field, until he promised to quit exhibition flying for all time. Reporters loved his discomfort. They plastered the story across the front pages of their papers.

Spuds admired Curtiss too much to criticize anything he did. Curtiss's flying stunt went unmentioned when he wrote to Chambers:

> ...Ely gave the prettiest exhibition of flying I have ever seen, but if he keeps on taking the same chances, he won't last six months....

On the last afternoon of the meet, the man with the megaphone told the crowd something of Curtiss's training methods. "The throttle is blocked," he explained, "so that the engine cannot develop enough power to get the machine into the air. Thus protected, the student drives the machine up and down the field until he can steer straight courses and has a feeling for the controls. Lieutenant Gordon Ellyson of the Navy, the first student of Mr. Curtiss's new class, will now show you this phase of training."

The engine sputtered. Spuds zig-zagged down the field. The engine sounded impressively loud when he opened the throttle. He was driving the machine for only the second time, but he felt he had the hang of it when he stopped on the cinder path at the end of the grass. No harder than steering a launch, he told himself as he got out, lifted the front wheel, and turned the machine around. Back in the seat, he blimped the engine to attract attention, then rolled back toward the crowd. He was watching the spectators when the block fell from under the throttle. When he banged the throttle open again, the motor jerked the plane ahead, roaring with all twenty-five horsepower. Spuds fell back in his seat, yanking the tightly held wheel with him. The machine leaped fifteen feet into the air, stalled, and crunched down on one wing. Spuds heard snapping wires, tearing fabric, and splintering wood as the propellor bit dirt. His first aerial demonstration had ended in a cloud of dust.

The engine died. Picking himself up, Ellyson fingered bruises,

Second Lieutenant John C. Walker, United States Army, Lieutenant T. Gordon Ellyson, United States Navy, and Eugene Ely at the Coronado Air Meet, 30 January 1911.

Spuds Ellyson, in blue dress uniform minus only his cap, starting his demonstration of Curtiss's training method on the Coronado Polo Field, 18 January 1911. A few moments after this picture was taken, he inadvertently made his first flight and crashed.

flicked dirt from his person. Then, remembering how Hubert Latham had gone through a fence in San Francisco and how others had crashed in the middle of Selfridge Field, he felt like a pro. Grinning, he stepped out of the settling dust. Running men slowed when they saw him on his feet. Curtiss reached him first, demanding, "Are you hurt?" Spuds said he was OK. Curtiss interrupted him as he apologized for wrecking the plane. "That's nothing, if you're all right," the inventor said. "Crack-ups are part of this game."

"I did worse dozens of times before I got the hang of it," Gene Ely said.

"I'm still awfully sorry I messed it up, Mr. Curtiss," Spuds repeated.

Curtiss fingered the crumpled wing. "Couple of hours will fix it," he said. "Don't worry about it."

Two days later, Ellyson laughed off the incident in a letter describing Curtiss's training system:

> ...In this connection I had a rather amusing experience the second time I was ever in the machine. I was running over the polo grounds at Coronado and on the run up the field everything went finely. On the run back the wooden block which had been placed under the throttle fell out and I unconsciously opened the throttle wide. Shortly afterwards I hit a bump causing me to fall back in the seat, at the same time elevating the forward control, and before I realized it I was fifteen feet in the air, and in making a landing broke one of the wings of the machine. To prevent such slips in the future Mr. Curtiss....

Gene Ely had left San Diego when Ellyson read in a letter from Chambers:

> I'm sorry you did not see Ely's flight to and from the *Pennsylvania*. Of course I know it was arranged for the spectacular, but the scheme of ropes stretched between sandbags to stop the machine seems to have worked well.

Spuds felt it would be poor tactics to obstruct a cruiser's guns to fly something as useless as the planes he had seen. Spuds considered Ely's shipboard flights to be mere stunts, with a bonus for the Navy of good publicity. He answered Chambers:

...As to Ely's flight I am sorry that I did not witness it but I do not think I missed learning anything thereby as I went over the whole thing with him the night before I left San Francisco, and it was I who suggested the use of the sand bags and the spacing of the same, and since the flight I have seen Ely and he told me all about it...

Spuds and several other men had convinced each other that they had devised Ely's arresting gear and had told him just how to make the flight. Undoubtedly the project was discussed in bull sessions, while Ely tested variations on the field. None of the kibitzers knew that, as an automobile race driver, Ely had used identical hooks to stop a car by picking up lines attached to hay bales.

CHAPTER NINE

Triad and Lizzie:

Hydroplanes and Training Flights

*D*iscounting the use of a flight deck, Chambers and Ellyson hoped naval aviation would develop from the "water machine" which Curtiss called a "hydroaeroplane" and which he assured them he would soon succeed in flying. The evening after Ellyson arrived in San Diego from San Francisco, he wrote:

> Today we commenced putting the hydroplanes and floats on the machine and inside of four days Mr. Curtiss will carry out his experiment of rising from and lighting on the water, which he hopes to accomplish before the meet here....

His estimate was optimistic. For the next nine days, Spuds smudged his face and wore grease to his elbows. The hydro's gasoline engine was smaller, lighter, and even more troublesome than the gas engines he had been familiar with in submarines. He learned to blow grit from its carburetor, replace broken valve springs and leaky hoses, solder radiator and water-jacket leaks. Each time he helped drag the machine into Spanish Bight's icy water, Spuds was wet to his navel. Again and again Curtiss failed to get into the air; after each try, Spuds and the others dunked themselves again while getting the contraption back to the barn.

69

They reshaped the tandem floats, tuned the engine, sanded the spray-pocked propellor, and tried again. The method was familiar; it was the same fix-and-try routine Spuds had learned in the *Shark*. The hydro finally flew on 26 January and again the next day. Each time Curtiss dragged the machine into the air, Spuds was as elated as if he had done it all himself. He envisioned naval aviation growing rapidly from these staggering hops, not realizing how slow that growth would be.

The repeatedly postponed Coronado air meet interrupted Curtiss's hydro experiments, but as soon as it was over he rerigged the machine with a single, scow-shaped float. The hydro flew better, but Spuds was disappointed because spray still chewed up the propellor. While they worked to solve immediate problems, Ellyson got so deeply buried in nuts-and-bolts tasks that he seldom thought of long-range developments. Chambers surprised him by writing that the Navy would want a two-man plane that could be hoisted aboard ship, one that could fly from both land and water. Spuds passed the word to Curtiss.

"We can hoist it aboard with the slings we use in the shop," Curtiss said. Then he showed Ellyson some unfinished fittings. "I plan to use these to attach wheels to the floats."

Ellyson reported that, if arrangements could be made, Curtiss would land alongside a ship, hoist aboard, then hoist out again and take off. The *Pennsylvania* lay in the harbor and Ely had made an aviation enthusiast of her captain, Charles Fremont ("Frog") Pond. Pond made the arrangements easy. The cruiser's log for February 17 included this report:

> At 8:45 Aviator Glenn Curtiss came alongside in his hydroaeroplane and was hoisted aboard with the machine by crane. At 9:05 he was hoisted out and left the ship, the experiment being accomplished without incident.

The "Pennsy's" crew did not guess that one of the men in rumpled khaki who assisted Curtiss under the crane, checked the machine on deck, and helped get it away was Lieutenant T. G. Ellyson, USN. The lieutenant described the stunt in a wire to the Department which ended:

EXPERIMENT PROVED AEROPLANE ADAPTABLE USE NAVY.

Glenn Curtiss's long, narrow, scow-shaped float, at Hammondsport. Curtiss first tried two floats under his hydro — one under the engine and pilot, the other in place of the nose wheel. He never got off the water until he built the float pictured above. The surfaces on the outer struts midway between the upper and lower wings are ailerons which Curtiss devised in an unsuccessful attempt to avoid infringing on the Wright brothers' all-inclusive patents for lateral balance of aircraft.

A week later he similarly reported flights from the field and water, with retractable wheels attached to the floats. He was sure this prototype would prove to be a machine the Navy could use right away. Curtiss called it the "Triad."

In 1911, fliers spoke of driving, not flying, their bamboo-tailed pushers. These tilting, tipsy "crates" were inherently unstable. Successful driving either on the ground or in the air required constant movement of controls. Few experts and no novices attempted this balancing act in any breeze. Because the air was still near sunset and in the early morning, Curtiss limited his students' practice to those hours. Spuds got up at five, to get the most out of the morning calm. His months of early rising in the *Rainbow*, for star sights, made it easy. He spent middays working on the experimental machine, or repairing the practice one that they called "Lizzie." Returning to his San Diego flat after the sunset practice and supper, he updated his journal and often fell asleep with his head on an unfinished letter to his family or to Chambers.

Before reaching San Diego, he asked the Bureau of Navigation for a typewriter, "as it is likely that many of my reports will be confidential." Later he explained to Chambers that he picked up valuable pointers in conversations with Curtiss that should not be passed through a stenographer. After that, each letter from the captain repromised the typewriter, and each of Ellyson's complained of its nonarrival. Late in February, he wrote:

> I am in serious need of a typewriter, because the one I have been using has been taken away from me, and the one I am at present using is very poor, besides I can only use it when I go to a downtown office. Will you please give me some information regarding the typewriter which was shipped to me some time in the past?

This phraseology is typical of Ellyson. All his life, as he avoided one word wherever more could be squeezed in, he multiplied his paper work. Three months after it was first promised, the typewriter reached him. He had it only one day, then shipped it back because he was leaving San Diego for the season.

Ellyson rarely gossiped about others, filling his wordy letters to Mamma with his opinions, ideas, plans, orders, escapades, and infatuations. Lizzie Ellyson enjoyed his confidences while telling herself his yarns were as exaggerated as the alarming ones he had

One of Glenn Curtiss's Lizzies at Hammondsport. The forward and after control surfaces were supported by wire-braced bamboo outriggers. The tail outriggers straddled the wooden pusher propellor driven by a four-cylinder water-cooled engine. Its radiator was just behind the pilot's head. The pointed cylinder above Spuds Ellyson's head was the gasoline tank. These wings were fabric covered only on the top.

sent her from the Cheesebox. Among the few letters she saved
from his Coronado period, one ended, "I believe I could be satisfied here the year round without ever going out at night. With
love, I am, your loving son, Gordon."

For a time he found flying and his strenuous schedule more satisfying than the stunts he had shared with Ken and Jakey in the
Orient. If he had thought about it, he would have been alarmed
because love and liquor seemed unimportant. But the phase passed
before he worried.

After Curtiss's students could steer a straight course across the
field, he had them make jumps of three or four feet into the air.
These little jumps were gradually extended as the students learned
to keep the Lizzie approximately level. Thereafter Curtiss would
show them shallow turns. In an early letter, Ellyson explained:

> ...Curtiss...says that he will have me flying inside of two weeks or a
> month at the outside. He is only willing to take the responsibility of
> teaching us to rise from the ground, make short straightaway flights,
> circle, and land. After that he says it is all a matter of practice....

Spuds soon realized he was going to need months of practice
before he would feel at home aloft. He urged Chambers to encour-
age the Navy to buy him a practice machine, expecting to be
turned adrift about the first of March. Then he wrote that if the
Navy bought a plane, Curtiss would be glad "to keep me under his
wing and teach me eveything that he can which will be of immense
value to me and the Service if I am any good..."

Two weeks later he wrote:

> Up to the present I have only reached the stage where I can raise the
> machine a few feet from the ground and keep it in the air from ten to
> fifty feet. In this machine Mr. Curtiss so cut down the power that he
> himself could only fly the machine with difficulty, and the longest
> flight which he was able to make was two hundred and fifty feet at a
> height of about ten feet from the ground. Then feeling sure that we
> would not be able to rise high enough to do any serious injury, he turned
> the machine over to us. Today he told me that he would put on more
> power and fix the machine so that it would fly. If we have good weather
> he promises that he will have me flying inside of a week.

The day after Spuds wrote the above, the Lizzie snapped her crankshaft. Spuds's progress stopped. No one practiced for two weeks, until a new shaft arrived from the east. While they waited, Ellyson and Charles Witmer, the only students interested in the hydro, worked with Curtiss. Occasionally Curtiss carried one of them along on a test flight. Spuds's admiration for the inventor rose steadily. Curtiss never said, "Do this" or "Do that," but rather "What do you think of this change?" He was always ready to listen to anyone's ideas but generally convinced them that his way was best. Ellyson wanted to continue working with him and learning from him as long as the Navy would allow.

On the other hand, Curtiss had appreciated Ellyson's Navy education and experience from their first meeting. As they worked together, he grew to also value Spuds's suggestions, opinions, and friendship. He became anxious to carry the lieutenant's training beyond his originally promised minimums. Besides the fact that they got on well together, he realized that Ellyson's enthusiasm was his best advertisement in the Navy Department.

The Lizzie got her new shaft, the students resumed practice, and Ellyson detailed each day in the monthly report he sent to the Department. A typical entry:

> March 1st...Made four flights over half-mile course, average length of flights four hundred feet, average height six feet. Found that machine could be balanced to a greater or less degree by use of the rudder.

Captain Chambers read such entries and wrote, "Congratulations on the fine flights." To less air-minded Department personnel, such reports seemed confirmation that flying had no naval value. How could flying four hundred feet just above the wave tops help the fleet?

Then, on 5 March, Spuds wrote Mamma Ellyson:

> Today I made my first real flights. Of course I have jumped off the ground several times before but only for fifty or a hundred feet. Today I made four flights of about a mile and a half apiece over a straight course. I kept an average height of ten feet and never went higher than twenty-five feet. This was simply straight-away flying and Mr. Curtiss would not let us attempt to turn or go any higher, in fact the aeroplane did not have enough power to carry us any higher....

Spuds Ellyson, his cap turned around in the style of some of the flying showmen, before his first attempt at driving the Lizzie. In Glenn Curtiss's control system, the wheel steered with the vertical rudder on the tail. The pole going out of the picture to the right tilted the forward elevators at the same time that cables from the bottom of the control column tilted the after elevators. The tubular frame around Ellyson's shoulders moved the ailerons when the pilot swayed in the seat.

Ellyson reaching the stage where he could "raise the machine a few feet from the ground and keep it in the air from ten to fifty feet."

That day Curtiss confided to Ellyson that he had bought his Hammondsport factory, which had been in the hands of a receiver. He planned to close North Island on the first of April and go east. Spuds figured that if Lizzie kept running, the best he might do before the camp closed was "to become proficient in the four-cylinder machine." He wrote Chambers:

> Mr. Curtiss has asked me to go to Hammondsport with him in order that he could teach me to become proficient in handling first the eight-cylinder machine, then the hydroaeroplane, and then the *Triad.* It is not likely that any of the Army officers will go with him, as yet he has not asked any of them, but says he may offer to take one of them; I would very much like to do this, and honestly believe it would be the best thing to do, but will the Department stand for the expense? There is no doubt but that I will become a better flier by sticking to him for a while longer than I will become if I have to learn the rest alone. Again I do not imagine that the Department will have an aeroplane inside of three months at the very earliest, and what will I do in the meantime? I of course am writing you the personal side of the question, but would like to know your views at the earliest possible moment, and also your advice....

Except for short interludes, Ellyson had lived with contemporaries until he went to San Diego to learn flying. In Richmond, he'd lived at home with six brothers and sisters; afterwards, he'd shared quarters with messmates and classmates. Naturally gregarious, he missed such company as he flew with Curtiss. Glenn Curtiss, who was wonderful to work with, offered no companionship off the job. Ten years older than Spuds, thinking only of his inventions and disliking parties, he lived quietly with his wife, Lena, who was even quieter than the inventor. The two men never achieved an informal "Glenn" and "Spuds" status. They always remained "Mr. Curtiss" and "Lieutenant" to one another.

The night after they left San Francisco, when Spuds found he had no one to "talk Navy" with, he sat in his room at San Diego's U. S. Grant Hotel and wrote his first long, chatty letter to Captain Chambers.

Ellyson had asked for flight training, expecting to share the experience with Ken Whiting, and he still hoped that Ken might join him. On 13 January, Ken had been ordered to Newport News as prospective commanding officer of the *Seal.* Because he had read

Whiting's orders in a newspaper, sympathy as well as his own loneliness inspired Spuds's paragraph to Chambers:

> Two Army officers are ordered here for instruction; why not two naval officers? Whiting has volunteered and is a most excellent man; why not get him out here, if Mr. Curtiss is agreeable, and I am sure I can get his consent? I have been with Whiting practically ever since we entered the Naval Academy, and I think his record will show the sort of man he is.

After consulting the detail officer, Chambers penciled below this request, "A bit too slow; besides, his present work important." Then he wrote Ellyson that only one officer had been sent because Curtiss had invited only one. If Curtiss asked for another, the Department would send one—junior to Ellyson—right away, but Whiting "can't be spared from his duty on the *Seal* now as that is very important."

Civilians Robert St. Henry and Charlie Witmer and Army Lieutenants Paul W. Beck, John C. Walker, and G.E.M. Kelly joined the North Island school before Spuds set his proposition before Curtiss. The inventor replied that he had about all he could handle with six students already in the school. "With only one Lizzie, none of you are getting enough practice now," he said. Spuds let the request ride. He wanted more practice, not less.

A few days later, Curtiss apparently realized that only Ellyson and Witmer shared his interest in the hydro or were curious to learn how his machines were built. Maybe Navy men were more his type than Army officers. He said nothing to Ellyson but had his agent, Fanciulli, invite Chambers to send another naval officer to the North Island school.

Chambers wrote that Ensign Charles Pousland would be immediately ordered from the destroyer *Preble* to North Island. Ellyson, who always evaluated people quickly, made up his mind about his Army classmates. He answered:

> ...I hope that Pousland's orders read so that he will have to report to me. My reason for saying this is because the three Army officers who are here are not doing the amount of work which they should. None of them have any idea of engineering or desire to learn the practical side of the care of the machine, which in my opinion are the most important. Their one and only idea seems to be to learn to fly. If I have authority over Pousland he will keep the same hours that I do, and will go into

The military students of the first flight class at North Island, posed with their instructor in front of one of his planes. *Left to right:* Lieutenant T. G. Ellyson, USN; First Lieutenant Paul W. Beck, USA; Glenn Curtiss; Second Lieutenant G. E. M. Kelly, USA; Second Lieutenant John C. Walker, USA. The class also included two civilian students not shown in the picture: Charles Witmer and Robert St. Henry.

the detail work with the idea of learning the best way for the proper upkeep of the machine. I do not know him personally but understand that he is young, smart, and willing....

Chambers promised that Pousland would report to Ellyson as "soon as a relief can be found." The slate was tight. In several letters this promise was repeated, then dropped. Told to choose between airplanes and command of a destroyer, the ensign withdrew his aviation request and took the ship.

By that time, Ellyson did not care. The Lizzie was overworked, and Charlie Witmer was his pal. Charlie, the second student to arrive, shared a flat with Spuds in San Diego's St. Francis Apartments. The two men began flight training first and were the closest to Curtiss. After the class grew to six, Curtiss gave Ellyson and Witmer permission to start practice early. They began rising before daylight so as to arrive at the barn in time to start Lizzie at dawn; they had done two or three hours' work before the others arrived about nine. On 1 March, the two moved into a bungalow at 320 1st Street in Coronado. With a boat for transport to the island, they slept an extra hour and still got in their dawn patrol. Spuds found cooking and housework a lark. Although Charlie neither smoked nor drank, Spuds found him excellent company and knew he would miss him when they eventually separated.

About the time Curtiss recovered his factory, the hydro split its float and sank in shallow water. He wanted to finish training his students before leaving San Diego, so he rerigged the machine as an eight-cylinder landplane and promoted Ellyson, Witmer, and Beck to work with it. "This machine is heavier, and a lot more sensitive than Lizzie," Curtiss cautioned them. "Just take off and land on the first few runs."

This is what I've been living for, Spuds told himself. Flying's easy. The only problem with keeping the Lizzie up was that dinky motor. With fifty horses, it'll be a cinch.

He was the first student to roll the eight to the barn end of the runway and point it toward the center of the island. He tramped the throttle to the footrest and was climbing before he caught his breath. Pushing the wheel as if to level Lizzie made the eight-cylinder flyer dive. Yanking the wheel zoomed him up from the grass tops. Squeezing fingerprints into the wheel, overcontrolling so the plane bobbed like a cork in the surf, he flew halfway down the runway before he tried to get down.

Left to right: G. E. M. Kelly, Glenn Curtiss, Paul W. Beck, Spuds Ellyson, John C. Walker – all in assorted flying costumes. The tail of the eight-cylinder machine was disassembled when this picture was made.

Closing the throttle, he eased the wheel forward, but the nose dropped like a rock. The landing gear beat two quick thumps and flung the machine back into the air. Ten bounces used the rest of Curtiss's longest runway before Spuds stayed on the ground. He sat very still for a long moment before he wiggled cramped fingers and wiped his sweaty forehead with a shirt sleeve.

Curtiss was right, he conceded. It's a damned tricky crate. But I flew it, so what the hell? He stepped from the seat, lifted the nose around, then took off toward the barn. The return run was slightly smoother, ending with only three bounces. He had never made a turn in the air, but neither had some exhibition fliers, so he felt like a real aviator. "Nothing to it. It's swell," he said when he stepped out to let Witmer have his turn.

With only one set of controls, dual instruction was impracticable, but after Ellyson's air work smoothed a bit, Curtiss put him in the passenger's seat and showed him how turns should feel. It looked easy. The expert's smooth banks made turns feel just like straight flying. When Spuds soloed, however, the plane slipped and skidded close to disaster. His luck held. He did not crash, and his airwork smoothed out. He was circling wide around the island before he got word from Chambers that he would be ordered to Hammonds-port, via Washington, when the camp closed.

The move was the sort of special consideration Ellyson expected, and usually got, even before he became the number one flyer. He never wondered why Captain Chambers was so like a fairy god-father, why the Department heeded the wishes of a mere lieutenant. He saw no reason to thank anyone when he wrote on 22 March:

> ...I have reached the point where I think that I will learn to fly after
> more practice. Today I made flights at a height of from 150 to 300
> feet, turning the machine with the rudder hard over and the machine
> well banked up, and made several glides from heights varying from 100
> to 150 feet with the engine stopped. Some of the flights and glides
> were made when the wind was quite gusty and the flying rough, and
> Mr. Curtiss expressed the opinion that we were flying in a wind that a
> good many aviators would refuse to fly in even at meets. I am not
> getting the opinion that I know how to fly, but simply want you to
> know the progress that I am making. I am more anxious than ever to
> remain with Mr. Curtiss as long as possible, because he made a sugges-
> tion after every flight which showed me just where I did the wrong
> thing, or how I could have done it better....

Next day the crankshaft of the eight-cylinder machine snapped. Witmer glided to a landing without any further damage, but no spare shaft was available. To get them out of his hair while he closed the camp, Curtiss sent the pair to a San Bernardino air meet with Hugh Robinson, telling them, "It will give you experience in unpacking and setting up the machine in the least possible time."

They had fun in San Bernardino, but Spuds was unimpressed by the three-man crew which took four hours to set up and repair Robinson's plane. He told Chambers he could train a six-man crew to do it in an hour and a half. Even that was too slow for the captain, who wanted a machine that could come out of a hold and be rigged on a cruiser's deck whenever a flight was needed.

After San Bernardino, Witmer left to fly for the Curtiss Exhibition Company. Lonely again, Spuds decided he would make it his urgent business in Washington to obtain a second Navy flier. On the last day of March, he addressed this report to the Secretary of the Navy:

> In obedience to the Department's order No. 5021-42 of December 23, 1910, I report that in my opinion, and that of Mr. Curtiss, I have qualified to fly a standard eight-cylinder Curtiss biplane under favorable weather conditions, but more practice must be had before I will be capable of flying in strong winds, making ascents in limited space, or landing on a designated spot. I have had no practice in flying the hydro-aeroplane.

He paraphrased this report in a personal letter to Captain Chambers, saying that he had delayed the report because he continued to learn something more on every flight, and explained:

> Since the Army officers who were under instruction here have all been ordered to San Antonio, for actual war maneuvers according to the newspapers, I have been worrying for fear that the Department would think that I was not making good on the job out here. In this connection, and I feel sure that Mr. Curtiss will verify what I say, when the Navy Department purchases their machine or machines, they will not find it necessary to call on Mr. Curtiss to send an aviator and mechanicians to their aerodrome in order to set up the machine and keep an eye on the Navy aviators, as has been the case at San Antonio.

Curtiss confirmed Ellyson's qualifications in a letter of his own. The two men broke their trip east for an air meet at Salt Lake City from April 4 to 10. At that time accounts of air meets were highly colored by the sympathies of each reporter. *Flying* magazine called this one "a successful exhibition" and credited Curtiss with "three flights a day in the hydro." Clippings from local papers, which Mabel Ely pasted in her scrapbook, showed that the local reporters were charmed by Ely's flying and disillusioned with the hydro. They called it a fake; they wrote that Curtiss could not get it off the lake. Ellyson told Chambers the machine seemed underpowered at that altitude, which made the captain want more horsepower in the first Navy plane. He wanted more power than Curtiss had ever built into any engine.

Almost from the day Ellyson reported to Curtiss at Los Angeles, his comments influenced Chambers's specifications for the early planes. Spuds's nature was to form strong opinions quickly and to fight for them. He knew his aviation experience was very small, but who in the Navy had more? And, if he were expected to fly the machines, should he not be heard?

Captain Chambers was also a man of positive ideas, but he realized he was working entirely from theory, so he listened to Ellyson's voice of meager experience. Spuds's experience was limited by the cut-and-try methods he learned from Curtiss, bound by what he thought the inventor could build and by the day-to-day nuts-and-bolts troubles he observed.

The captain, with impracticable but broader vision, saw flying as similar to steering a boat or riding a bicycle. He thought of a scout plane as a high crow's nest. The periodicals he read seldom distinguished between real accomplishments and crackpot proposals. Only a few fliers sensed a relationship between power, weight, and wing area. For example, nonflying scientists praised Chambers's design for an auto pilot, too heavy for anything but a steamship. But, even before the first hydro flew, Chambers wrote Ellyson that the first Navy plane had to be a hydro that could develop into an all-purpose Navy amphibian. He wanted all training done in hydros, so naval air would need no shore facilities.

Spuds was wedded to Curtiss's training system even before his own training was well underway. He argued that a man should learn to fly a "standard machine" before trying a hydro or any other special Navy-type plane. Before the standard, the flier needed experience in a low-powered Lizzie. "If I had been in an eight-cylinder machine with plenty of power the day I left the ground at the polo grounds in Coronado, there would have been a serious accident," he said in mid-February.

Both Chambers and Ellyson made judgment errors because of limited knowledge. As long as they listened to each other, their varied viewpoints minimized mistakes. In April 1911, when they met in Washington, they agreed to order two planes—a Lizzie, and a high-powered, two-man machine that could be rigged alternately as a landplane, hydro, or Triad. Chambers would write very broad general specifications. Ellyson, as inspector, would authorize all practical improvements during the building of the planes.

From the day Ellyson arrived in San Francisco with Curtiss, newspapers and aviation periodicals mentioned him frequently as "*the* Navy flier." Articles about Curtiss's school, advance air-meet publicity, and reports of meets at San Bernardino and Salt Lake City all built the Ellyson legend. Thereafter, the governor of Idaho asked the Secretary of the Navy to send "the Navy flier" to air meets in his state. Secretary Meyer refused. For most of 1911, the press headlined the activities of "Lieutenant Ellyson, the Navy flier." The reason for this unique reference is not apparent since Navy Lieutenant John Rodgers began training at the Wright brothers' flight school in Dayton, Ohio, in March.

The press had made Ellyson a celebrity before he reached Washington in April. Captain Chambers helped the build-up, to further his designs for a naval air service. Spuds began to see a long, bright future ahead as senior aviator. In the State, War, and Navy Building, beside the White House, Chambers showed Ellyson off to the friends of aviation, sent him to convert others. To the detail officer, Spuds said, "The Navy's buying two Curtiss planes; it needs a pilot for each of them."

Agreeing, the detail officer exhumed the old flight training request of Lieutenant junior grade John Henry Towers. "He's the *Michigan*'s fire-control officer. She's in Europe, but I'll get Towers back and send him to Hammondsport for you to train," he promised.

[CHAPTER TEN]

Hammondsport:

Testing

*O*n the first of May, at Hammondsport, Spuds found Curtiss still reorganizing his factory beside Lake Keuka. The promised hydro was not ready. Itching to fly it, to get Navy planes and a Navy student, Spuds puttered for three days, then wrote:

> ...I hope the order for our two planes will be placed at once and as soon as it is, he [Curtiss] will start work immediately....About Towers, he [Curtiss] says get him up here whenever I can and I can start training him immediately....

A week later, having no plane order, hydro, nor Towers, Ellyson went with Curtiss to a Bridgeport air meet, wiring Chambers from New York City:

> WILL GO TO BRIDGEPORT TOMORROW WITH CURTISS RE-QUEST ORDERS IF ADVISABLE ADDRESS HERE HOTEL CUMBERLAND

Back in Hammondsport on the fifteenth, he sent Chambers a wordy report on the meet, details of planes he had inspected at Mineola (including an all-metal one), and Lieutenant Beck's letter to Curtiss about the fatal accident of G.E.M. Kelly at San Antonio.

Spuds discussed the technical aspects of this crash, ruling out materiel failure; he expressed no personal feelings about the death of his fellow student.

The new hydro waiting on the ramp was the current focus of his interest. Impatiently, he waited for Curtiss to balance it. During assembly, the factory suspended a plane with a man in the seat and balanced it statically. Then, after each test flight, mechanics moved the engine, pilot's seat, or the float until the balance in the air suited the test pilot. Curtiss spent two days making these adjustments on the new hydro, then said, "It was nearly right that time, Lieutenant. One more check and I'll take you up."

The pontoon had developed a small leak, but its repair could wait until the next day. Spuds helped drain the float and launch the machine. He stood watching, with John Cooper, as Curtiss lifted from the lake and circled for five minutes. The two men heard the engine slow, saw the nose dip into a landing glide. They watched to see it flatten out close to the water; instead, the nose dropped farther. The machine dove into the lake, flipping onto its back. Flung from his seat, Curtiss crashed through the forward control surfaces and splashed fifty feet in front of the wreck.

The watchers dashed into the shallow water. Before they reached Curtiss, he limped toward them. Ashore, wiping blood from the gash above his right eye, he said, "The forward controls did that. I'll put them down on the float when we rebuild it."

Curtiss had been unable to lift the nose after water ran forward in the float, so he put in watertight bulkheads when he rebuilt. Thus the crash brought progress, by the fix-and-try system, while it delayed Ellyson's hydro instruction.

Spuds talked Curtiss into beginning the manufacture of parts for the Navy planes while they waited for the order. He learned to drive Curtiss's automobile, instructed Curtiss's three new students, and overworked the word "immediate" in daily letters to Chambers urging more speed on the requisitions and the orders to transfer Towers, "so he can catch up with the class."

"These people are as crazy to learn as I was at the start," he wrote before his mania for early rising chilled their enthusiasm. A few days later, he opined, "They have not had much practice. Towers can easily catch up." Four days later, his letter read:

> All this crowd is pretty lazy though, and only once have they been up
> before seven o'clock and they miss the best part of the day for flying
> which is between daylight and seven. As soon as he [Towers] gets up

Glenn Curtiss and Spuds Ellyson in a Triad at Hammondsport. After Curtiss's crash at Hammondsport, he moved the forward control surfaces down onto the float "out of a man's way when he gets tossed," as shown above.

here we will start in work at daylight every morning and I hope I will
have him flying as well or better than they do in a very short time,
for he is a hard worker and I believe he will pick up the game very
quickly.

Towers reached Hammondsport on 26 or 27 June and moved
into the boardinghouse where Spuds lived. Four months earlier,
Ellyson had written:

A man should become thoroughly familiar with the machine before he
even makes any attempt to make runs on the ground...should be made
to work around the machine in the capacity of a regular mechanic...then
should be allowed to run over the ground in a machine that cannot possibly fly....

He planned to follow such a program when he had students of his
own. If he remembered this conservative plan in June, he found
several excuses for an exception. Maybe he believed his own prop-
aganda that two planes needed two pilots even if one plane was
only a Lizzie. The Navy planes were assembled, waiting for their
engines to come off the test block. Spuds expected to move them
to Annapolis as soon as they were flight-tested. Until that move he
could train Jack in Curtiss's Lizzie and profit by the inventor's advice about his first student.

At first light, the morning after Jack reported, the two were at
Curtiss's hangar in a corner of the little pasture that served as a
flying field. Pushing aside several odd relics, Spuds pulled out a
thirty-horsepower Lizzie that any three men could have carried.
As he moved, he did all the talking, telling wide-eyed Towers how
the various machines were supposed to work. He fished a jackknife
from his pocket, picked up a piece of wood, and whittled as he
continued the monologue. He fitted the whittling under the Lizzie's
throttle and started the engine. "I'll try it first," he said, as he
flopped into the seat. He taxied down the pasture to the lakeshore.

Driving back, he stepped from the low seat and left the engine
idling. "That block fixed it so you can't take off. Get aboard and
try it. Steer it down to the lake, lift the front wheel around, and
steer back here," he told Towers.

For the first time, Towers understood that Ellyson, not Curtiss,
was to be his teacher. He had never even sat in a plane, but was
too in awe of "the Navy aviator" to question his orders. Gingerly

he settled into the seat, grasped the wheel, and gave it a tentative twist. Scared to go, more scared to disobey, he pushed the throttle wide open.

Ellyson had made no allowance in blocking the throttle for the fact that he was twenty pounds heavier than Towers. Halfway to the lake, the plane leaped twenty feet into the air, stalled, fell off on a wing, and cartwheeled into a ball of broken sticks and wires.

"My God. I waited till the second time before I did that," Spuds told himself as he ran toward the crash. Jack crawled out of the mess—scratched, bruised, dirty, and dragging a broken foot.

Ellyson and Curtiss planned to flight-test the A-1, the Navy's first plane, on 1 July, the first day money became available for naval aviation. When Captain Chambers arrived for the occasion, the new machine glistened in the sun beside the factory. Spuds explained they had installed a borrowed fifty-horsepower engine in it for the occasion because the A-1's larger one was being rerun on the test stand after several failures. No one guessed how many more times it would fail.

Curtiss asked the officers to pose with him in front of the A-1 for photographs to commemorate the historic occasion.

"Ditch your crutches in the grass where they won't show," Spuds told Jack Towers when he saw Curtiss frowning at the sticks. "Don't want anyone to think they might get hurt in one of Mr. Curtiss's machines."

Charlie Witmer, who was in Hammondsport for a plane overhaul, muttered something about Spuds's Coronado performance as he manned the camera and snapped the picture.

In the sunset calm, Curtiss lifted the A-1 from the glassy water to circle the lake. Chambers was delighted; Ellyson was impatient. When Curtiss beached, Ellyson took the passenger's seat, and the inventor took off again, then stepped ashore after that hop. Ellyson, preparing to solo, announced he would now fly for his license. He had put off the test so the Navy's first aviator could qualify in the Navy's first plane.

Climbing to the prescribed altitude, Spuds made the required figure eights around the pylons, glided to land alongside a marker, took off, and repeated the performance. Perfect. "Nothing to it," he told himself as he taxied to the beach.

Doctor Zahm, the official Aero Club of America observer, deflated him, saying, "Sorry, Lieutenant. I can't certify you for a license on those landings. Your engine must be stopped before you touch down."

Spuds's face flushed. "This is a hell of a time to say that. Why didn't you tell me before? You said stop beside the marker. I did. You never said I should kill the engine."

Spuds's face got redder, his voice louder, as the scientist insisted that a dead engine was the rule. Zahm may have felt an explosion coming. "Possibly my instructions were unclear on that point," he conceded. "Let's try it again in the morning. The light's too far gone now."

"At daylight, then," Spuds said, his ears still red.

In the morning after Spuds satisfied the observer, Curtiss took the plane to give Captain Chambers his first flight. Later in the day, Chambers agreed that the two Navy fliers should accept Curtiss's invitation and operate at his factory until the machines were operating perfectly and Navy facilities were ready at Annapolis. "We will learn a lot just being near Curtiss," Spuds said. "And the doc says Jack can begin training again in a couple of weeks."

On the following morning, Ellyson told Chambers not to take the noon boat up the lake. "I can fly you to Penn Yan after supper, in plenty of time for your train. It's only twenty-two miles up the lake." The old man was easy to convince. He had liked his ride with Curtiss and looked forward to going back to Washington to tell of the Navy plane and pilot that flew him to the train.

Nobody considered that Chambers was bigger than Curtiss and that Ellyson was heavier still. When the two tried to take off in the still evening air, the borrowed engine was too weak to lift them in the heavy machine. Spuds ran it wide open until the radiator boiled and the engine smoked, but he couldn't pull the plane into the air. On the beach he found a can and refilled the radiator, then tried again. The plane was still on the water when they reached Penn Yan in time for Chambers's train.

Minus his passenger, Spuds took off easily for the return flight. Fifteen minutes into the flight, he felt the engine labor and slow, and he sniffed hot oil and metal. He nosed over and landed. The light was failing when he beached at the town of Keuka. He spent an hour buying oil and filling the radiator, then took off into the starlight.

In the soft, warm, smooth air he felt as though he were drifting effortlessly through a fairyland, detached from the world and its cares. Flying seemed much easier at night than it ever had in sunlight—until he glided in to land on the black lake beside the dark factory.

He thought he was still some thirty feet in the air when the nose

Demonstration of the Navy's first plane (the A-1) on 1 July 1911. Glenn Curtiss, who tried to make a photographic record of everything he devised and of everybody he had any connection with, asked these people to pose with the machine. *Left to right:* Charlie Witmer; John Cooper; Dr. A. H. Zahm; McClaskey; Jim Lamotte, a Curtiss employee; Curtiss; Spuds Ellyson; Captain W. I. Chambers; John Towers; Moore; unidentified.

of his pontoon slapped the water, jarring his spine and sending the machine rocketing toward the stars. He opened the throttle, leveled off, circled, glided again. Another bone-shaking bounce. Again he put on power and leveled off, looking around for some reference point to help him find the level of that deceptively black mirror, the lake. Finding no lights near enough to be of help, he decided to feel for the surface. Holding the nose up very slightly, he eased the throttle until he felt the machine settling. Slowly he went down into the blackness. The factory was far behind when the heel of the float kissed the water. He snatched the throttle back and breathed easy again when the machine coasted to a stop without bouncing. Spuds had just invented the power stall landing.

Next afternoon a wire from mechanic George Hallet reported that Witmer was in Pittsfield's House of Mercy Hospital after a crash had broken nearly everything but his spirit. With a friend in trouble, Ellyson did not stop to consider regulations nor to ask for permission. He took off, with Curtiss, to help. As he left town, he wired Chambers:

WOULD IT BE POSSIBLE FOR ME TO GET LEAVE FROM JULY FIFTEENTH TO TWENTY FIFTH AND FLY HYDROPLANE NOW IN THE WEST FOR CURTISS AT SEATTLE WASH WITMER WAS TO FILL DATE BUT WAS HURT TODAY AND NO ONE ELSE HAS FLOWN HYDRO OUR MACHINES WILL BE COMPLETED WITH ALL TESTS BY THE TENTH WILL ACCEPT ONLY EXPENSES WILL NOT REQUEST LEAVE IF YOU HAVE ANY OBJECTIONS OR IF YOU THINK IT BAD POLICY

Though Ellyson's actions underlined the loyalty he felt for friends, the wire also revealed another facet of his nature—he was a ham who wanted to fly the test. That impulse was partly inspired by his desire to help Curtiss out of a jam. Afterwards he explained to Chambers that he went to Pittsfield because Witmer "is a particular friend of mine and I thought that I would run the risk of taking a day off without permission."

In that same letter, he reported the accident in detail and opined it was "due to atmospheric conditions." If he was aware of Hallet's statement that the crash was due to the plane's not being properly balanced after the factory overhaul, Spuds's loyalty to Curtiss kept him from mentioning it.

When he got back from Pittsfield, the Navy's big engine was still on the test block. Again and again, it would run for twelve minutes;

Captain W. J. Chambers and Spuds Ellyson in the A-1 as they prepared to attempt a flight from Hammondsport to Penn Yan.

then fouled plugs would make it stutter and shimmy. Spuds became the serious researcher, glad he had not gone to Seattle.

Jack Towers discarded his crutches ahead of schedule and suggested he begin again to learn to fly. Spuds watched him limp on his stiff right ankle and for once curbed his own impatience. "We'll wait until it's all well," he said—and waited two whole days. By that time Jack convinced him that toeing a throttle was easier on the foot than walking. The big engine was ready in the A-1, so Jack ran Curtiss's Lizzie, and Spuds drove his dream boat.

The afternoon mail brought Jack orders to Washington for promotion examinations. "Just when I'm getting going," he complained.

"I'll fix that," Spuds said, and telegraphed a request for delay until 1 August. "This will enable ten days of practice and save wear and tear on our machines...." He expected that they would be shipping the planes to Annapolis by 1 August and that Towers could learn in Curtiss's machines in the meantime. He put another optimistic, quick judgment into a letter on 11 July: "The engine is a wonder." He stuck to this opinion through weeks of failures.

On 13 July, Curtiss and Ellyson each flew the A-2, the Navy's Lizzie, for three minutes. Then Spuds asked the Department's permission to accept the two planes. He reported forty-one flights in the A-1, totaling nine and one-half hours, during which all rigs were tested. Since the A-2 was identical except for power, he felt justified in saying, "The machines have passed all tests." Next day the big engine was back in the shop with melted bearings. Spuds passed lightly over that fact in his evening letter to the captain and boasted about his student's progress. Jack was making hops the length of the field; he practiced early and late, working with Spuds on the A-1 in between.

While the bearings were being rebabbitted, Spuds decided to shift the A-1 onto its landplane gear. "We can get a lot more work done if we don't have to beach it after each hop," he said. Jack reminded him that from the tiny field it could take off only toward the lake and that it often did not fly long enough to get back over the land.

"We'll put on some emergency floats, like Ely had," Spuds said. "Let's try them on the four first." That day, Jack had logged twenty one-minute flights in the A-2. They fastened a cylindrical tin float under each of its wing roots and a splashboard, like a small water ski, on the front landing gear. Spuds took it off the field and two minutes later made a landing in the lake to test the floats.

The splashboard flew off. The machine dove. Spuds slammed

into the wheel, breaking its bamboo pushrod. When he straightened up, he was sitting up to his neck in the lake with the plane's tail high behind him. Damage was minor. The machine was fished out, and Spuds flew it twice more before sunset for one-minute hops.

Three days later, he put on a new splashboard with better bracing and put the machine into the lake again. The board held, and "the machine floated in a horizontal position as soon as the operator left his seat." "I'll put the same setup in the A-1," Spuds said.

Towers went back to practicing in one of Curtiss's planes, for the A-2s performance was discouraging. Spuds had had Curtiss make its parts interchangeable with the A-1s, so that it was too heavy for its little four-cylinder engine. Even Curtiss could not get it above twenty-five feet or keep it in the air for more than three minutes. He offered to put an eight-cylinder engine in at no extra cost, for he wanted the Navy to be satisfied with his work. Spuds put him off. The machine was built the way he had ordered it. It was the Lizzie he had advocated all spring. He did not want to admit he was wrong. "It is simply a case of the engine being improperly adjusted," he wrote in late August, hoping he was correct.

Ellyson had neither accepted nor rejected Curtiss's offer when Chambers wired orders sending him to Chicago for "the purpose of observing the characteristics of the various aeroplanes, aeroplane motors, and the aerial observing instruments, foreign and domestic, in use at the Aviation Tournament...on August 12 to 20." Spuds promptly wired for permission to take Towers, at Tower's expense. No answer came by train time. "You go anyway, on my responsibility," he told Jack. "No sense staying here. You couldn't do anything with everyone else away."

In his six months of aviation, Spuds had been on stage with the stars at a dozen or more small air meets. Chicago was the big show of the year. This time he went as a recognized pro, with Aero Club of America license number twenty-eight in his pocket. Meets were aviation's big business—the payoff. Ely, for instance, had grossed more at some meets than Congress had voted for a year of naval aviation. Spuds was ham enough to enjoy being on stage, but he wished the Navy would let him enter some of the events. His flying could win the Navy some good publicity and put some of the prize money in his empty pockets. His orders said "observe," and he knew others had been refused permission to enter competitions. So he merely observed without making any earthshaking discoveries. After the third day, he left Chicago because Hammondsport wired that his big engine was ready for a retest.

Spuds Ellyson and Jack Towers in the A-1, rigged as a landplane, with one of the emergency floats showing under the wing at the left. One foot throttle shows clearly under Ellyson's right foot. Note the throw-over wheel, which allowed either man to fly.

A week later he sent Chambers four pages of comments on the accidents at Chicago. "Stone's accident...due poor handling... Johnstone...started directly for trees...Coffyn was trying to land.... Martin landed at the wrong end of the field....Hammond...three miles out in the lake....Simon...in the lake....McCurdy...struck high-tension wires....Johnstone...wings folded....Badger...the machine seemed to fly all to pieces...." His only mention of successful flying was a paragraph of praise for Beachey's daring stunts. The remainder of his letter concerned his activities after the meet, including the fact that the big engine needed new cylinders.

A couple of days after writing that letter, Spuds judged Towers ready to solo the big machine, but the engine sounded suspicious. Five solo hops reassured Spuds. "Come on, Jack," he said. "We'll go around once together, then you can take it alone."

The engine lost power as Spuds lifted the machine into the air at the end of the little field. He flew straight ahead, fighting for enough altitude to turn around. Some two miles from the factory, he dropped a wing and started to turn. The engine stopped cold. As he glided toward the water, he remembered how the A-2 had floated level on the tin cans after he was out of the seat. "She'll stop suddenly," he yelled to Jack. "Hang on, then dive clear as soon as we land."

When they touched the water, the plane stopped even more quickly than the A-2 had done the first time. The splashboard shattered; the plane flipped onto its back and carried both men down with it.

> We both reached the surface in about ten seconds and found the machine floating upside down. Neither of us were hurt in the least. We could not right the machine until a motorboat came to our aid, and then we had to sit on the tail bamboos in the water to keep her from capsizing. We were in the water for two and a half hours while towing the machine ashore, but some kind friend brought us a pint of whiskey so we did not freeze nor have either of us any ill effects from the ducking.

Towers later told how they reached shore stiff with cold, and men propped them up beside a small fire. After a good pull on the pint, Spuds's knees folded, and he fell flat on his face in the fire.

That summer most landings were forced landings. After 21 July, troubles came too fast for Ellyson's notebook. At the end of August he wrote:

> No record was kept between the above dates because the engine failed
> in so many respects that it had to be rebuilt. All breakages to engine
> and machine while experimenting or practicing were repaired or re-
> placed by the Curtiss Co., without charge to the government....

He then filled three pages of the plane log with a summary of the
major failures.

By September Hammondsport's fall weather was interrupting
flying. Chambers had told Ellyson to move to Annapolis at his discretion, but Spuds hung on hoping each day would solve his engine problems and let him finish an experiment they had been preparing all summer. The breaks went against him. On 2 September,
he wired:

> USING POOR JUDGMENT MADE FLIGHTS TODAY IN TWENTY
> FIVE MILE WIND AND ROUGH WATER   IN SIXTH FLIGHT
> WHILE ATTEMPTING TO TURN ON THE WATER PROPELLOR
> BROKE BREAKING TAIL BAMBOO COMA ENGINE BEDS AND
> CONTROL WIRES WILL COMPLETE REPAIRS MONDAY
> WEATHER NOT SUITABLE FOR EXPERIMENT BROKE BOAT
> BY POUNDING ON THE WAVES

While the A-1 was being fixed, Ellyson borrowed an eight-
cylinder engine for the A-2. Towers used it to win his license from
the Aero Club of America, and Spuds boasted of his student's ability.

The day after Jack qualified, Spuds flew the A-1 for half an
hour, then sensed something wrong. He cut the engine, landed on
the field. When he tried to restart the engine, it clanked like a can
full of rocks. A sheared bolt had mangled most of its insides.
Spuds said this was "pretty disheartening," but he still had "the
greatest faith in the engine."

After a period of indecision, Ellyson sent Towers, their two recently acquired mechanics, and the two planes to Annapolis. The
A-2 went with its small engine, although by that time Ellyson
thought it would "be useless to us at Annapolis" because of its
low power.

Ellyson himself waited to see A-1s engine rebuilt. To fill time,
and his purse, he flew a borrowed plane at an Ithaca air meet and
unofficially asked Chambers about leave to enter a Brooklyn show
with a rented plane. Chambers answered:

APPLY FOR LEAVE TO OCTOBER FIRST DONT SAY WHAT
FOR OK I THINK

Spuds wired his request and headed for New York. Then remembering that Richmond papers reported air meets in considerable detail, he thought of Mamma. Never do to let her hear of his stunts first from the press, he decided, and wired her:

MY ADDRESS TILL OCTOBER FIRST BRESLIN HOTEL AM
FLYING EVERY DAY IN MEET AT NASSAU BOULEVARD
WON CROSS COUNTRY RACES SATURDAY AND AGAIN
TODAY AGAINST SEVEN COMPETITORS AM ON LEAVE
AND FLYING AS AN INDIVIDUAL WILL BE CAREFUL

CHAPTER ELEVEN

Aviation Camp at Annapolis:

Airplanes in a Cornfield

*I*n 1911, air-meet promoters posted large cash prizes to attract big name fliers who would draw rich gates. At Nassau Boulevard, Spuds Ellyson—the Navy flier—enjoyed evening drinking and bull sessions with fliers like Gene Ely and Harriet Quimby, the first woman licensed as a pilot and the first woman to fly the English channel. But, like all the others, Spuds was at the meet primarily for the cash he could use to meet his current and past summer's expenses.

Sizing up his competition, he picked the daily cross-country events as his best chance for gain and frittered away no engine time on long shots. This strategy won him $700, which was less than Army fliers Thomas D. Millings, Paul Beck, or Hap Arnold collected. They in turn were outpriced by the Englishmen, T.O.M. Sopwith and Graham White. Spuds felt comfortably solvent on 4 October when he reached Annapolis.

Jack Towers had a room waiting for him in Carvel Hall and told him, "Both planes are set up and running. I've flown the A-1; it's fine as a hydro. Tuned up the A-2, but the field's too small to fly it with this engine."

Spuds tossed his bag into the room, then walked with Jack down Maryland Avenue to the Academy boat landing to board the motor launch Jack had obtained to ferry aviators over the Severn River. Its engine was an extra-stubborn specimen of an ornery breed. Mechanics Percie Coffey and Duffy spelled each other in yanking the starting rope wound on its flywheel. Jack watched them glumly. "Got this boat only because nobody else wanted it," he said. "Old Captain Gibbons, the sup, doesn't like aeroplanes or aviators." Twelve minutes of rope yanking got the motor running irregularly. "Started easier than usual," Jack said as they headed for the Experiment Station.

There Ellyson reported "for duty in connecion with the test of gasoline engines and experimental work in development of aviation...." The officer-in-charge, Captain Thomas Wright Kinkaid, had offered Towers office space and asked for a weekly aviation report he could send to Washington. A pleasant man, he was more interested in aviation than Superintendent John Henry Gibbons, but just as ignorant of it, and he had problems of his own.

Having made their manners, the fliers boated along the Severn's north shore past the rifle-range dock to the little beach near a three-bay hangar and the aviation field. Spuds was surprised at how small the field looked when cleared of the cornstalks that had covered it in April when he and Chambers had chosen the site.

In early summer, field work had lagged, and Chambers had suggested operating temporarily with the Army fliers at College Park. Similar training, service opposition, and mechanical troubles were forging interservice friendships among fliers, but Ellyson turned down joint operations. College Park was always in the papers. It was visited by too many reporters who were ready to stir up Army-Navy competition to make news. Spuds usually enjoyed competition but not while he was developing the Navy-type airplane Chambers wanted. Spuds saw the task as months of cut-and-try, such as Curtiss had put into the Triad. For such a job he wanted an isolated place like North Island, insulated by a bay and without distracting competitions.

No highways reached the Greenbury Point campsite; the Severn River shut off unhelpful visitors. In July Spuds was glad that Curtiss's hospitality had allowed him to wait for the site. Then Chambers's letters made him wonder if Washington realized they had to do more than rake the old stalks to make a flying field of a cornfield. "Take a look at it while you're down there," he said as Jack started for Washington and his promotion examination.

Towers's report made Ellyson jump a train for Washington. After choosing the site for the hangar, he convinced Chambers the place needed smoothing and rolling. He was back in Hammondsport two nights later.

In October, after experience with the A-1, he thought the field disgustingly dinky, but he was stuck with it. The hangar held the Navy-Wright plane. Its pilot, Lieutenant John ("Jang") Rodgers, had left it in care of Electrician, first class, Dale Sigler while he helped a civilian cousin fly across the continent. When Towers arrived, Sigler was glad to have company and helped with the Curtiss machines.

The Wright machine and its pilot complicated the status question within naval aviation as soon as the Wrights began teaching Jang Rodgers to fly. Commissioned two years ahead of Ellyson, Rodgers was ordered to naval aviation three months after Ellyson; he had won his ACA license two months later than Spuds. Until he died, Ellyson insisted that his earlier qualification made him the senior naval aviator. He, and others, held that commission dates should determine seniority only in nonaviation affairs. In air matters, the qualification date should rule. Rodgers neither agreed nor forced the issue. As long as they both flew, this unresolved question divided naval aviation.

Though the Navy was never directly involved in them, the Curtiss-Wright patent suits widened this split. The Wrights sued Curtiss for patent infringement soon after he began flying and continued to hamper aviation development until, during World War I, the government forced the Wrights to accept a cross-licensing agreement. Early in that contest, the Wrights developed a personal hatred of Curtiss that splashed over onto everyone remotely connected with him. At the Chicago meet, for example, they threatened to fire Frank Coffyn, one of their best pilots, because he gave Towers a ride in spite of the fact that he knew him to be a Curtiss student. This feeling restricted Rodgers and the other Navy fliers to casual contact at Chicago and led Chambers to operate the two types in separate camps until after Rodgers left aviation for ship duty in 1912.

During his first Wednesday at the hangar by the Severn, Ellyson heard several "pzing pfts." He asked what made the noise. "Ricochets from the rifle range," Jack answered. "Somebody put this hangar right in the line of fire, behind the butts." Spuds wondered if they were dangerous. "Before we got here," Jack said, "Somebody told Sigler they were harmless. He chalks where they hit."

"I've found over thirty," Sigler volunteered. "All high under the eaves. They hit only on Wednesdays and Friday afternoons when the midshipmen are shooting."

After that, the pzing-pfts were ignored until the Friday Percie Coffey dropped his wrench and yelled, "Jesus! I felt that one's whiskers." They had all heard it. Along the rear wall, Sigler found chest-high, freshly splintered holes in the planks and the storeroom door.

"That kind's not harmless," Jack said.

"Knock off and get out of here," Ellyson ordered. Next morning they found bullet holes in the A-1's wing. "From now on, everyone will leave the field whenever midshipmen are firing," Spuds decreed.

En route to Annapolis, Ellyson had convinced Captain Chambers that he should fly the A-1 from Annapolis to Fortress Monroe "to determine and eradicate the weak points in the machine, to determine the physical strain caused by a long trip, and to thoroughly test the shift controls." Unofficially he also wanted to set a hydro distance record and show the rest of the Navy what his machine could do. "The captain promised me orders but said we didn't have to wait for them," he told Jack. "We'll get going as soon as we can." Four days later he wired his mother:

TOWERS AND I WILL START FLIGHT TO OLD POINT TOMORROW IF WEATHER IS FAVORABLE TORPEDO BOAT WILL FOLLOW ALL OVER WATER WILL WIRE

He did not want the newspapers to give Mamma the first word. They got off three and a half days late, landed twice to secure parts that shook loose, then ended the trip seventy-nine miles south of Annapolis where the engine's bearings all melted. The torpedo boat *Bailey* found them sitting in the dark between the machine and a fire they had built on the beach and returned them to the Experiment Station.

Ellyson expressed the engine to Curtiss for rebuilding. Junking it, Curtiss sent a replacement. He knew when he was licked. In the interval, the fliers put an eight-cylinder engine into the A-2. One eight-minute flight convinced Spuds the field was too small for even an eight-cylinder machine. He pushed the plane into the hangar's middle bay where it finished the year as a source of spare parts.

In spite of previous hard use, the replacement engine flew satisfactorily on Jack's first test flight, but the wind buried a wing and broke it when he turned after landing. Repairing it overnight, Jack and Spuds took off again; this time, a wave shattered the propellor after Spuds landed.

They had been trying for Fort Monroe for three weeks when that was fixed. On 25 October, a cold north wind slapped spray into the boat while its crew struggled with the starting rope. Near noon, when they got A-1's engine roaring, the wind was stronger— the sort of weather that had twice wrecked them after air tests. Why take a chance on doing it again? Spuds scribbled on a paper and handed it to Coffey. "Go over to the Academy and wire this to Captain Chambers, if we get off and head down the bay," he said. Coffey looked at the message.

HAVE STARTED TRIAL FLIGHT IF WEATHER FAVORABLE
WILL PROCEED OLD POINT ELLYSON

Spuds headed into the wind in the lee of Greenbury Point and opened the throttle. The wind took them nearly straight up. He turned south over Chesapeake Bay's blanket of whitecaps. For two hours the wind booted them along faster than they had ever traveled before. The air was as rough as the bay. Arms began to ache after a few minutes of fighting the controls to keep the machine right-side-up, headed in a southerly direction. Every ten minutes they threw over the wheel and swapped the job. Several times, while Spuds flew, Jack disconnected his shoulder yoke, knelt on his seat, and reached back to tighten leaky water connections. In spite of his work, the engine boiled its last water out and put them down some 112 miles south of the Severn.

For two hours they patched, then got into the air for another twenty-five minutes. Fort Monroe was in sight, six miles ahead, when the engine quit and dropped them into rough water. The pontoon split as Spuds drove the sputtering machine through a six-foot surf to the beach. He wired Chambers:

ARRIVED BUCKROE BEACH SAFELY WATER GROUNDED
MAGNETO

At the same time he wired for two mechanics to bring a new float and spare radiator. Before these arrived, temporary repairs let

Jack snatch the lightened plane into the air inside the surf and solo it to the fort.

Ellyson spent the next three days changing his mind. They set up the machine when the parts came, but poor gasoline prevented a takeoff. When they got better gas, the weather had soured; a long storm was forecast. Spuds dismantled the machine, sent Towers and the men to Annapolis, and asked the superintendent to send the Academy tug for the plane.

Captain Gibbons, who disliked planes and pilots, remembered that Ellyson's orders said, "...without the assistance of tugs or boats, if possible." He decided to let the fliers sweat it out. Spuds was still waiting for an answer when the weather cleared. He recalled Jack, set up the plane, and took off.

The trip south had won the good publicity he wanted. He was thankful that aviation publications ignored his return trip—a grim sequence of forced landings and foul weather that proved little except the ingenuity and persistence of the two fliers. Years later, when he was a retired admiral, Towers summed up the flight:

> We came back in a week. We forged and machined four water-pump shafts. I don't know how many times we soldered the radiator. We lived in Negro cabins. The Negros would all run into the woods when we taxied upon the beach. We couldn't get anybody to help us....When we finally got back to Annapolis, it was a very cold day in November. We pulled up on our little beach and waited for the mechanics to come out. We wondered, "Well, why doesn't somebody come out? We're heroes," and so forth. Then all of a sudden we saw two little spurts of sand right in front of us. The midshipmen were at it again, so we cleared out.

From then on, winter winds and rains slapped Greenbury Point. The pilots flew when they could but spent much more time starting the reluctant boat engine. On one of November's few decent days, Ellyson's Manila playmate, Jakey Fitch, visited Greenbury Point to see what his old chum found more interesting than liquor and women. Spuds sent him up with Towers in the A-1, making him the first nonaviation officer to fly in a Navy plane. Jakey never forgot his shock when, looking down between his knees, he saw the top of the Greenbury Point lighthouse.

Three days after he had initiated Jakey, Ellyson got word that Donald, his youngest brother and favorite relative, was dangerously ill in a Richmond hospital. He telegraphed Washington to request

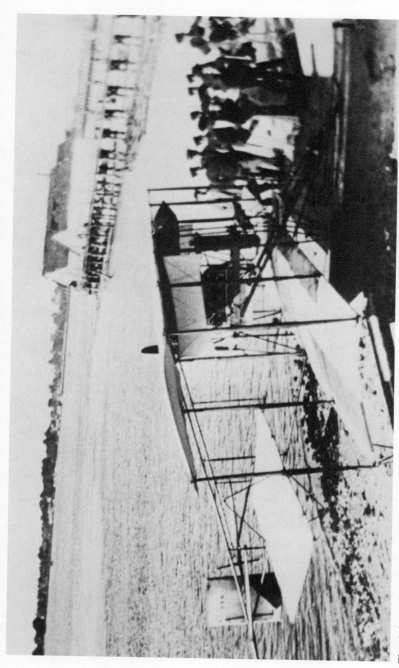

The A-1 on the beach at Fort Monroe after the first flight from Annapolis. Jack Towers said afterwards, "We went down in a day and took a week to get back."

ten days leave and took off. A few hours later, John Rodgers returned to Annapolis and to his plane, the B-1.

Spuds had been in Richmond for three days when he read Jack's wire about crashing. It ended,

SHAKEN UP A BIT NOT SERIOUSLY INJURED

which was 1911's understatement. Spuds thought little about it until several days later when he heard that Jack was still hospitalized. Writing Chambers that Donald was out of danger, he asked if he were needed in Crabtown. Chambers had been there, knew the plane had fallen two hundred feet into the icy river. Jack, bruised and sprained, had clung to the wreckage for nearly an hour before John Rodgers and the mechanics coaxed the temperamental boat to run long enough to reach him.

With Jack in the hospital, the engine in the shop, and the plane nothing but wet junk on a dock, Chambers told Spuds to relax for the three remaining days of his leave. Returning to Annapolis, Spuds assembled spare parts around the A-1's engine and nameplate. When the machine was flyable, the weather was not.

Ellyson had begun urging Chambers in October to accept Curtiss's invitation to winter naval aviation on North Island. Chambers hesitated. He was in a dilemma, wanting someone to follow Curtiss's development work and also wanting the fleet at Guantanamo to see planes in the air. Spuds said they had insufficient tools, spares, and men for two separate camps. Believing Curtiss's design, especially his control system, to be far superior to the Wrights', he did not want the fleet to see a Wright machine flying without a Curtiss beside it.

Spuds argued the Navy would profit if he worked beside Curtiss. Towers should be with him, for flying the A-1 was a team job. The two were a team with exceptional faith and trust in each other and should not be split up. Ships at San Diego were on an easier schedule than at Guantanamo; hence they could offer more cooperation. Spares could be shipped there more quickly, and Rodgers would get along all right with Curtiss in spite of the Curtiss-Wright feud.

The clincher may have been a wire from Curtiss that Ellyson quoted to Chambers on 14 December:

WE HAVE DOUBLE CONTROL COMPLETE WITH SAME ADVANTAGES AS WRIGHTS EXPERIMENTAL WORK COMMENCES

NEXT WEEK ON NEW HYDRO REGULAR HYDRO HERE NOW
COME OUT AS SOON AS YOU CAN

When fitted with floats, the Wright machine had failed to take off
with two men aboard. Curtiss's wire revived Chambers's hope that
dual instruction would soon be practicable in a hydro. Orders to
move to San Diego came two weeks later.

Ellyson's orders show how the question of seniority was avoided.
They detached him from the Academy and directed him

> ...to establish a naval aviation camp at North Island at a place designated
> by Mr. Curtiss, who has offered the land....You are entrusted with the
> care and control of the Navy Curtiss machines, the Navy Wright machine
> being independently under the control of Lieutenant John Rodgers....

The day after New Year's, when Spuds started the Curtiss gear
west in a sealed freight car, he had everything he wanted except a
ticket to California. In those days, an officer was required to carry
out his travel orders, then claim his expenses. No government
transportation orders yet existed, no credit cards, no "go now-pay
later" plans. "A dead horse," or an advance in pay, could be drawn
legally only when an officer was ordered overseas. Spuds was in
debt to the government, because his account had been checked
$400.00 for some ancient overpayment. He had used up his local
credit. The claim for expenses on the Fort Monroe flight had just
been corrected and submitted for the third time. While it remained
unpaid, Spuds was broke and stranded.

CHAPTER TWELVE

California:

Wintering with Curtiss

Since Captain Chambers felt flying to be so wonderful and so important to the future Navy, he was convinced that his young fliers could do no wrong; they deserved all possible favors. Ellyson shared these opinions. Chambers fought the pilots' battles against Washington opposition and found solutions for their problems. Because at North Island and Hammondsport they were remote from service opposition, the fliers met antagonism first in the person of Captain Gibbons, the superintendent of the Naval Academy. The captain's dislike of aviation soon taught Ellyson to bypass the Academy administration and carry his problems directly to Chambers. The bypass practice was established before New Year's of 1912, so Spuds tossed his ticket problem to Chambers without mentioning it in Crabtown. Loyal Chambers had to go to the Secretary of the Navy to get a special "dead horse," which Spuds accepted, matter-of-factly, as the due of the Navy's most important lieutenant.

Ellyson and Towers were the first of the fliers to reach San Diego. They checked in with Curtiss, then rented a bungalow at 731 Adella Lane—across town from the one Spuds and Witmer had shared—and made a call aboard the U.S.S. *Iris*.

Like Spuds's old *Rainbow*, the *Iris* was an ancient merchantman whose conversion to a distiller ship had come too late for the

Spanish-American War. In 1912 at San Diego, she served as the submarine and torpedo-boat repair ship and as flagship for Lieutenant Commander Louis Clark Richardson, commander of the Pacific Torpedo Fleet.

The Department had told Richardson the aviators would receive mail through him. He was to support them with supplies and the shops of the *Iris* and by approving their requisitions for parts "after consulting the Department by Western Union code." Hoping naval aviation and his torpedo fleet could help each other, Richardson lent Spuds a motorboat and provided lighterage for the planes from the railhead to North Island. Spuds appreciated the help but declined to concur in plans for a joint sub-air base, not wanting aviation to be merged with another type command, especially one he felt to be a departmental stepchild.

Four of the aviation enlisted men arrived from Annapolis a few days behind Ellyson and Towers. Fifty years later, one of them recalled the arrival:

>...I have always considered Ellyson, Rodgers, and Towers as three of the finest men I ever knew or worked with. In uniform, and on the field, we were always "officers and man." When the working day was over, or in "civvies," we were a bunch of good fellows. One incident that I remember well will illustrate this: We four enlisted men, H. H. Weigand, a chief gunner's mate with a sleeve full of gold hash marks, Percie Coffey, Judson Scott, and myself all "first-cruise" electricians, first class, made the trip together from Annapolis to San Diego via the Santa Fe Railroad. When we got off the train in San Diego Ellyson and Towers were there to meet us. Rodgers and Victor Daniel Herbster were still in the east. The first question from Ellyson was, "Have you had supper?" Our answer was negative as, at that time, the Santa Fe did not carry diners, but stopped for meals at railway stations along the way. "Well, we are just going to eat, better come along," was his next observation. We four were in uniform, though Ellyson and Towers were in civvies. They led us to the U. S. Grant Restaurant, then, and probably still, "tops" in San Diego. Enroute they told us that the place was noted for its steaks, and suggested that we try them out. When we were seated and gave our order, all for steaks, of course, Ellyson turned to the waitress and said, "Put all of this on my tab." While we were eating, one of the officers asked if either of us bowled—said they were planning to have a few games after supper. Coffey and Scott were enthusiastic bowlers, so Wiegand and I provided a gallery, while the other four spent the entire evening in a most enjoyable tournament.

Next day Spuds put the four on the *Iris*'s payroll and set them to work at the Curtiss-Navy camp. He quartered Weigand and Coffey in tents on the island, while Scott and Sigler waited in the *Iris* for the arrival of Rodgers and the Wright machine. When the Curtiss car arrived on 25 January, Ellyson had canvas hangars, fresh from Mare Island's sail loft, waiting to house the machines.

Spuds and Jack flew the A-1 five days after it reached San Diego. True to its reputation, the A-1 brought an end to their fun when its boiling radiator forced a landing. Another water-pump shaft had sheared. Apprehensive about the start of another fix-and-try season such as the Hammondsport summer had been, Spuds hoped the water would be warmer if they had to take more dunkings.

During the busy summer of 1911, while Spuds had worked with Curtiss, he had skipped two quarterly walking tests. General Order Number 27 required officers to prove their physical fitness each quarter by taking, and reporting, a walking test. The test was Secretary Meyer's idea, and he himself kept tabs on it. Jack and Jake got Spuds out for the tests in December and January, but he neglected to report completion. In February, his neglect brought a departmental query. Why had he not complied with General Order Number 27? Believing himself above ordinary officers' rules, Spuds replied that he had been too busy with aviation. Calling this excuse unacceptable, the secretary admonished him. Spuds began to walk.

Assistant Naval Constructor Holden Chester Richardson, known as "Big Dick" because he tipped the scales near 200, arrived in San Diego soon after the planes. Some six months earlier, at Philadelphia, he had tried his hand at designing airplane floats. Chambers encouraged his efforts and sent him to Annapolis, where he was a passenger on one of A-1's last flights of the season. At that time Richardson told Towers that model basin tests showed long, slim, sharp-nosed floats, like torpedo-boat hulls, should give a plane the most speed on the water with the least power. Towers opined such floats would dig in, instead of planing for takeoff, and would be hard to balance in the air. Ellyson and Curtiss concurred with his view.

Ignoring the fliers' experience and betting on experiments that had neglected one essential fact, the Department built Big Dick's floats and let him go west to see them tried. He wanted not only to see the tests but to learn to fly, so he could try out his own aviation ideas.

Naval Constructor Holden Chester Richardson as Jack Tower's flight student at North Island in 1912. Known as "Big Dick" in those days, he served with naval aviation even after retirement. He was later known affectionately to all naval aviators as "Commander Dick" and later still as "Captain Dick." He became the world's foremost designer of aircraft hulls and floats and piloted one of the NC planes that attempted the Atlantic crossing in 1919. After his retirement, a desk was kept for him in the Bureau of Aeronautics, and he returned on several occasions to attend to patent matters.

Thus he became Ellyson's guinea pig in a test of Chambers's dream: dual instruction in a hydro. Impracticable with the A-1s original throw-over wheel, the technique appeared possible with the double control Curtiss had built. After rigging it in the A-1, Jack and Spuds made two hops to try it out. Then Spuds wrote:

> ...The operator uses the left seat, as he is in charge of the machine and would always rise and make landings, though this can and has been done equally well from the right seat. The only difference between this and the dual control is that the steering post is Y-shaped, and there are two steering wheels. The seats [that is, shoulder yokes] are connected as before with detachable clamps.

The chance that a student or passenger might grab the wheel at a critical moment had prompted Ellyson's original insistence on the throw-over wheel. After some experience, he discounted that danger and now said, "It will be satisfactory for instruction." He never gave a reason for the seniority he ascribed to the left seat. It probably arose because Curtiss first carried passengers to his right. In any case the custom has persisted into the jet age.

Before beginning Big Dick's instruction, Ellyson and Towers took turns giving three other officers short hops. A mile off shore, the engine stopped as Spuds taxied out with a fourth. An internal bolt had come loose, wrecking the engine. The machine was grounded for five weeks; Ellyson never again flew it in California.

Because of the delay, Spuds started Richardson's training on the field, using one of Curtiss's Lizzies. At the same time, Wiegand and Coffey began setting up the A-2. Since the machine had been cannibalized in Annapolis, the job took them a month. By the time they finished on 13 March, Richardson was making grass-cutting hops on the long runway.

That night, showers washed the air. Morning came fresh, still, cool, and unusually clear. No wind stirred. No cloud marked the sky. Big Dick wanted to go, but weather-wise Curtiss suggested an air test first. "I'll try out the A-2 at the same time," Spuds said and took off. He landed almost at once, amazed that air could look so still and be so bumpy. Before ten, he made two more quick jumps, finding conditions no better for a novice. The fliers sunned themselves by Curtiss's barn, watching little dust devils form, wander about the breathless island, and die. Near eleven, when Jack went up, everyone near the barn could see the air was even rougher than before.

After an early lunch, Ellyson said he would fly low above the two-mile straightaway, land, turn around, and fly back low, as Richardson would in practice. With no wind, he thought it just had to be smooth near the ground. Towers recounted what happened next in a letter sent to Captain Chambers the next day:

...he went down, all right, but got badly tossed about. He had gotten about a third of the way back when he took a sudden drop, recovered, then a second one caused him to shoot straight into the ground at an angle of about 45° and from a height of about twenty-five feet. It was so sudden that he did not have time to do anything and there was not enough room to recover anyway. The machine plowed an awful hole in the field, then turned over. As near as I could tell from conditions, Ellyson was thrown from his seat through the forward controls to the ground, striking on his helmet, then over and striking on his back and hips. The machine sort of scooped him up when it turned over. I fortunately had my motorcycle there and when I got to the wreck he was lying half in the wreck, the lower part of his body on the top engine section and his head and shoulders just a few inches from the radiator. The helmet and his face were completely covered with earth and the first thing he said when he began to regain consciousness, which was three or four minutes after I got there, was that he couldn't see, which was no wonder for his eye sockets were completely filled. I got some water from the radiator and washed them out and went over him and found that apparently no bones were broken, and then got him out of the wires which were cutting him. He then fainted again, and about that time the others came up, so I went after a doctor and some whiskey. The doctor from Coronado (U.S. Army, retired) got over in a very short while, and we put Ellyson on a cot and by boat and machine brought him to the house. The doctor called in a trained nurse, who has been here ever since. I tried then to get hold of the doctor on the *Iris* but couldn't till this morning. All day yesterday and most of last night they gave him morphine to ease the pain in his neck and back, which seems to be the worst, but which the doctor does not think will turn out to be anything serious. The other damages are multiple bruises and badly skinned places, also a sprained ankle. The danger of a rupture of anything in the head showing up will be over after tonight, so if nothing turns up there is nothing to be alarmed about. He will probably be in bed for a week, perhaps two weeks.

Had hoped to hear from you today telling me to go ahead and order the spares required to rebuild the machine. There is not much additional expense required except to purchase the eight plane sections, for we have nearly all the braces required, also wheels, skids, diagonals, etc., and if they are not used on this machine they would probably never be used, for the models are changing all the time. I personally

Spuds Ellyson demonstrating the double controls devised by Curtiss and installed in the A-1 at North Island in the spring of 1912.

am anxious to rebuild it at once. Motor, radiator, and gas tank are
unhurt, also tail and ailerons. Have not been able to talk anything over
with Ellyson, for the doctor wants his brain to rest. As a matter of fact
I don't believe Ellyson realizes how much damage was done to the
machine.

Probably no one realized how much damage had been done to
Spuds. He had poked his head hard into North Island, and his neck
was kinked for the rest of his life. Richardson wired the Department:

ELLYSON FELL TO GROUND FROM 25 FEET IN LAND MA-
CHINE TODAY APPARENTLY NOT SERIOUSLY INJURED AC-
CIDENT DUE TO BAD AIR CURRENTS

Lizzie Ellyson was visiting Spuds's sister Bessie in Chicago when
Spuds asked Jack to wire her to allay her possible alarms. Towers
must have thought of the wire he had sent after his own crash
when he sent one off to Lizzie:

GOT SLIGHTLY BRUISED AND SHAKEN UP IN SPILL THIS
MORNING NOTHING SERIOUS IF YOU SEE ANYTHING IN
THE PAPERS IT WAS PROBABLY EXAGGERATED   GORDON

For five days, pain and dope kept Spuds muttering nonsense. At
intervals he twisted, squirmed, and groaned until the nurse calmed
him with a gentle touch. "She was a marvel," he told Mamma afterwards. "For the first four days she never got farther than ten feet
from my bed....I simply had the feeling that I just wanted to touch
someone, and I think that for the whole time she held my hand...."
On the fifth day, he was rational for awhile. In snatches, he dic-
tated a letter which Jack typed and sent to Mamma:

...I was thrown out and landed on my helmet which prevented further
injuries than twisting my neck and a general shake up, also a few
scratches and bruises. The doctor insisted on keeping me in bed for a
week....I will be ready for duty by Monday next....

He was too stiff and weak to sign where Jack typed "Gordon" so
Jack added in longhand:

The wreck of the A-2 at North Island, 14 March 1912. The "X" marks the hole made by Spuds Ellyson's head. Ellyson never flew again at North Island but was back in the air at Annapolis early that summer. The A-2 was rebuilt and put back into service.

Dear Mrs. Ellyson:
   Gordon asked me to write this and send it to you. He telegraphed
last week about the accident but I must have got the wrong address.
As regards his injuries he is getting along nicely. As we have to be away
part of the day, we have a nurse. No bones broken and he will be out in
about a week.

                                         Sincerely,
                                         J. H. Towers

Mamma had received the telegram. She had probably discounted
it; Gordon always made a good story out of whatever happened
around him. But the letter with Jack's postscript alarmed her. She
saw the wire as an understatement and telegraphed that she was
going to San Diego; did Gordon need money? Ellyson had been in
the Navy for ten years, but, to his red-haired mother, he was still
merely one of her children, in trouble.

Spuds was much more comfortable eight days after his crash,
when Mamma's wire arrived. He did not want her replacing his
hand-holding nurse and bossing him around. He framed this message:

I WAS BADLY BRUISED AND STRAINED ABOUT THE NECK
AND BACK BUT AM GETTING ALONG FINELY SITTING UP
TODAY NO BONES BROKEN OR PERMANENT INJURIES
WOULD NOT ADVISE YOUR COMING UNLESS YOU SO DESIRE
IF SO WE CAN PUT YOU UP HAVE TWO DOCTORS AND A
NURSE AND AM WELL LOOKED AFTER AM NOT IN NEED OF
MONEY   GORDON

Once aroused, Lizzie Ellyson was hard to soothe. Towers answered her next day's query with:

GORDON IS GETTING ALONG NICELY AND WILL BE OUT OF
BED IN A FEW DAYS NECK IS STILL SORE AND STIFF HE
HAS NOT BEEN DELIRIOUS FOR TWO DAYS AND IS VERY
CHEERFUL NO BONES BROKEN AND HE WILL PROBABLY
WRITE IN A DAY OR TWO   TOWERS

That message held her. Two days later, Spuds typed three pages
which began:

Dear Mamma:

I haven't written before this because each day I thought that the next day I would be able to use a pen, and I know how you hate to receive letters from me written on the typewriter....

He followed this opening remark with his version of the accident and his injuries, then reported on his nurse, his doctors, and his finances—all were wonderful. Then he wrote:

...[the plane] will be rebuilt as a hydro and in the future all flying will be done over the water, so there will be no chances of another accident. It has been my hobby for a long time that all instruction flying as well as practice flights be made over water, but it was not until after my accident that I was able to push it through. It was the accident together with the double control which we have developed out here.

Perhaps the bump on his head made him forget his months of insistence on Lizzie training and his opposition to Chambers's idea of hydro training.

His letter to Lizzie Ellyson ended:

I am sorry that I have caused you so much worry and will try not to do so again in the future. With lots of love, I am,

Your loving son,
T. G. Ellyson

Then he added a postscript:

As I was all right when I received your telegram about coming out here I did not think you cared to waste that amount of money.

He took the sheet out of the machine, turned it over and scrawled:

Keep this for me and please do not allow newspaper men to get news from my letters. Ellyson has had enough of that kind of notoriety. You can evade my questions, why not theirs?

The letter said he was back on the job; actually he stayed home under the doctor's care for nearly another month. He was uncomfortably nervous alone, so a nurse came in during the hours Towers was at the island. In the evening Spuds listened to Jack's recital of his day's work. He was testing this and that and giving Big Dick instruction in the A-1. Richardson's pontoons proved as bad as the two fliers had prophesied, but Big Dick's flying was going well and he understood how to improve the floats.

Five idle weeks bored Spuds. Too nervous to sit still, he was still too sore to get around comfortably, let alone fly. His fingers twitched. When he could stand it no longer, he sent a wire to Captain Chambers:

REQUEST ORDERS PROCEED EAST IMMEDIATELY MY NURSE LEAVES MONDAY [22 APRIL] AND WOULD LIKE HER ATTENDANCE AM DOING NOTHING HERE AND REQUEST IMMEDIATE ORDERS IN ANY EVENT ANSWER HOTEL ALEXANDRIA LOS ANGELES IMMEDIATELY

He never reread his telegrams, never learned to cut extra words. His three "immediates" in this one brought him telegraphic orders next day. He was to report to the Bureau of Navigation for temporary duty with Captain Chambers. Chambers had been moved out of the secretary's offices and ordered to the Bureau of Navigation, because that bureau had received the first $25,000 appropriation for naval aviation. Rear Admiral Victor Blue had little interest in aviation. He told Chambers to do his work at home because the Bureau of Navigation had no desk space for him. Instead, Chambers found a desk and moved it into a cubbyhole underneath the stairway in the State, War, and Navy Building (later the executive offices of the president). From that stand he tried to look out for the slowly growing naval aviation.

Halfway across the continent, a train butcher sold Spuds a newspaper that reported Big Dick's wreck of the A-1 on his second solo hop. Spuds showed the article to a fellow traveler. "See? He got only a ducking. That proves what I've always said. Training in hydros is safe."

CHAPTER THIRTEEN

Annapolis:

Specifications for a Flying Fleet

*W*ashington newspapers noted the arrival of the Navy's pioneer flier, Lieutenant Gordon Ellyson. He was a lion in the State, War, and Navy Building. Acquaintances greeted him in the corridors, admirals stopped him with curiosity, captains flattered him by asking his opinion. Spuds enjoyed their recognition. His stiff neck served as a battle scar; he was everybody's friend.

He wrote a chapter on naval aviation for *Curtiss's Aviation Book.* Viewed from the atomic age, his chapter seems to show limited vision, but it was written thirty-three years before the atom bomb flattened Hiroshima, when the opinions expressed in the article marked both Ellyson and Chambers as radicals in the State, War, and Navy Building. Furthermore, his optimism had been tamed by a year of forced landings. He expected that years of fly-fail-fix-fly procedures would be needed to produce reliable engines. He outlined the features he felt desirable in a plane which would serve the Navy most effectively:

> The ideal naval plane should carry two men for four hours, at not less than 60 knots, take off from a ship, land in the water alongside, and carry a good wireless.

Spuds felt night-landing lights and a self-starter should be added to
the planes but expected such machines could not be built for some
time. The water takeoff capability was needed only for training.
All training should be done in hydros with double controls because of the greater safety.

That June, as Chambers began to write specifications for new
Navy planes, he asked the pilots to give him their consensus re-
garding certain features. In general they agreed with Spuds's descrip-
tion, though most thought fifty knots was the best speed possible
at that time. Ellyson thought a climb of 100 feet per minute was
adequate, or believed that Curtiss could do no better. Rodgers
wanted to specify 150. Richardson suggested flexible specifications
with rewards for improved performance. Towers wanted some sort
of enclosed body to shelter the pilots. Captain Chambers would
not consider that suggestion. "Anyone should know a scout has to
sit up in front of everything, so he can see, like a ship's masthead
lookout," he said.

Despite the generally held conviction that only a pusher hydro
could serve as a naval scout, Chambers expected that, momentarily,
some radical improvement would make all current planes obsolete.
Hence, after the first of July, he ordered only a new hydro and the
first flying boat from Curtiss. Later he added another boat from
W. Starling Burgess, a Marblehead yacht builder who was making
planes under a Wright license. Thereafter, trips to Hammondsport
and Marblehead as traveling inspector and test pilot punctuated
Ellyson's Annapolis flying.

The hydro was delivered in October 1912, but the boats, the
first of their kind, took much longer. As the boats took shape,
their builders continued to modify them, adding changes they had
devised or that were suggested by Ellyson, Richardson, Towers,
and others. Some of these alterations improved the machines, but
all delayed the jobs. Spray froze on the control wires and their
sheaves during Spuds's final trials of the Curtiss boat. Curtiss slushed
them with grease cut with glycerin, finished the job after Thanksgiving, and expressed the machine to Washington, with one of his
mechanics riding the car to be sure the boat did not get shunted
aside en route. By that time, it was obvious that Burgess would
miss his contract date of 1 January 1913 by several months—a
delay that may have modified Ellyson's career.

On 24 May 1912, Ellyson had joined the other fliers at Annapolis,
and the broken planes arrived from North Island. He and Towers
were invited to live in Ogle Hall, an unofficial bachelor mess organ-

ized in a colonial house by five of Ellyson's classmates who were instructing at the Academy.

Captain Chambers, unable to get more officers detailed to flying, arranged approval for spare-time lessons for volunteers. So Spuds broadcasted invitations to visit the camp and try flying. Ken Whiting's midshipman brother and more than a dozen officers crossed the river to try a ride. Several followed up with requests for lessons.

The miserable engines made instruction deadly slow work; more flights were aborted than ever took off and most that made it into the air ended in forced landings. June Week was typical of the season. Spuds tried for three days before he could stay in the air long enough to circle the fleet vessels anchored off the Academy. All three machines went down trying to fly to a battleship anchored off Baltimore. Most volunteer students tired of wasting their free time in waiting at the camp for lessons that were repeatedly postponed. Only Ogle Hall members Isaac ("Ike") Dortch and Laurence North ("Fuzzy") McNair stayed with the training until they soloed.

In July, after new-plane inspections began calling Spuds out of town, he turned the instruction over to Towers, then got back into the picture in the fall, when Ike and Fuzzy were ready to try for Aero Club licenses.

In refusing Ellyson's request for test observers, the Aero Club wrote that new rules required at least one landing on land. No field or landplane was available at Annapolis that season, and the candidates had flown only hydros. Ellyson boiled. He strongly protested the decision, then wrote to Chambers: "...I am desirous that we get a U.S. Navy pilot's certificate immediately, and disregard the FAI [Federation Aeronautique Internationale, the world governing body for aeronautics, based in Paris] entirely as far as our work is concerned." He suggested requirements for a Navy air pilot's test. Within eight months, the Secretary of the Navy approved them, with slight modifications. They went into use immediately, but a bureaucratic hangup occurred. The order said that a student had to be tested and passed by qualified naval air pilots, but no one would say how to get the first one qualified. Hence the first naval air pilot certificate was not issued until 1915. Shortly thereafter, an appropriation bill used the title "naval aviator" in providing flight pay. After some months of confusion, the issuing of naval air pilot certificates was stopped, and fliers were redesignated as naval aviators, a term that continued to be used for many years.

The detail officer relented that fall and ordered a few officers to the camp for training. In later years, Ellyson and his legend builders claimed that all were his students. Actually he was busy with other matters; Towers did most of the instructing.

In the spring of 1912, when the aviators reached Annapolis from North Island, John Rodgers arranged with the Ferry Realty Company for camping privileges on their beach just north of the Experiment Station, where only a small dock separated the Wright and Curtiss camps. After the tent hangars were up and the wrecked planes stowed in them, Rodgers set up more tents and obtained permission to move all aviation men to the camp from the *Hartford,* the Academy station ship and let them feed themselves in the camp. The camp soon became a happy, ragtime place where everyone dressed and lived as they pleased. Administration was simple, since Ellyson and Rodgers ran separate teams, bypassed nominal superiors at Annapolis, and carried any problems directly to Captain Chambers.

This irregular method became so firmly established that Ellyson became indignant when Captain Kinkaid at the Experiment Station questioned his free-wheeling travels with neither orders nor leave. "We have authority," he told the captain, "to go to Hammondsport on duty, paying our own expenses, whenever we obtain Captain Chambers's permission and tell you we're leaving."

Kinkaid, a mild gentleman, did not think the matter important enough to get heated up about. His new assistant, Lieutenant Ernest Joseph King, may have felt differently. Already unhappy about his ragtime neighbors, Ellyson's freedom further irked him. King never saw eye-to-eye with Towers or Ellyson after that summer.

Besides being clear of the midshipmen's rifle range wild shots, the new campsite offered a money dividend; it relieved the pilots of most of the cost of supporting naval aviation—which had been coming out of their pockets. Aviation had no allotment, or appropriation, in the general supply system and was not recognized by the Bureau of Supplies and Accounts. Hence no supply officer could accept an aviator's chits for any materials. Curtiss was generally helpful. Chambers arranged to buy major repair parts, but no provision was made for day-to-day needs. The fliers had been buying most of the odds and ends required to keep the planes flying, sometimes even the gasoline. The mechanics had to obtain their own tools. As Towers said much later, "Of course the Experiment Station had all kinds of stuff, and what they wouldn't give us, we, with our mechanics who had been highly trained by that time, could obtain by 'twilight requisitions.' "

The North Island wrecks were rebuilt and flying again when naval aviation's first tool money became available. Ellyson got an open-purchase order for the allowable $50 and told top chief Wiegand to list needed tools. Wiegand was a well-meaning man who had been in the Navy a long time, but if he had been the sharpest man in his ship, nobody would have sent him to aviation. He asked each mechanic what he wanted and scribbled the answers in pencil with a tired hand. Spuds checked the list, gave him the purchase order, and said, "Go to that hardware store over on Main Street and get as much of this as fifty bucks will buy."

The blacksmith, electricians, gunner's mates, and the cook who all worked as mechanics, clustered around when the boat brought Wiegand back. He seemed embarrassed as he unloaded a big box. Before it was open, he said, "I lost the list. Musta fallen outa my pocket. At the store I couldn't remember anything that was on it. So I bought these. We're always using them." Braxton ("Blackie") Rhodes, the blacksmith, knocked the box open. It held only cotter pins and safety wire—fifty dollars' worth.

"Good God! Those'll last ten years!" Blackie yelled. Twilight requisitions continued to fill the need for tools for a few more months.

Ellyson was away from Annapolis the first week in August 1912, when John Rodgers was suddenly sent to nonflying sea duty. Spuds returned as the undisputed senior flyer. He inherited both the incomplete radio and engine tests Rodgers had been doing and the administration of the two camps. Between his next several trips, he tried in several ways to simplify the administration. Early in October he unified naval avaition—on paper. In the process he sensed troubles ahead. "Would it be possible to have orders issued so that I would be put in command of the camp...so that I will be able to order surveys, and expedite business...? I hope you know I do not care anything for the title...but unless this is done I'm afraid we are going to run up against a snag....I have no official status...," he wrote Chambers, then dashed off on another inspection trip. This was the first attempt to make naval aviation an organized unit, and it failed.

When he returned ten days later, he found his unification had produced three rivals instead of two. Vic Herbster, Rodgers's ex-student, insisted on being the Wright camp. Alfred Austel Cunningham, the first Marine flyer, who had arrived after receiving flying lessons at Marblehead, lone-wolfed as Marine Aviation. Towers's new students called themselves "the Curtiss fliers." In spite of Ellyson's best efforts, he never eliminated the Curtiss-Wright schism which persisted some two years after he left flying duty.

Nothing came of his request for official status. Aviation continued to be administered inefficiently. Each of Spuds's successors, frustrated by the same problems he had faced, repeated his request. They got no response until late in 1914, when Ken Whiting was made officer-in-charge of the Navy Aeronautical Station at Pensacola, Florida.

During the summer of 1912, Ellyson's letters told of additional projects that got nowhere, including unsuccessful flight instruments he put together with the help of an Experiment Station chemist. He qualified with Wright controls at Marblehead and never flew the type again. At Annapolis, thinking an altitude record would show that a hydro could fly high enough and long enough for scouting, he got Dr. Zahm to install an official barograph. Then his engine quit at eight hundred feet. Inaccurate reporting of his activities in an Annapolis newspaper raised his redhead's temper. Failing to find the paper's source, he blew off steam in a letter to Chambers, saying in part:

> ...I have no desire to attempt any records, but am solely looking for information. I have flown long enough not to want to be a fool and I do not think there are two "safer and saner" fliers in the country than Towers and myself.

Three weeks later, Mr. Fanciulli asked Ellyson to fly the Curtiss entry in a proposed hydro race from Newport to the fleet flagship anchored in New York harbor. The invitation transformed Spuds from the misunderstood researcher to the avid performer. Sponsored by the *New York World,* the race looked to Ellyson like fun, acclaim, and easy prize money. Not knowing Chambers had already turned down a bid for Navy participation, Spuds accepted, "unless Chambers objects." Spuds thought any objection unlikely, since he saw the flight as "good Navy publicity."

For several days Ellyson planned happily for the race, supposing Chambers's silence to be consent. When the captain's objections arrived, after a delay in the mail, Spuds was surprised, hurt, and angry. Chambers's diplomatic explanation that Navy pilots stood high in Washington because they tended to Navy business instead of going in for sensationalism did not cool Spuds. He jammed paper into a typewriter and began a reply: "I do not agree with you that it would be sensational...."

After Chambers read this long, impassioned letter, he soothed his pet pilot with a careful explanation of departmental attitudes, skillfully blended them with praise of Ellyson's past feats. The six-page longhand draft of this letter found among Chambers's papers shows extensive scratching and revision in an effort to insure the desired effect.

Spuds always cooled as quickly as he blazed. In a day or so, he simmered down, forgot show business, and turned his attention to the catapult.

[CHAPTER FOURTEEN]

Washington:

A Successful Catapult

*A*ll early naval aviation advocates assumed naval planes would
fly from Navy ships. A catapult was the third method tried. Ely
had demonstrated the first, but platforms that masked a cruiser's
guns were obviously unacceptable for launching an occasional scout.
After the San Francisco show, Captain Pond of the *Pennsylvania*
had proposed launching from "a monorail or taut wire" with a
water landing alongside the ship after flight. Thereafter, Curtiss
and Ellyson discussed various cable arrangements and promised
Chambers they would try one at Hammondsport. One thing and
another postponed the trial until near the end of the summer of
1911.

When the cable was finally stretched from a twenty-foot post to
the water, both Navy planes were out of commission. Curtiss and
Ellyson fastened a metal channel to the keel of one of Curtiss's
hydros and pulled the plane to the top of the cable. Spuds thought
he was headed for a cold ducking when he climbed into its seat.
Afterwards, he described the attempt:

> As we were worried over the question of lateral balance, as we felt
> assured that the experiment would be a success if there were a head
> wind, and as we knew that aboard ship we could always get a head
> wind by getting underway, we decided to wait till there was a north

A metal channel centered under the float to center the machine on the cable while it was hauled up to the platform (right) and while it gathered speed down the wire for launching. Notice that cylindrical wing-tip floats with splash boards have been added to Glenn Curtiss's hydros to steady them on the water, especially in crosswinds.

Spuds Ellyson flying easily after takeoff from the taut cable at Hammondsport, 7 September 1911.

wind or, in other words, a wind that blew directly up the wire. Today [September 7, 1911] we had such conditions. I was afraid that at the last minute Mr. Curtiss did not want me to try the experiment, but he finally consented.

The engine was started and run at full speed, and then I gave the signal to release the machine. The machine gained headway so rapidly that the people holding the ropes could not have used them even if there had been any necessity, but the balance was under perfect control from the start. I held the machine on the wire as long as possible, as I wanted to be sure that I had enough headway to rise and not run the risk of the machine partly rising and then falling back on the wire outside the groove. Everything happened so quickly and went off so smoothly that I hardly knew what happened except that I did have the use of the ailerons and that the machine was sensitive to their action.

Chambers and Ellyson were enthusiastic about the system's possibilities. Curtiss suggested further trials at North Island, followed by a shipboard test. "The wire can be stretched from either the bow or stern to the superstructure of a battleship..., can be rigged and unrigged in a very short time...," Chambers wrote in an article printed in the November (1911) issue of *Aircraft*. Soon after he wrote the piece, he had second thoughts. Would it be smart to balance a plane on a cable, high over a ship rolling in a seaway? Suppose the ship had to steam cross wind with the plane perched up there? Before Christmas, he delayed further tests of the method and told Curtiss he planned to build a compressed-air catapult from an old torpedo tube. When he mentioned the scheme to the Wrights, they offered the detaching hook used with the falling-weight catapult for many of their early flights. Chambers talked the plans over with Naval Constructor Richardson near Christmas and started to build the catapult at the Gun Factory. After Big Dick Richardson came back from North Island, he took over the project, finished the catapult, and took it to Annapolis.

In June 1912, the aviation mechanics helped Richardson install it on the Santee Dock. "Hope to try it tomorrow," Spuds wrote on 20 June. Not until the last day of July, however, was he in town when the catapult engine and plane were simultaneously ready.

At eleven on the morning of the test, he flew the A-1 to the Academy side of the river. Before it was hoisted to the catapult car, Captain Gibbons, the superintendent, told Spuds to get into uniform; working khaki was nonregulation. Gibbons required all

The A-1 on the car of Big Dick Richardson's first compressed-air catapult which was mounted on the Naval Academy's Santee Dock awaiting test flight, 31 July 1912.

Spuds Ellyson, the capsized A-1, and three would-be rescuers drifting upstream with the flood tide after the first catapult shot. The catapult car floats in the foreground.

officers inside the walls to wear the uniform of the day as an example to the midshipmen. Each morning the aviators walked to the dock in starchy whites, changed into old khaki for work and flying at the camp, put the whites on again to go home at the end of the day.

Spuds asked to test the catapult in his working clothes, but the superintendent refused. Big shots coming to watch the experiment must observe a regulation post. Legend has it that Ellyson wore his white dress uniform, gloves, and his sword and medals that day. Old photos confirm the white uniform but neither the sword nor the gloves; he rated no medals at that time.

Before three that afternoon, townsfolk, Washington officials, faculty, and midshipmen crowded the dock. They watched Doc Feldmeyer, the local Kodak representative, set up a special, high-speed camera to record the historic event. Dead-load shots had proved the catapult's end speed, so Ellyson was confident when he climbed aboard the A-1 and started the engine. Neither balance nor a slight cross-wind blowing up the river worried him, as they had during the wire-launch experiment. The broad pontoon sat solidly on the catapult car.

Spuds opened the throttle wide and listened to the motor's smooth, satisfactory roar. He gave the agreed hand signal. Big Dick tripped the air valve. The catapult whomped the plane, and the plane kicked Spuds like a mule. It jammed him back in the seat, freezing his fists and the steering wheel to his chest.

Starting along the track, the machine reared on its stern like a frightened horse, then rolled slowly to the left and splashed into the Severn River.

Feldmeyer's trick camera jammed at the critical moment, but a couple of plebes recorded the event in snapshots. "We all knew what was wrong as soon as the car started to move," Blackie Rhodes said afterwards. "The plane acted like a standing man, tackled low from behind."

Nobody had thought it necessary to fasten the plane to the car, although fifteen years earlier Langley had published an account of similar trouble, and its cure, when he successfully launched his unmanned "aerodromes."

The plane bobbed to the surface, bottom up. When Spuds surfaced without his white blouse, the crowd cheered. He grabbed a wing, worked his way to the pontoon, and rode it as the tide swept the machine upstream. A quarter mile away, a steam launch caught up with the plane, and Ellyson bossed the salvage job.

When Richardson saw Ellyson snap back in the seat and the plane's nose go up, he began to plan improvements. Even before the steam launch caught up with Spuds, Big Dick was considering a new valve and the addition of a hold-down fitting. Next day a reporter quoted Ellyson as he told Chambers he was all right: "A bump like that was nothing to a good aviator." The *Annapolis Evening Capital* reported that Ellyson had said that "...a change in the valve would be made, so that the propelling force would gradually accelerate rather than shoot the machine out with a sudden impact." He also explained that the side wind was a strong obstacle to a successful start.

Big Dick Richardson had made the catapult his own, but if Ellyson mentioned Dick's part in making improvements, neither writer recorded it. Spuds left the repair of the A-1 to Towers, took three days' leave, then headed for Hammonsport.

Two months later, the complications of the hot summer and Ellyson's impatience showed in the letters he wrote to Chambers from Annapolis concerning a test of the remodeled catapult in Washington. He was especially eager to fly to Washington, rather than ship the plane. Would a ramp and a hangar be ready for him at the Navy Yard? Mechanics should be sent ahead. He couldn't understand why Richardson could not have the catapult ready before 9 October. The A-1s present engine had been used by Curtiss's race pilots before the Navy put 132 hours on it and dunked it six times. Recently, no one had kept it flying for more than eleven minutes, so he "had not the confidence in it to start a long flight... [but was] ready to fly up in the A-2 as soon as ordered."

For some reason, when orders came for this flight, he decided to use the A-1 after all. With Fuzzy McNair, he tried for over an hour without getting off. First the engine was too weak, then the wind got too strong. Next day he tried again with Lieutenant Bernard L. Smith, the second Marine aviator. Heading toward the beach, Ellyson dragged the loggy machine into the air but climbed too slowly to go over the trees. When he banked into a turn, the plane settled until it hit in "a skidding landing" and flipped. Hauled from the river, Ellyson and Smith were only cold and wet, but the A-1 was finished. Ellyson's favorite plane had dunked him once too often. He wrote it off without a qualm.

Riding the train under changed orders, he reported for temporary duty in the Washington Navy Yard, testing the catapult with a new hydro being shipped from Hammondsport. He found quarters

The AH-3 leaving the catapult on 12 November 1912. Note the car dropping into the water after releasing the plane.

Spuds Ellyson testing the Navy's first flying boat, the C-1, in Lake Keuka (at Hammondsport), November 1912.

aboard the *Sylph,* the Secretary of the Navy's yacht, and faced a further delay of more than three weeks.

On 12 November, Curtiss, Chambers, and other notables stood beside the remodeled catapult on a barge anchored where the Anacostia River joins the Potomac. The barge swung to aim the catapult into the wind. The new hydro, the AH-3, was secured to the car by Richardson's new hold-down.

Ellyson pressed himself firmly against the seat back, stiff-armed the wheel, opened the throttle, and waited for the kick when Richardson opened his new valve. The plane whacked Spuds a stout blow, but easier than the one before. At the end of the track, a cam dropped the car into the river as Spuds soared up in an easy spiral.

Curtiss called it "the greatest aviation advance since wheels replaced skids for aeroplane landing gear." The *New York Times* said the Navy planned to put catapults on battleship turrets—maybe one at each end so a plane could be started in either direction.

Ellyson was in Hammondsport testing the flying boat when the *New York Herald* said a Boston man claimed the Navy catapult infringed on his patent, and the German Embassy asked Curtiss for the patent number of the catapult. Thereupon Spuds urged Chambers to patent the device jointly for the three of them. Chambers had conceived it; Richardson had built it; Ellyson had tested it. The captain never followed up on the suggestion. He may have believed the device to be unpatentable, or he may have thought the Germans were only trying to find out how it worked. He did nothing after the judge advocate told him the Boston man had no claim.

On 17 December, Ellyson flew the C-1, the Navy's first flying boat, from the catapult on the barge. He called the flight "routine," but it was the last catapult takeoff he ever made. He was on non-aviation duty for more than two years before anyone else rode Big Dick's "cat."

Ellyson's catapult tests were the beginning of a long series of catapult improvements. Richardson and others modified and enlarged the cats, and they were used on cruisers and battleships throughout World War II. A highly developed form is in use on aircraft carriers in the 1970s.

CHAPTER FIFTEEN

The Girl at Last:

Marriage

A few persons who were in Annapolis in 1912, and more who were not, helped build the legend that the Navy's 1912 aviators were fast, hard-drinking hell-raisers. This allegation has been emphatically denied by those who knew them well. Fuzzy McNair wrote in 1961:

> ...Annapolis was chock full of bachelors; they were young, gay, and full of life....There were also an attractive group of young marrieds, with many visitors constantly visiting town, as well as many attractive men and women living in the village. With so much youth and beauty close at hand there were naturally many parties and the old town was famous from New England to Florida for an unbounded hospitality. As for the drinking I would not call it excessive, especially among the aviators who were dedicated men, loving their work...the men I flew with, Ellyson and Towers, were calm, cool, and steady in the air at all times. I feel the reputation they unwittingly gained was due to some writers trying to overdramatize the era; you know—the good old days, or them was the days....

Other sources confirm that Ellyson was dedicated to his work that summer, but not as exclusively as when he was learning to fly. He was busy, but not too busy to find heart interests from Annapolis to New England. *The* girl changed her face regularly, as of yore. Where,

how, or exactly when he became engaged to a Miss Kennedy of
Atlantic City is unclear; she remains a shadowy figure, for his letters contained only scattered references to her. Her domineering
mother, however, so impressed Spuds that long after the affair was
over, he dreamed the old lady had him in court for breach of promise. This engagement was in his mind, but unmentioned, when he
ended one of his long letters to Captain Chambers:

> I am unqualifiedly against the extra-pay proposition, because it would
> result in many officers being ordered to this duty on account of in-
> fluence. I am heartily in favor of a suitable pension for the person de-
> pendent on the aviator. For instance, why should I be barred, or any
> of the bachelors who are on this duty, from being married? If any of us
> thought that we were likely to be killed we would all quit. Just the
> same, in case we should marry, our families should be looked after.

Spuds, still Miss Kennedy's fiancé, was living aboard the *Sylph,*
waiting for his second catapult test, when he took time out to usher
at Lieutenant Russell Crenshaw's Richmond wedding.

Crenshaw, from Richmond, had finished at the Naval Academy
two years behind Ellyson. In 1912, when the fliers camped on the
beach of the Severn, Crenshaw commanded the *Stringham,* torpedo
boat number 19, which was based next door at the Experiment
Station. He tried an airplane ride with Spuds that June but never
joined Ike and Fuzzy in the spare-time flight class. Polly Robbins
may not have wanted to risk her fiancé in one of Curtiss's planes,
but she approved of the fliers he brought to Richmond to serve as
groomsmen at her wedding on 30 October.

That visit was one big party for Spuds. Lizzie Ellyson had scarcely
ten words with her son, but she hoped this busy social life was a
happy omen. She knew some, and guessed more, of Gordon's love
life. He had written something of the southern Philippines, of
Manila girls, and of the women on the homebound transport. She
remembered his San Diego detour at the end of that voyage and
knew that his celibate spell during the next year in Coronado had
been brief. His letters had raved about more girls than she could
remember. She took comfort in their numbers, not realizing he
had been close to marriage on several occasions—nor did she know
of Miss Kennedy.

Her Gordon was twenty-seven now—old enough, she thought, to
settle down. Any Richmond girl in the wedding party would make

a lovely daughter-in-law. He had known most of them all his life.
Maybe this visit one of them would charm a proposal out of him.
A wedding like Russell's, with Gordon as the groom, would be
wonderful. The Navy could not keep him away so permanently
with a Richmond wife to drag him home occasionally. She scarcely
noticed the bridesmaid from New York, Helen Glenn.

After the wedding, Helen Glenn visited a sister whose husband
was an army officer stationed in Washington. Ellyson, back aboard
the *Sylph* to wait for the catapult test, saw a lot of Helen.

Helen was probably inconspicuously present aboard the barge
on 12 November when Ellyson made the first successful catapult
takeoff. Two days later, on the fourteenth, he was ordered to
Hammondsport to fly the acceptance trials of the Curtiss boat, the
C-1. He may have argued that the weekend would be wasted if he
arrived on Friday. Certainly he avoided his real reason when he
asked Chambers for a delay. The orders were recalled; a new set
was dated the sixteenth.

When Ellyson proposed to Helen, he told her of his previous
fiancée and his fear that Miss Kennedy's mother might sue if he
and Helen married. He toted up his four-figure debts, bared his
love of alcohol and cards, and promised to mend his ways if the
two were wed. For better or worse, on Friday, 15 November 1912,
Helen Mildred Lewis Glenn married Theodore Gordon Ellyson in
the rectory of Christ Church at Alexandria, Virginia.

Before leaving to honeymoon in Hammondsport, Spuds asked
a friend to send this night letter addressed to Mamma:

WAS MARRIED FRIDAY NIGHT AS PER LETTER WROTE YOU
LAST NIGHT MY WIFE AND I LEAVE FOR HAMMONDSPORT
TOMORROW NIGHT WE WILL BE DOWN FOR THANKSGIVING
[to let you] SEE MRS GORDON

The wire did not get filed until Monday and was not delivered before Tuesday, the nineteenth. Lizzie Ellyson may have had to wait
even longer to learn her daughter-in-law's name, unless Spuds's
letter beat his wire to Richmond.

The happy pair did not visit Richmond for Thanksgiving. The
Hammondsport winter was closing in, and Spuds made two test
flights on the holiday, trying to finish the trials before the lake
froze.

When he considered it, Ellyson realized that Mamma Ellyson was hurt and angry at his elopement, but her coolness hurt his bride, and he felt more irritated than sorry at the breach growing between them. He hoped time would teach the two women to appreciate, if not to love, each other. In the meantime, he was very much in love, and Helen made him happy.

Six months later, his continuing hope for a truce showed in a letter to his wife which included these words:

> I wrote Mamma...that my one regret for being married as we were was that she, knowing me so well, and knowing that I have been "crazy" over so many girls, would think that I had been unduly hasty in my marriage, and that I could cause her worry because she perhaps thought it was just another case...that it was not, for I had not made love to you, or kissed you, until I asked you to marry me.

Lizzie Ellyson never softened, nor did Helen.

Later, when the time came for Ellyson to transfer to Norfolk, his orders and rail travel would have allowed him to stop over in Richmond. He was traveling alone, but since Richmond had not welcomed his wife enthusiastically, he took the night steamer *Southland* from Washington directly to Norfolk.

Sleepy little Hammondsport had no night life. The great Curtiss was just a local neighbor, and his flying machines were old stuff. The famous Navy flier Ellyson was just one of Curtiss's boys who had stayed in the same boardinghouse off and on for a long time. Spuds thought Hammondsport an ideal spot for his honeymoon, except that his work kept him away from Helen all day. Since he feared she was lonely, he borrowed a hydro and consoled her with her first flight.

While they honeymooned in Hammondsport, Helen's mother was still writing her to come home from Washington, urging her to hold off on an engagement until she knew Mr. Ellyson better. Nearly a week passed after the marriage before Helen's family and Captain Chambers all had news of the wedding. Captain Chambers wired congratulations. Mrs. Glenn invited the pair to New York.

After the flying boat was expressed to Washington, they stopped over with her. Helen had diplomatically prepared her mother; Virginia friends had helped with praise for Spuds and the Ellyson family background.

Mrs. Glenn had sometimes worried about her too-adventurous daughter. Recovering from the initial shock of the announcement, she realized the elopement had saved her the expense of a wedding and that a husband would take the worry duty for Helen's future escapades. Gaining a famous son-in-law was a satisfactory arrangement. When Spuds turned on his well-practiced charm, it worked; he was calling Mrs. Glenn "mother" before the end of the second day of the visit. Because she never tried to boss him, he always found her company easier than Mamma's.

Ellyson sent Chambers word of his stopover "to meet my new family" and promised to be in the Department on Friday morning in time to receive the flying boat. He asked the captain to summon mechanics Wiegand and Saar from Annapolis and asked when aviation would sail for Cuba in the *Sterling*.

Chambers thought he would give his newlywed pilot a break, hold him in Washington, and thus extend his honeymoon. He wired:

STERLING WILL NOT LEAVE BEFORE CHRISTMAS STOP YOU WILL REMAIN UNTIL BURGESS BOAT IS RECEIVED

Spuds failed to understand the old man's attempt at generosity. He was enjoying life with Helen but had never believed that marriage should modify duties. Something was wrong. He had counted on commanding the naval aviators when they made their debut with the fleet at Guantanamo. Could that Burgess boat entrap him as the *Seal* had snagged Ken?

Helen, who disliked Towers from the beginning, was sure he had pulled a fast one to maneuver Spuds out of the job. Ellyson would not believe it. Jack wasn't the type. They were pals. Still, some recent letters had been hot with misunderstandings about material. Could Helen have a point? No, but the seed of doubt she planted persisted.

After four days at Mrs. Glenn's home, Ellyson took his bride to Washington where on 17 December he flew the flying boat from the catapult.

Mrs. Glenn was happy to have Ellyson for a son-in-law, but she also wanted her daughter's services and company. She found frequent needs for Helen's presence. Illness, business, dental troubles— the excuse was always stated so that Spuds agreed Helen should go to help her. Each time Helen went home, her mother found new complications to extend the stay. This routine began during the newlyweds' New York stopover, when Mrs. Glenn made Helen promise to come back before Christmas.

Two evenings after the catapult test, Ellyson put his wife on the night train for New York to keep her promise. Once again, he took up quarters on the *Sylph*. In love and lonesome, he wrote Helen a long letter as soon as he boarded the yacht. It began, "I don't like this living alone." He promised to go to New York "tomorrow night, or there will be some row in the Navy Department."

He arrived without a row, then after a four-day Christmas had his pockets picked in the Pennsylvania Station while waiting for the Washington sleeper. Before it pulled out he found time to report the loss in a love note to Helen, "Every cent I had in the world except about four dollars in change...but never mind, a good time...." Next morning, he stopped in the post office beside the Washington station to write another love letter before checking in at the Navy Yard. Every day until Helen joined him, he wrote at least once, usually twice, sometimes more.

He made a quick trip to New York over New Year's, expecting to bring Helen back to the flat he had rented in the Farragut, across the square from the Army and Navy Club. Mother, however, found some pressing need for her daughter and, at 7 o'clock on the morning of 2 January, Spuds arrived alone in Washington.

During these separations, Spuds found living on the *Sylph* cheaper but little less lonesome than his wifeless apartment. His friend, the yacht's bachelor skipper, seldom spent an evening aboard.

Lizzie Ellyson's son drew a solid line between a bachelor's legitimate fun and that of a good husband. He found it easy to conserve cash, stay sober, and look only at Helen when she was with him. Old friends and bachelor habits attacked his determination when she was not. He wrote that he "needed her, not physically, but for moral support."

Cards and bars were expensive and as natural to Spuds as eating. If he stopped in town for supper after leaving the office, chums tempted him in the bar of the New Ebbitt House or the cardroom of the club. If he took a walk to break a lonely evening in the *Sylph*, he gravitated to the same places. When he resisted temptation, he added a boast in his next letter to Helen: "Just ran into a friend from Richmond whom I had not seen in ten years. He had a beautiful bun and I had a drink with him—French Vichy." "No drinks" was the underlined postscript on another letter. "Just came in here for supper," explained one letter written on letterhead that proclaimed the New Ebbitt House to be "Army and Navy Headquarters."

Ellyson said he had married the world's one perfect woman; therefore others were no longer of interest to him. The theory made him feel disloyal whenever he found himself admiring a lovely lady. Then he hated himself, for he sincerely wanted to be a good husband.

The Saturday after New Year's, Ellyson helped the *Sylph*'s skipper, C. L. P. Rodgers, entertain the daughters of the Secretary of the Navy at lunch aboard the yacht. He enjoyed the afternoon, though it kept him from a planned visit to Helen's sister. Feeling a bit guilty, he explained, "It was policy for me to be there, as they had asked Rodgers to ask me."

Helen got to Washington a few days after that luncheon. The Ellysons had ten days in their Farragut love nest. Then Spuds wrangled orders to report on the aviation exhibits at the New York automobile show. "The Army tells me it will be even better than the Aero Club's show you sent me to last year," he told Captain Chambers.

Just after midnight one night in the middle of January, Spuds and Helen raced through Washington's Union Station after their redcap. With only seconds to spare, they tore down the stairs to the platform. Six steps from the bottom, Ellyson's feet flew out from under him, and he landed in a heap. Two strangers helped him to his feet, but he took only one step before he yelled, "Ow! Turned my ankle, I guess." He was glassy-eyed and paste-white when they eased him into a seat just at train time. Helen wanted to get off and find a doctor. Refusing to move, Spuds mumbled, "Gotta go. Orders. Just turned ankle. Get over it."

After pulling Spuds's shoe from his bulging foot, Helen asked a trainman to find a doctor. "Too late to get one now," he said. "We're due to pull out."

"Let me phone for one to meet us in Baltimore," she said.

"I'll wire for one," the man promised. Something held the train in the station for forty minutes. No doctor showed at Baltimore. Spuds was dopey. Helen raised hell. At Wilmington a doctor came aboard, said the foot was broken, and tied a pillow around it. Spuds remembered nothing between his fall and that pillow.

Helen wired her mother's doctor to meet them at Mrs. Glenn's apartment with a bone specialist. After Dr. Albert S. Morrow examined him at the flat, Spuds thought of the size of the New York specialists' fees and had Helen call the Brooklyn Navy Hospital.

Surgeons Bogart and Morris, who were on duty there, were old friends.

Informing him that the Navy would be unable to pay Dr. Morrow, they put Spuds on the sick list and reported to the Department: "...deformity reduced under anesthetic at 1:30 P.M. at his temporary residence, 265 West 81st Street, in consultation with Doctor Albert S. Morrow, whom he had called in....When able to travel, Lieutenant Ellyson will return to Washington."

He got back to the State, War, and Navy Building in about ten days but was forced to use crutches until late in April.

In the meantime, immobilized in his mother-in-law's flat, his right foot in what Dr. Morris called a "Stimson moulded plaster stirrup splint," Spuds worried about the exhibits he was ordered to see. He phoned Ken Whiting.

After two years' work at Newport News, New London, and New York, after uncounted trials, dives, breakdowns, and tows, Whiting had commissioned the *Seal* as the G-1 at about the time Spuds waited for his second catapult shot. She was still far from reliable, and Ken had her in New York for more work. On the phone, Spuds explained his problem and asked Ken to come meet his bride. Then he scrawled a string of aviation questions about the show.

Ken brought rye. "Purely medicinal. Best-known cure for broken bones in head or foot," he said. After the treatment, Spuds handed over his questions and asked Ken to go to the show to record the answers.

Next day, Ken returned without answers. The show had consisted entirely of American automobiles. It held no aviation exhibits. "Sorry I was misinformed by the Army," Spuds wrote Chambers.

Flying experience during 1912 rapidly changed many of the aviators' opinions, which often diverged from what Chambers learned in his reading. Misunderstandings grew, because Ellyson either could not or did not give reasons for his own shifts of opinion. New ideas came out as if he had always held them. In Washington after his West Coast crash, he advocated an East Coast aviation establishment which would use hydros exclusively, speaking as though he had never asked the Navy to buy North Island, a Lizzie, or a "Standard Curtiss" landplane.

As he wondered about this apparent instability, Chambers noted the pilots disagreed not only with him but among themselves as they discussed plane types, control systems, and preparations for the winter cruise. He began disregarding all of them and made decisions that, to a nonflier, seemed logical.

Since he was not going, Ellyson left the loading for Cuba to Towers and spent Christmas in New York. Back in Washington on 29 December, he wrote Helen, "I may have to go down to Annapolis tomorrow but I hope not, and am not going unless compelled to."

Nobody compelled him. His next letter noted, "I have not done any flying since I arrived here, but it would seem as if Captain Chambers is counting on keeping the flying boat here all winter. I am working against that and think I will succeed...."

Some impulse controlled Ellyson after his New Year's in New York. The day he returned, he made seven flights, totaling about two hours. Shortly after the last one, he went to bed with what he thought was food poisoning, blaming a bad oyster at lunch.

At that time Captain Chambers began to use Ellyson in the Department as his assistant and prospective relief. Months later, he realized Spuds was not the type for a Washington desk job. Spuds Ellyson never became a happy desk man, but he was especially unhappy in Washington. He was sure he had answers and knew what should be done. Why did Chambers piddle around waiting for concurrence from everyone in town before getting on with the job? Such normal bureaucratic procedure zoomed his blood pressure. With twinkling eyes, Chambers watched the impatience of his favorite pilot. As an old Washington hand, he knew the system always beat down the man, if he stayed around.

Ellyson found it progressively more difficult to change what the old man considered matters of policy; he argued for days before he was allowed to ship the C-1 flying boat to Towers in Cuba. He did not try to hide his anger when he lost an argument over Lawrence Sperry.

At Hammondsport in 1912, Sperry, a seventeen-year-old mechanical genius, worked on an airplane gyro stabilizer, the granddaddy of jet-age autopilots. Spuds became his booster after flying with the device. During his first visit to Mrs. Glenn's, he talked with the lad's father, Elmer, who wanted to send Lawrence to Guantanamo with the Navy planes to perfect the instrument. He promised credit to the Navy, said nothing of cash.

The next month Ellyson brought the Sperrys and Chambers together in Washington. To his surprise, the captain was "most insulting to both Sperrys," whereupon Elmer sent Lawrence to San Diego to work with Curtiss.

Ellyson called this "a great blow to me, because the Navy deserves the credit for developing this [device]...." Months later, the day before Ellyson left Washington for sea duty, Rear Admiral Victor Blue, Chambers's young boss, signed an agreement with Curtiss and Sperry to test the gyro stabilizer in a Navy plane. Spuds's part in this contract is unclear.

In spite of such official differences, Ellyson still liked Chambers. As he lay crippled in New York, he was sincerely sorry he was not helping the old man. After 1 February the Ellysons returned to the Farragut flat, and Spuds's professional disagreements with his boss became more frequent. The crutches he was forced to use shortened his already quick temper. With Helen frequently in New York to answer some SOS from her mother, restless nights made him testy on the job. Sometimes all of Chambers's policies seemed wrong to him. Did the captain really understand what the problems were? Could even the best-intentioned nonflier ever understand them? Spuds was in no mood to make allowances when the captain announced his decisions in a papa-knows-best manner.

Chambers later wrote:

> I never lost faith in Ellyson, notwithstanding the fact that he lost his
> head far enough one day to go to the Chief of the Bureau and state that
> he did not agree with my policies, without ever mentioning to me the
> points wherein he differed....

That March, change entered Washington along with the Democratic Party. Josephus Daniels, the new Secretary of the Navy, announced that, before promotion, officers must have at least two years' sea duty in grade. Those who had long served in the Navy Department panicked. Rear Admirals Andrews and Cone asked for sea duty in their permanent lower grades. Friends told Ellyson and Chambers they should get to sea and qualify. Chambers insisted the work they were doing was more important to the Navy than a few months' sea duty could ever be.

For some time, Spuds could not decide what to do. Aviation was coming back from Cuba, but for unstated reasons he did not want to rejoin them at Annapolis and did not think he would have to. At the same time, he liked to fly. He did not like working in the Department and he did not want to succeed Chambers.

With Helen in New York again, he tried to forget his problem on a weekend at the Indian Head Proving Ground with his classmate Bruce Livingston Canaga. On Monday he went to Annapolis to meet the returning fliers. He found Towers somewhat upset after having talked to Chambers over the weekend. Their discussion left both pilots unhappy. Back in Washington on Wednesday at noon, Spuds spilled his irritation in a long letter to Helen before he checked in at the Department.

His afternoon with Chambers was as unsatisfactory as Jack's talk had been. That evening he sent Helen another letter filled with anger:

> ...I have decided to quit flying for good and all, that is never to get in a machine again for any reason. Things have come to such a pass here that I had to decide, either to go to Annapolis and take charge of the camp or quit for good. I have not told anyone yet of my decision, nor will I for the present. I cannot do the job halfway....I hope you approve.

The specific disagreement that inspired this letter was not mentioned.

Ellyson felt better after Helen returned to Washington and he had shed his crutches, but he stuck to his resolve to stop flying. The Burgess boat was ready in April, but he left its testing for someone else. Near the end of that month he was ordered to the dreadnaught *South Carolina* as first lieutenant, with the detail officer's promise that no senior would be sent to rank him out of this lieutenant commander's billet. The promise adds credence to the suspicion that his transfer was the result of an oral request. The legendary Ellyson had been able to pick and choose.

On 29 April 1913, he was detached from naval aviation. He took Helen to the train to New York, closed their flat, adjourned to the Army and Navy Club, and wrote her a letter:

> I am on my way to catch the boat in a very few minutes....Only ten days till I see you again.....It won't be so hard for me this time as it was when you went to New York before, because I will have work to do aboard the ship during the day and companionship at night, neither of which did I have during our other separations, and best of all I don't, and won't, feel like drinking.

CHAPTER SIXTEEN

Back at Sea:

The *South Carolina*

*E*llyson reported to the *South Carolina* and wrote Helen all about the ship. For the rest of his life, whenever they were separated, he wrote her an overlong daily letter in which he detailed his day's activity and poured out his thoughts, opinions, problems, and troubles with the frankness he thought essential to a successful marriage.

During each cruise he numbered the envelopes consecutively, so Helen could open a batch in sequence and tell if any were missing. He remained extremely regular in this program, with very few lapses, long after the letters changed gradually from love letters to those of duty. Most were filled with trivia, but his character, impulses, and beliefs came through between the lines. A few hint at disagreements with Helen and escapades or actions he may have regretted.

At Norfolk, Ellyson found that the four and a half years since he had left the *Rainbow,* his last surface ship, fell away as he sniffed the odor universal to ships — a unique blend of soap, paint, stack gases, oakum, and men. Watertight doors closed behind him with their own peculiar solid clunk. The hand chain clanked familiarly as he swung down a ladder. He did not analyze his feelings, but all his senses reacted to old, unnoticed items; he was

home again in a new ship. On his second day aboard, he followed
the skipper on his regular Friday afternoon inspection, then wrote;

> ...I have just finished a three-hour walk going through all the ship's
> compartments. I believe in making a reputation as a hard worker at the
> start and showing up at odd, unexpected times, for this keeps everyone
> on the jump and accomplishes more with less real work. I think I am
> going to like this duty immensely but I can tell more about it when I
> know my job better....

The crew was making the *South Carolina* shipshape after her
yard work. Most of this cleaning up was part of Ellyson's new job;
a first lieutenant was in effect the ship's head janitor. Working
through the division officers, he was responsible for the maintenance
and cleanliness of the hull and fittings outside the engineering
spaces. Spuds jumped into this work with all the enthusiasm he
had once applied to learning to fly.

In those years, Atlantic fleet ships usually stayed in the Caribbean
from January until June, made a ten-day visit to New York, then
alternated drill periods at sea with visits to coastal cities until November. Since following these ships in the summer was expensive
and gave small returns and was impossible in the winter, most fleet
wives stayed at home except when the ships visited their home
yards from Thanksgiving until Christmas or for overhaul. Spuds
and Helen started with an extra dividend of ten days in Newport
in mid-May and a few more days in New York at the end of the
month. On Memorial Day, Spuds put on his full-dress uniform,
mounted a horse, and rode up Fifth Avenue as an aide to the grand
marshal of the holiday parade. He felt he was the most important
man in the city; the parade was more fun than anything since his
last air meet.

The ship moved to Annapolis for June Week and to pick up
midshipmen for their training cruise. Jack Towers wrangled a
room in Carvel Hall for the Ellysons, in spite of the June Week
crowds; and Helen arrived for four days. Together the Ellysons
visited Jack's aviation camp and borrowed its uncertain open boat
for a trip to the *South Carolina,* lying out in Annapolis Roads.
True to the camp's ragtime tradition, the boat's coxswain, Bourdon,
was dressed in nondescript civilian clothes. On the return trip a
thunderstorm drenched the party and drowned the engine. It was
dark before Ellyson managed to signal a passing boat, convince
them he was in the Navy, and get them to tow the disabled boat to

The USS *South Carolina*, battleship number 26, was commissioned three years before Spuds Ellyson joined her. She was 441 feet 3 inches long, 76 feet 3 inches beam, and displaced nearly 15,000 tons. She rated 40 officers and 772 enlisted men. The *South Carolina* was the first American battleship classed as a dreadnaught, or all-big-gun ship, with a battery of four twelve-inch guns in four turrets. Spuds Ellyson served first as her first lieutenant, later as her gunnery officer.

the Academy. Soaked and half frozen, Spuds took Bourdon with them to Carvel, gave him a stiff drink, and arranged an overnight berth for him. Years later, the sailor boasted he had been the first enlisted man to sleep in the exclusive old hotel.

Their fun at Annapolis ended when Helen went back to her mother's and the battleship carried Spuds toward Mexico. Each day he munched chocolates from one of the dated packages that Helen had stowed in his room to last until he could expect a mail steamer to bring letters and packages from her.

Eventually the ship anchored, transferred the Academy "mids" to a northbound ship, and rolled the summer away, watchfully waiting in front of Vera Cruz and Tampico. President Woodrow Wilson's foreign policy permitted little more than official contact with the beach, no liberty, and little recreation.

Every ship that went north carried a batch of Spuds's daily letters to his bride. Financial problems were woven through the letters almost from his wedding day; they never changed in that respect. Those from his last cruise were, with regard to finances, like those from this first trip in the *South Carolina*. Debts he had acquired before marriage salted the early letters. As he struggled to shed old debts, he acquired new ones. Less than a month after his wedding, he wrote for the first time, but not the last, "I put a monthly check in the bank, so the check I gave you is now OK." Three months later he was pleased to recover some of the money that had been charged against his pay account the previous year but objected to the fee the law firm of King and King was charging for pushing the claim through the court of claims for the group of officers, including Spuds, who had been adversely affected by the original comptroller's decision. A week later his bank account was overdrawn again. His first letter after leaving Newport noted, "I sent C. E. Mullen a check today so scratch him off our debt list." On the way to Tampico, he asked Helen what they owed for storage and promised to pay it when he got some money on the first of the month. In August, he told of swimming at Y Barra, then supposed it would be his last swim there, for he promised not to go ashore except on duty. "I paid off two more bills this afternoon," he added. He counted that as $163 paid off since he had left Annapolis. He was still resisting King and King but supposed he would have to pay them in the end because "those people are shysters and it is their business to stick people."

In September he decided on a new plan to speed his payments, put it in effect, then typically asked Helen what she thought of it.

Today I made out another allotment for $100 and I will write the Riggs
bank to place it to your credit. The first payment will be made December
first. This will cut me down to $60 a month which is the very bottom I
can get along on. In another envelope I am enclosing letters I have
written to the other people telling them of the arrangements I have
made. I did not make the allotments to them direct because some
months we might get in a pinch and if the allotments were going to
them I could not stop it. This will cause you a little trouble, sweetheart,
but do you mind sending them a check once a month? My intention is
not to touch this money except for debts but there is a loophole in
case we get up against it. I have intended doing this myself but I find
out when I have the money there is too much temptation to spend it...

Three days later he figured he still owed $2,331.35, having paid
$368 since 19 May. Marriage had changed some of Ellyson's ideas
about money. As a bachelor, in September 1912, he had told
Chambers he was against extra pay for flying. The captain complimented him on this stand and said the scheme was being pushed
by Army officers to set up "a system where a fellow can be ordered
to a soft job, with big pay, swell around and loaf so long as his
influence works." Hobbling about the Department on crutches in
March, when Congress authorized the first flight pay, Spuds did not
want to ask Chambers to make him one of these loafers. Nevertheless, as a married man pursued by creditors, he was deeply disappointed not to be one of those designated to draw the extra money.
A week after extra-pay orders were issued to the other fliers, he
asked for sea duty.

Off Mexico in July, he heard that Captain Chambers had been
"plucked"; that is selected for retirement in order to speed promotion in the junior ranks. He's gone, so a request won't embarrass
him, Spuds thought, and made an official request for flight pay
from the time of its authorization until he had been ordered to
sea. His request ended, "I was the only officer on duty at the
aviation camp who did not receive such orders."

As the request went through channels, it found its way to the
desk under the stairs where, as a retired officer, Chambers was
still running naval aviation in the same old way. In August, when
the orders came back to Ellyson, he was embarrassed to find that
the captain had summarized his role in naval aviation with flowery
praise, recommended approval of the extra money, and clinched it
by adding that Ellyson's name had been "inadvertently omitted
from the original list." Spuds sent the papers on to Helen, telling
her, "This means we will get about $150 in back pay."

No back pay, promotion, or raise ever solved Ellyson's money problems, which were built in for life. Months after his death, creditors were still asking the Department for his address. When he had money, he spent it on cards, his family, on parties, drinks, and fun. When he had none, he signed chits. Impatiently, he also paid out a lot unnecessarily in the line of duty. Only a few of his many trips between Washington, Hammondsport, and Annapolis were made on travel orders. He seldom waited for a piece of paper. When a problem was hot, he bought a ticket and hopped a train. He usually had the problem solved before a request could have brought orders, but the practice kept him broke.

Because he was habitually careless about receipts, he was at least once the target for one of the unscrupulous shopkeepers who increased his shop's take by making double claims against Navy men, who often settled to keep his complaints off their records. In Spuds the chiseler misjudged his victim. Ellyson refused to be intimidated. When the Department asked, he said the claim was unjust and that he would not pay it unless a court judgment was brought against him. The Department backed him, and the claim died.

Off Mexico, the *South Carolina* gave Ellyson his first taste of the gunboat routine typical of the banana wars of those years. Most of the time, the ship stood by, like a policeman on a quiet corner, waiting for something to happen that seldom did. Ships lay within sight of the beach for weeks, with their captains unable to grant liberty. The bored crews drilled and polished, coaled and cleaned up. Each coaling scarred a ship's paint and spread black dust from doublebottoms to topmasts. By the time her men had scrubbed away the coal dust and retouched the paint, more coal would arrive.

According to Spuds, coal never arrived at a convenient time nor in the proper amount. The first time the new collier *Jason* came alongside, he was unhappy about the battering her green crew gave his ship with their big clamshell buckets. A bit later, he complained that the *South Carolina* needed 1,200 tons of coal, but the admiral would let her take only three hundred tons, claiming that other ships needed the rest of the collier's cargo. "Three hundred tons will get us just as dirty as 1,200, and this is the third time in succession we have gotten the short end of the deal."

When the *Jason* was due again, he was glad the bunkers were practically full. They would not have to take any, nor dirty up the ship he had shined in anticipation of the admiral's inspection. He was happy for three days, until the ship received word to be ready to take on 360 tons at 5:30 next morning. Where could they put it? Only 180 tons had been burned since the last coaling when they had stored forty tons on the fireroom floorplates. "I almost cried when I heard this," he wrote to Helen that night. "For there is my nice clean ship all dirty again, and I haven't the cleaning gear or paint to put her in first-class condition before the admiral's inspection."

Though he could be bitter about his routine troubles, they still could not expend all of his energy. He reorganized his job almost weekly. He volunteered for extra work. When Adolphus Staton, the gunnery officer, became a special pal, Spuds took on the spotting work for the turret guns. He organized fishing-boat trips for the men, became athletic officer and arranged shows and boxing matches. He talked a group of volunteers into a daily physical drill. "Swedish will get you in shape," he told them. "It's a new kind of exercise inaugurated at the Academy last year. It looks foolish, but it's really strenuous." He was sure that they would all keep at it for the duration of the cruise, but as it often did, his interest flagged after he had the drill underway. Spuds was a starter, not a steady plugger. He did his routine work satisfactorily, without much flair. But when a new idea caught his fancy he threw himself into it with an enthusaistic burst of energy. That enthusiasm usually lasted long enough to get the idea going, then sloughed away.

When Ellyson first joined the *South Carolina,* only the watch stayed aboard after working hours. Ashore, the other officers scattered about Norfolk, making the most of their few remaining days with wives or sweethearts. The city offered no gathering place such as the club in Manila. Remembering the China Station, Spuds decided his new messmates were socially a total loss. By the day before they were due off Tampico, he knew better. That murky, wet, Saturday afternoon, officers sat around the wardroom and talked of all manner of things—"hot-aired," Spuds called it, and enjoyed the afternoon.

His evening letter noted, "It appears that the Consul's wife at Tampico boasts that she has kissed every American officer who has been in Tampico, and we were betting on what her batting average will be on here."

Letters of that period no longer carried little postscripts like "No drinks." Drinking was not mentioned at all. But the Navy was still wet, and shipmates remembered that Spuds drank anything the others did. The wardroom's favorite during the cruise was described as "a delightfully fiendish" cocktail of Bols gin and Italian vermouth, after which ordinary martinis tasted like distilled water. All hands were proud of the ship's reputation as a "heavy drinking, many-party" vessel. When they had a chance to play, her officers played hard. Spuds joined their fun and forgot he had ever thought them dull.

The junior officers, who thought of the first naval aviator more as a hero-friend than as a boss, welcomed Spuds to the card game which usually ran in the steerage mess from midmorning until midnight. He found the wardroom simpatico, too, except Lieutenant Commander William Scott Whitted, the engineer, with whom he seldom agreed. Younger members of the wardroom soon elected Spuds the mess caterer-treasurer, and he became one of the most active party organizers.

Navy Secretary Daniels had not revoked Meyer's hiking order. Soon after reaching Tampico, Spuds, the captain and the doctor, and one other man landed some seven miles up the beach and walked the railroad tracks into the city, finishing their quarterly stint by 8:30 A.M. Spuds limped to a sidewalk cafe. His first hike since discarding his crutches had raised new corns. While waiting for an eleven o'clock boat, beer cut the dust from his throat but did little for his sunburn and sore feet. At boat time, the men were joined on the dock by three attractive American girls, luncheon guests of the steerage mess.

Admiring them, Spuds felt like a small boy with his hand in the cookie jar. "Do you think they'll stay that perky crossing the bar," the doctor asked him, "or be seasick like most lubbers?"

Spuds snorted. "Their silly chatter bores me," he said. Refusing to join the others in the cockpit, he flopped into the steamer's bow and rode alone.

At lunch in the stuffy wardroom, he thought the chief engineer had countermanded one of his orders. Flushing through his fresh sunburn, Spuds called down the table to point out brusquely that, by regulations, only the mess treasurer gave orders to the attendants during a meal. "As long as I'm treasurer, I'll run this mess," he yelled. "If you want to give orders here, I'll have to be relieved first."

The engineer raised an eyebrow in surprise, then reddened. "Ellyson, that is no way to speak to a superior," he began. Angry words flicked back and forth until the executive roared for both men to pipe down.

Spuds, "mad clear through," seethed silently through the meal, then dashed off an official letter to the captain demanding redress because he was "entirely in the right and backed by regulations." Knowing Ellyson, the executive held the letter for a cooling-off period, then made peace. Spuds withdrew the letter "because there is no use starting bad blood aboard ship if there is any way to avoid it."

The *South Carolina* saw other Ellyson outbursts, all aimed at seniors. Junior officers and enlisted men were never his targets. He took on the chief again when mess night became a current enthusiasm. "One of the prettiest old customs I know of," Spuds described it. "But it is rapidly dying out. Ten or twelve years ago, every ship observed it. Each Saturday night, in home port or at sea, every member of the wardroom mess was required to be present in dress uniform. Wives and fiancées were invited in some ships, but no outsiders were allowed." Spuds wanted the mess to adopt the custom. He had argued for so many innovations by that time that he thought someone else should suggest this one. He chose C. C. Hartigan, a popular and persuasive officer. But when Hartigan proposed mess night, the engineer immediately said, "I won't stay aboard for any such thing unless I feel like it. The regulations don't require me to. The whole business will just be useless extra expense."

Spuds grabbed the ball. "There won't be any extra expense as long as I'm mess treasurer," he said. "It's a pity that some senior officers here won't build a little spirit in the mess to get everyone together. A happy mess always leads to a happy and efficient ship." He expanded on the theme with quotes from various admirals.

The engineer glared down the table at Spuds. "There are eighteen other members in the mess," he said, "and the ship has gotten along all right since commissioning without any such foolishness."

"What's she ever done since you and the other seventeen have been running her, except stand wooden in gunnery and engineering competitions?" Spuds demanded.

Before the argument got more personal, the executive cut it short by calling for a vote. Only the chief voted against Spuds's proposal. "He was the only one who had been aboard long enough to affect the efficiency of the ship," Spuds told Helen in his evening account of the squabble.

During the summer Spuds wrote a dozen times that the ship was starting home. Each time the orders were changed or his rumor proved unfounded. Nevertheless, in mid-September, when new orders arrived, Spuds helped organize another farewell party. Invita-

tions to a stag party went to American civilians in Tampico. One
man, missing the word "stag," brought his mistress along, intro-
ducing her as his wife. Outraged, Spuds wrote, "She was attractive
and conservative but we all knew who and what she was. Besides it
was no place for a woman." Two days later he forgot mistress,
man, and party when the *South Carolina* finally sailed for Norfolk.

Ellyson never mentioned mess night after the ship reached the
Navy Yard at the end of the month. The routine quietly died while
Spuds and Helen spent his two weeks' leave in New York. The
leave was pleasant, but he was glad to get back to his ship. He
wanted to keep an eye on the Navy Yard work, and he found his
shipmates more fun than New Yorkers.

The wives of the *South Carolina*'s officers found themselves
competing with Harry Tabb's bar where their husbands usually
stopped on their way home "for oysters and daiquiris. Not too
many oysters and maybe too many daiquiris, for which we may
have caught hell," Max DeMott wrote years later. "We played a lot
of bridge with the Ellysons that fall. Our wives persuaded us to
become Christians and we were confirmed together as Episcopalians
by the Bishop of Virginia. That was quite an event." The bishop
survived it. The reactions of the Baptist Ellysons in Richmond is
not on record.

The "straight dope," or "scuttlebutt," inaccurately forecasts a
crew's future. Built on hearsay, impermanent plans, and false logic,
it moves through a ship like wind and is seldom accurate. It changes
often, but some men fasten on each fresh bit as immutable fact,
no matter how often the "straight dope" has misled them. Ellyson
was one of those. When the *South Carolina* headed south in January
1914, Spuds sent Helen back to her mother's with the ship's winter schedule in her bag. "It's the straight dope, honey; you'll know
exactly where I am all the time," he assured her. "It shows I'll be
back long before our baby is born."

Did Mars laugh at the optimism of the father-to-be?

CHAPTER SEVENTEEN

Caribbean Maneuvers:

The Vera Cruz Landing

"*A*s junior captain in the division, I normally command the landing force regiment," Captain Robert Lee Russell reminded Ellyson the night before they entered the Caribbean. "Basset in the *Delaware* is regimental adjutant, but I want a permanent adjutant in the ship with me. It's easier to get out parade orders that way. When we anchor at Culebra tomorrow, go over to the flag and tell the chief of staff that I want you to be the adjutant."

"But, Captain, I haven't drilled since I left the Academy," Spuds protested. "I don't know anything about infantry. Never did."

Russell smiled as Spuds continued to give him reasons for someone else to take the job. When he ran out of excuses, the captain said, "I want a competent aide. I think a man who can operate both under the sea and over it can operate a regiment of sailors for me."

Spuds knew he was hooked, but he struggled a bit more. "Thank you for the kind words, Captain," he said. "But I've noticed that such compliments always go with a job that is a particular lemon." Next day, he was Adjutant Ellyson. His first assignment was to draw up all orders for an assault landing exercise scheduled for four days later.

Ellyson was grimly determined to do his best in the foul job, but he had no idea where to begin. Nor did he believe the skipper knew where to start either.

163

He borrowed several books from the ship's marine officer and found others in the ship's library and office. Several outlined model orders for a landing which he began to adapt by changing dates and names. But he soon found himself stuck, hopped into a boat, and went to the flagship to gather more data.

Lieutenant Claskey of the staff outlined the problem for him. The information on preparing landing orders was being printed as fast as possible; though it was a rush job, the materials were not yet ready. "Go ahead on your own—and send me a personal signal if you get stuck or if the dope doesn't come fast enough for you," he said in parting.

Back in his own ship, Spuds exploded into the job, grabbing order forms from this or that book and fitting his data into them. He wished for a map of the island, but without one he used the sea charts. As he finished each order, he gave it to the officer-of-the-deck for wireless transmission to the other ships of the division. He knocked off at three in the morning. After breakfast, papers from the flagship invalidated half his night's work. In the midst of revision, he thought of Claskey's parting words, scribbled a message, sent it to the officer-of-the-deck, and went on with his writing.

Tired of Spuds's long dispatches, the officer-of-the-deck sent the message along to the wireless room with only a glance.

That evening Captain Russell's face was as red as the explosive flag when Spuds answered his summons. "Look at this," he roared holding out a message blank. "Consider yourself informed."

Spuds read:

RADIOGRAM 2X SIGNED BY LIEUTENANT ELLYSON IS EN-
TIRELY IMPROPER NO REFLECTION OF THIS KIND UPON
ORDERS RECEIVED FROM PROPER AUTHORITY CAN BE
TOLERATED AND YOU WILL PLEASE INFORM HIM SIGNED
BADGER CINC

"Why in hell did you ever broadcast anything like this? The whole fleet got it. No wonder the admiral's sore," the captain said, thrusting another paper at Spuds. The radio room had broadcast his personal message to Claskey as:

DELAY IN RECEIPT OF WRITTEN INSTRUCTIONS FROM CINC
HAS RETARDED EFFICIENT DEVELOPMENT OF ORDERS
AND THE LANDING FORCE AS A WHOLE TWO SETS OF OR-
DERS ALREADY ISSUED ARE VOID OWING TO ARTILLERY

ORDER MARINES ARE CATCHING ALL SIGNALS PLEASE EX-
PEDITE ORDERS   ELLYSON

"I wanted that sent as a personal—a visual, as Claskey requested—
not broadcast by radio," Spuds said with rising temper. The whole
fleet had read his bawling out from the admiral too. He deserved
neither that nor Russell's anger because some communicator had
goofed. Rather he should be getting praise for day-and-night work
on a stinking job. "I want to see the admiral personally about this,"
he said. The captain demurred, but Spuds insisted until Russell
told him to go over in the morning.

Next day, after he had called on Admiral Charles Johnson
Badger, Spuds said, "The admiral told me he was exceedingly glad
I had seen him, that he was sorry he had to send such a signal, that
he thoroughly understood my explanation and congratulated me
on the very good work I had done in organizing the regiment...."
When he wrote Helen of the episode, he told her, "It was probably
all for the best because the commander-in-chief does not hold it
against me. It brought me in personal contact with him and brought
attention to the work I had done, and it always pays to advertise
with those higher up if it is done the right way. This was."

That afternoon the battalion commanders attended a conference
in the *South Carolina* and complimented Ellyson on the clarity of
his orders. On top of the admiral's kind words, this praise sold the
job to Spuds and convinced him he had all the answers for any am-
phibious assault. The operation began at 3 A.M. the next morning.
A formation of fifty-six launches, without lights, tried in the dark
to reach an unmarked, unexplored beach to surprise its defenders.
They never found it until the defending Marines began firing at
their white uniforms. Once ashore, they milled in confusion until
dawn. Nevertheless, Ellyson was elated because the umpires ruled
they had captured a beachhead, instead of ruling them out of action
before they beached.

Later, when shown the Marines' defenses, he thought it wonderful that they had made the island "impregnable" in only eight
days. Fortunately for the American troops of World War II, not
everyone else shared his opinion. Wiser men developed better ways
to attack and defend beaches.

The ships moved to Guantanamo to train for target practice.
Three days later, Haiti's president absconded with the national
treasury. The American minister cabled for Navy protection.

Orders from Washington blasted the schedule Spuds had given Helen and hurried the *South Carolina* to Port-au-Prince.

She steamed into the harbor with her landing force, including Adjutant Ellyson, ready to storm ashore. Spuds was disappointed to find that the *Montana* and a German cruiser had each landed seventy-five men the day before; his group was not needed. He went ashore with Captain Russell to see shuttered shops in a quiet city patrolled by vigilantes who were mostly foreigners. Later, to keep the minister happy, ten Marines were sent from the ship to serve as a legation guard. Neither ship nor guard did anything. Spuds was sure their stay would be short and that they would soon be back on schedule. Instead, the ship settled into the same deadly routine he had known off Mexico. Once again he organized smokers, fishing parties, and wardroom fun. He took over the wine mess, campaigned for new members, and diversified its stock.

"My God, Spuds, where do you get all that energy?" Gunboss Staton asked him.

Spuds would not admit even to himself that he was working to keep from thinking of Helen, to make himself tired enough to sleep without love. He gave a double-barrelled answer. "I think an officer should always go into anything assigned to him for all he is worth...and few officers have the incentives in their wives that I have."

"I guess you're right," Staton said. "Maybe I should find an incentive like that."

Incentive or no, Ellyson's energy varied like other men's. One week he did nothing about his routine janitorial work, then basked in the captain's compliments during weekly inspection. Another week he double-checked everything and went into a depression because the captain found fault everywhere. That afternoon he was in high spirits again; fish were biting and he was catching more than anyone else in the boat. For five weeks he alternated between deep depression and elation.

On the day he thought would be his last in Port-au-Prince, he was depressed. He had hoped to avoid coaling, since the ship was nearly full, but they were ordered to fill up before going to Guantanamo. Everyone expected an admiral's inspection at Guantanamo, so the crew hurried through the coaling and began the cleanup before lunch. After lunch, when the captain discovered the record showed the ship could hold seven more tons of coal, he ordered it taken aboard. Spuds argued against the second coaling and lost. He was surly even after the extra coal was aboard.

Then Russell cancelled the cleanup, or field day, Spuds had expected and made the men follow the fleet routine which called for scrubbing hammocks that afternoon. Spuds blew his top. He felt the admiral had the skipper bluffed, never realizing that his arguments made the old man oppose him.

The inspection Spuds feared never came off. After three days in Cuba, State Department alarms sent the ship back to its gunboat routine at Port-au-Prince.

Only scanty, stale news of the world reached the ships at Port-au-Prince, but rumors were fresh. In New York the same scanty news was expanded, exaggerated, and generally pepped up to help newspaper circulation. Helen read hints of war with Mexico. She wrote to ask what would happen to Spuds if war came.

"First, I would not volunteer for aviation there, for very little good could be done there on account of the nature of the work, and there are as many men as there are machines, all of whom are better qualified than I would be on account of their familiarity with the new type of machines," he wrote. He would stay in his ship; the battleship's duties would be to keep the lines of communication open until the Army arrived. "I am regimental adjutant; I would probably land but would remain in the coast towns. The two most important points on this coast are Vera Cruz and Tampico...."

That letter was one of his most accurate forecasts, but he thought it merely a theoretical dissertation, believing Wilson's watchful waiting would never change to action. War could not happen. For thirty-three more days, the *South Carolina* swung at her Haitian anchorage, where there were no women to make Spuds uncomfortable. He wrote daily of his activities; he asked Helen to pay his life insurance premium—though he had not had a bill, it was due. His bank account was overdrawn again. Would she borrow $35 and send it to the bank? He passed on the rumors that they might be ordered home and his opinions on garbled news from Tampico, where a boat from the U.S.S. *Dolphin* had blundered into the flank of a Mexican battle.

When cabled orders to sail for Hampton Roads arrived, Ellyson, the lover, was happy again. The orders were for Hampton Roads, not the Southern Drill Grounds—a Navy name for an area of the Atlantic east of Virginia. They would probably skip target practice and go right into the Navy Yard. He would be with Helen in less than ten days. As they steamed north, some of the radio reports about Mexico concerned him a little, especially the one that asked

Admiral Mayo if he had enough strength to take and hold Tampico. "Could be serious," he told Edward Cook Raguet, who was on his way to relieve the watch.

Raguet had been officer-of-the-deck for about five minutes when a wireless operator brought him a message:

PROCEED KEY WEST FOR COAL AND JOIN FLEET ENROUTE MEXICO

As the ship swung around in the white-flecked, dark blue sea, Spuds could see no silver linings in the cotton-ball clouds overhead. A radio news flash about a fleet "demonstration" disgusted him. What good where demonstrations? They never changed anything in Mexico. The Mexicans were not easily bluffed. The delay was annoying because it was useless, but he felt he would be home within a couple of weeks anyway.

Beyond Key West, the ship was ordered to Vera Cruz to reenforce the landing party already ashore. This order transformed a depressed lover into a busy adjutant who forgot everything but his immediate job, which was clear sailing this time; Culebra had made him an expert, at least in his own opinion. The *South Carolina* anchored after midnight on 22 April and sent her landing force ashore before daylight. Spuds went with them and served for two weeks on Captain E. A. Anderson's staff. Anderson's command included the *South Carolina* and the *New Hampshire*'s battalions. Back aboard ship, Ellyson described the first day's experience ashore in a letter to Helen:

> ...Our regiment was the only one ashore that did not have one or more war correspondents attached to the staff, and that is why we do not appear in the papers. During the fighting on April 22, we were the only regiment mixed up in it at all, that was around the Naval Academy, Military Barracks, and Preparatory School, and during the scrap we had more men killed and wounded than all of the rest of the force ashore added together during their entire stay. Yet the *Arkansas* and the *Utah* received the credit for the work. We were ordered by Captain [William Rees] Rush to proceed and clear out a certain district and were informed that the route along which we were to march had been cleaned out. Nevertheless the way we marched was suicidal, down the street in column of sections, that is half of the company in solid lines with the staff leading as shown.

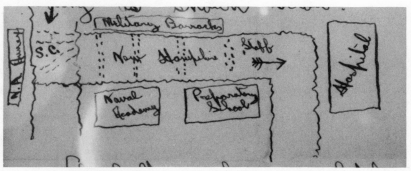

The buildings shown on sketch were those said to have been cleaned out. Before we started out I asked permission to take out a scout and work from building to building, making sure that the roofs and inside were clear, and have the regiment follow at supporting distance, but my request was refused, as Captain thought these buildings empty. I then suggested that we go through in open order with skirmishers well in advance, but was again turned down. I had talked to the people who did the fighting the day before, and they had run into the same sort of trap, hence my suggestions. When we were in the position shown in the sketch, fire was opened from the Naval Academy and immediately taken up by the other buildings, there being over three hundred men and two machine guns in the five buildings. The worst of it was that we could see nothing to shoot at, for all the fire came from loopholes. The *New Hampshire* retreated rather precipitately to the open field, losing three men killed and five wounded, and the only reason more were not killed was because the Mexicans were poor shots. It was thought that they simply stuck their guns through the wall and fired without aiming. We took position in the field, and opened on these places with our field pieces (hand-drawn 3 inch cannon), this being followed later by the guns from the *Chester* and *Prairie*. We then advanced in open order and took the buildings in succession. The greatest surprise of the day was the good work done by [Roman Burchart] Hammes. He had the 3 inch field piece and his work was superb. He worked his piece with the greatest skill, and was at all times in the open and under fire of the snipers, while the rest of us were under shelter. A puff of smoke would come from a window, and five seconds later he would put a 3 inch shell through the place, which was the end of whoever happened to be there, and not once during the day did he miss a shot....

Ensign Hammes was a retired captain when he first heard of these compliments. He modestly said the accuracy "was the work of my gunner's mate; I merely designated the target and he did the hitting. On that first day I escaped at least three would-be direct hits above the neck. One got an artilleryman who happened to step into the line of fire. The second got a man next to me, through the hat and above the hair, and a third [which otherwise would have hit me in the eyes] was deflected by the ammunition box on the gun carriage. There were other narrow escapes, but it must have been my lucky day....I suppose it is safe now to make a confession that I kept 'top secret.' One of the shots from the field piece went into the ice plant, and the resultant fumes did rout some Mexicans. However, a few days later when we were in the bars there was no ice, and everywhere I heard 'Who shot up that ice plant?' "

Ellyson's story of the ambush continued:

> When the fire first opened I was at the head of the column talking to the captain, and as he didn't run I couldn't, but I sure did want to. It was anything but pleasant, for it was the first time I had ever been under fire. We were the last to get out of the street, and after that I never even realized that we were being fired on as I grew used to it as one does to everything else. After this experience the rest of the fighting was done as I had suggested in the first place.

They were still in the open field when Lieutenant Sinclair Gannon, giving first aid to a sailor, was shot through the body. Spuds had seen a puff of smoke from a window just under the Greek flag on the Greek consulate (not shown in the sketch) and was sure that shot had felled Gannon. He "surrounded this building and made prisoners of all the inmates, six men and twelve women. The latter I allowed to depart, but the former, although one declared that he was the Greek consul and could not be arrested, I sent to the military prison, because I saw that shot."

The general fighting ended on that day. Some sniping still occurred, but no further casualties were reported.

A couple of days behind the *South Carolina,* the antique battleship *Mississippi* reached Vera Cruz with most of the naval aviation unit aboard. Lieutenant Commander Henry Croskey Mustin put planes ashore in a camp near the harbor entrance from which Patrick ("Pat") Nisson Bellinger flew scouting missions on request. War correspondents, hard pressed for copy in the pacified city, found Pat's camp the coolest place to concoct fictional dispatches that would satisfy their employers. Learning that Ellyson was in the landing force, and remembering his aviation fame, they put his

Patrick Niesson Lynch Bellinger, naval aviator number eight. Bellinger commanded the submarine C-4 before Jack Towers taught him to fly in 1912 at the Annapolis aviation camp. He served continuously thereafter in naval aviation. Among other duties, he was the first commanding officer of the Naval Air Station, Hampton Roads; he commanded Patrol Wing 2 at Pearl Harbor when the Japanese attacked on 7 December 1941; and he later commanded the aircraft Atlantic Fleet.

Captain Henry Croskey Mustin, naval aviator number eleven. In 1913 he was a lieutenant commander and the first lieutenant of the cruiser *Minnesota* at Guantanamo when Towers gave him unofficial flight instruction. A few months later, he wangled orders to aviation duty and soon was the pilots' champion when they had technical misunderstandings with their nonflying superiors. In May 1915 Mustin was the first commandant of the Naval Air Station, Pensacola, and, in 1921, the first assistant chief of the Bureau of Aeronautics.

name into some of their yarns. Such published fictions fattened the Ellyson legend. "He was in charge of the wounded," is one completely false example. That "Ellyson commanded the *South Carolina*'s landing force" is another myth, for the ship's log shows that his friend Staton was in command. Bob Murray, who told of winning Spuds's hat at poker, was quoted as remembering at Vera Cruz, "I waited until a heavy seaplane had come spattering and swishing into shallow water and the pilot had climbed to the mooring float...." According to Murray, the pilot was Ellyson. Actually Ellyson visited the camp to talk to Pat but never flew in Vera Cruz.

Spuds was not flying, but Chambers still listed him as an available pilot. Helen knew he had quit in a flash of temper, then rationalized his decision after he cooled down. "Flying's a new skill that may soon be added to the others required of all line officers, but you don't have to marry the girl," was one way he put it to his shipmates. It was time to have other duty, such as head of department of a capital ship, in order to become a complete naval officer, prepared for any command.

Nevertheless, he felt aviation was his private discovery and tried to keep track of it. In June 1913, Herbster, Helen, and others gave him the story of the crash that nearly finished Towers, who was a passenger in the B-2, and killed the pilot, Ensign William DeVotie Billingsley, on 20 June 1913. The following month, when the ship visited Galveston for ten days, he spent most of his time ashore drinking beer and talking aviation with Roy C. Kirkland, an Army flying pal who was camped at Texas City.

He found it difficult to be correctly informed for Helen's letters mixed aviation rumors, gossip, and facts, as did the newspapers and magazines. For example, in September he believed B. L. Smith had left aviation. In January he was delighted to find him flying with the Marines at Culebra. "I was sorely tempted to go up with him to get an idea of what Culebra is like, but decided I had no right to with present responsibilities since I am not in the game at present. Another thing, I do not like to go up when anyone else is doing the driving."

In October 1913, the "Chambers Board" met in Washington to consider "providing an adequate air fleet for the U.S. Navy, the fleet to include dirigible balloons, and aeroplanes with the necessary shore stations, shelters...." Ellyson, enjoying life with Helen in Norfolk, was not a board member, and the board's report was not approved and published until after he returned to the Carribbean.

When he heard at Port-au-Prince that naval aviation had moved
to Pensacola, he was sure the move must be temporary and that
the fliers would all go up to Annapolis in the springtime. In his
regular correspondence with Glenn Curtiss, he expressed his indig-
nation when the courts found for the Wrights in the long Curtiss-
Wright patent litigation. But though his interest in the field was
lively, Spuds was drifting away from aviation.

Shortly before the Vera Cruz landing, Chambers wrote to
promise Ellyson a Navy air pilot certificate and to waive the prescribed flight test. "This is quite a courtesy on his part," Spuds
told Helen, "and I appreciate it." Then he gave her explicit instructions about which picture she should send for the certificate.
He need not have hurried. Nearly a year passed before the ticket
reached him, with this covering letter from the Division of Operations, Navy Department:

> ...I desire to inform you that this certificate was issued upon recom-
> mendation of this office and special recommendation of Captain
> Chambers. It was considered that owing to your very excellent work in
> connection with aeronautics in its very infancy in the Navy that you
> were deserving of the first certificate issued. It gives me great pleasure
> to forward this to you.

At Vera Cruz, after the Army relieved the naval landing force,
Spuds lunched aboard the old battleship *Mississippi* with her
skipper, Lieutenant Commander Henry Mustin. The *Mississippi*
had been made the aviation ship, because she was so obsolete no
one else wanted her. In her, Mustin had moved the aviation camps
from Annapolis to the abandoned Navy Yard at Pensacola, Florida.

When the Mexican crisis occurred, Mustin obeyed orders from
the Navy Department and sent the 1st Aviation Detachment under
Towers to Tampico in the cruiser *Birmingham*. It contained all of
the flyable planes. A few days later, Mustin assembled a few more
planes and sailed with the rest of naval aviation in the *Mississippi*.
While the *Mississippi* lay off Vera Cruz, Mustin learned that
Richardson's improved catapult had reached Pensacola. He was
eager to work with it, so he pumped Spuds about his own catapult
experience. Mustin was nine years senior to Ellyson, but in an
afternoon of aviation talk, Spuds took the role of the elder states-
man. On or off flying duty, he remained, in his own opinion, the
Navy's senior flier. That night he wrote that Mustin was "very

bright and a hard worker, just the man needed for the job he holds."

Ellyson and Towers missed each other at Vera Cruz. Jack, in charge of the 1st Aviation Detachment, was at Tampico in the *Birmingham* until a few days after the *South Carolina* sailed for home via Key West.

The *South Carolina* was a day out of Vera Cruz when a radio message put Spuds on the spot. It asked if he wanted immediate orders to aviation. He had enjoyed flying, but at Vera Cruz he had seen that the planes were practically useless. He was certain the future was brighter for a battleship officer than for an aviator. Besides, he did not want his pregnant wife worrying about his neck. On the other hand, as the Navy's senior flier and aviation expert, he felt honor-bound to fly whenever he was needed. If he was needed, why did the Department ask instead of ordering? If they did not need him, why the "immediate" in the message?

He talked his problem out with Captain Russell. The skipper wanted to keep him in the ship but eventually agreed he should answer "yes."

After Spuds radioed his "yes," he wrote several letters to Helen, though mail would not leave the ship before Key West. Each was a running account and rehash of his hopes, fears, and concern for her feelings. The captain was sure Spuds would be detached at Key West. Spuds hoped and believed the men in Washington could not work that fast.

"It is hard for me to do a thing which I fear will hurt you," he wrote to Helen. "Some people will say I cared more for my profession and good name in the service than I did for you, else I would not have gone back into aviation at such a time...you will not think this....you would not have respect for me if I turned down this offer when my services are likely to be needed, nor would you if I allowed people to say 'Spuds was needed and offered the duty but as usual when a man gets married he is worthless to the service unless he has the proper sort of wife.' I have...."

Spuds relaxed when the ship left Key West without receiving his orders. Then a radio message said the question had been directed to Staton, not to Ellyson. Staton later wore the Medal of Honor, but he wanted no part of flying. Neither did Ellyson at that moment. Elated at this reprieve, Spuds told Helen he was "glad and happy, for I know it will relieve you of a lot of unnecessary anxiety, and I did not want to go back for I need the battleship duty, am perfectly contented and happy here, and am not as keen about aviation as I used to be, but suppose I would be just as keen once I were back in it...."

The mix-up occurred because Captain Mark L. Bristol, who had succeeded Captain Chambers in Washington, had combed the officers' files for possible fliers. He found Staton's 1910 request for orders to observe an air meet and wrote the radio message that was somehow garbled from Staton to Ellyson. He also uncovered Whiting's original request and invited him too.

Ken Whiting was delighted. The "Gone," as he called the G-1, was as good as anyone would ever make her, and routine operations were a bore. He had never lost interest in aviation. Bristol sent him to Dayton, where he was the last naval officer taught to fly by the Wrights. After his qualification in September, he went to Pensacola as the senior officer of an administrative and physical mess.

The armored cruiser *North Carolina* had become the aviation ship when the *Mississippi* was sold to Greece. She was at Newport News, Virginia, in August 1914 when the war broke out in Europe. She immediately dumped her planes but kept her aviators as watch officers when she was rushed across the Atlantic to look out for Americans in the Near East. She had left a detachment at Pensacola consisting of a student, Ensign Clarence King Bronson; instructor, Ensign Godfrey D. C. Chevalier; a handful of men; and the Navy's airplanes. Ken found the detachment living as squatters in the abandoned Navy Yard, without records or pay accounts. They had no authorized mess and had not been paid since June, but "Chevy" had kept his men eating and his planes flying.

Whiting found a kindred pragmatist in young Chevalier. Both thought straight and big, concentrated on essentials, ignored details and dull routine. They both played rough and drank too much—too often. Neither gave a hoot for regulations, customs, or stuffed shirts which got in the way of anything they thought important. Chevy taught Whiting to fly Curtiss-type planes, while Ken kept the undermanned, embryo air station alive. When the other fliers returned from the Mediterranean in January 1915, Mustin relieved Whiting as officer-in-charge; Ken remained as executive officer.

In the meantime, before the ink was dry on Whiting's orders to Dayton, a consul yelled "help." A radio message rerouted the *South Carolina,* sending her hurrying to Puerto Plata, on Santo Domingo's north coast. Spuds was philosophical about the change. No longer a newlywed, he settled down to the inactive waiting and watching that was gunboat routine. For five weeks the ship lay anchored off the sugar port. Spuds filled the first ten days with routine work, topping it off with sailing, fishing, bridge, and a bit of poker.

Then he relieved Adolphus Staton as the ship's gunnery officer—an appointment he considered an important promotion, for the gun-boss was normally a dreadnaught's senior department head. Spuds threw himself into his new work with the burst of energy he always mustered for a new project. He was soon deviling the captain to arrange underway drills for his turret crews, but he never got all he wanted.

He asked to be relieved as athletic officer because it interfered with his gunnery duties. Captain Russell agreed, then changed his mind. Bitterly Spuds wrote, "[it was] because I took an interest... the only way to act here is not to do anything, for the more one does, the more he is expected to do, whereas those who do nothing of their own accord are not given anything to do." In spite of this gripe, he continued to drill his gun crews and organize recreation for both officers and men. A few compliments were all it took to start him on another round.

Early in July, at the request of William Jennings Bryan's State Department, the ship moved west to Cape Haitien, but her routine was the same. Each day an officer, usually Ellyson, went ashore to get a report on conditions from the consul, who never had anything to report. On this duty Spuds got to know the Americans who ran coffee plantations in the hills and the forty-mile railway which served them. Soon he had invitations for ship people to visit the plantations. Since shore leave and liberty were prohibited, Spuds wrangled authority to take groups ashore, under his control, to accept these invitations. Forty years later, his shipmates recalled these "supervised trips" as most welcome changes with "plenty of rum, beer, and food...very, very pleasant."

Even before the Vera Cruz landings, Ellyson worried about rumors that Secretary of the Navy Daniels, a prohibitionist, was going to outlaw wine messes aboard ship and forbid officers to wear civilian clothing at any time. Spuds did not like the clothes rumor, but the wine mess one was alarming. "He [Daniels] is certainly using the Navy to further his own personal political aspirations without a thought of the good of the service," he wrote. Five weeks later he noted, "Our radio news informs us that the Secretary has issued an order...that 'no officer shall drink intoxicating liquors or wines on government property ashore or afloat.' It seems to me that this is more or less a criticism of the President, for he serves wine at all official parties...it is likely to cause misunderstandings when entertaining foreigners because both the English and Germans take offense if their sovereign's health is not drunk on such occasions. Our mess has a very small stock, except cigars and tobacco, so even if we were required to throw overboard all wine stores, it would not hurt any member seriously."

Off Haiti, the dread order arrived in the mail, but Captain Russell "saw fit not to have the letter opened or brought to his attention. At any rate the mess continued in full operation until September," according to William Keen Harrill.

Late that month the ship anchored briefly in berth 2, Hampton Roads, just off Fortress Monroe. Shortly before she got underway for target practice, Ellyson put Ensign Harrill into a boat with instructions, funds, and a large empty suitcase. The ensign returned with the suitcase full of wine mess supplies. Two weeks later, en route to Philadelphia, General Order 99 was officially received on board.

Thereafter, according to Harrill, "the *South Carolina* was never exactly dry...her officers had the reputation of being a hard-drinking outfit, nonpareil...she was a happy ship and her officers very congenial. For this I attribute more than a proportionate share to Ellyson."

Ellyson had gone south as an expectant father. He took his status very seriously—when he thought of it. Whenever his wife's letters mentioned the expected child, her symptoms, or her obstetrician, Spuds answered with appropriate comments. While he was off Vera Cruz, she asked about sponsors for the child. "If a boy I would suggest Billy [Helen's brother] and [Jack] Towers or Donald [Spuds's favorite brother], having no choice between the latter two, except possibly toward Towers, for he has been a true friend," he answered in part.

When the child was born on 21 July, however, it was a girl, and Helen chose her own sponsors for Helen Garrard Glenn Ellyson. Spuds got the news off Cape Haitien. He had to wait until October to meet the two Helens in Philadelphia. The three of them settled into a Spruce Street apartment for four months while the Navy Yard modified the *South Carolina*'s turrets.

Spuds needed practice in the role of father and husband. Soon he discovered Helen Garrard could be an appealing miss—and a demanding one. Being her father was a new adventure. Nevertheless, the Philadelphia interlude was less exciting than Norfolk had been a year earlier. His favorite playmates, Max DeMott, Adolphus Staton, and Oscar Smith, had left the ship for other duty. Ship parties were no fun without a wine mess. City nightlife took too much cash for a young family bedeviled by creditors. In February 1915, when his ship headed south again to join the fleet in the Caribbean, Spuds was ready to go.

Spuds wrote Helen daily, as usual. Many of his letters were addressed to Helen at her mother's flat on New York's West End Avenue. Others went to her at the Chamberlain Hotel on Hampton Roads. Helen did some ship-following.

The *South Carolina*'s log shows routine operations—no banana wars, no gunboat duties. She had a new chief engineer; Spuds had fewer wardroom quarrels. She spent the winter and spring months drilling in the Caribbean, divided the summer months between New England and the Southern Drill Grounds. She made three brief calls at New York and was in the Philadelphia Navy Yard each June and December. Helen was in Philadelphia for Christmas in 1915, when Spuds sent in a request for duty at the Newport Torpedo Station upon completion of his three years' sea duty, which would end in April. That station belonged to the Bureau of Ordnance.

Many people believed the "gun club," the officers connected with the Bureau of Ordnance, ran the Navy and enjoyed the surest chance of promotion. Spuds's two years as the *South Carolina*'s gun-boss seemed like a foot in the door. He had worked hard, had used one of the first gun directors which fired all the ship's guns in salvo, but had never been able to make a high score at target practice. Captain Charles Butler McVey, Jr., chief of the Bureau of Ordnance, may have looked at Spuds's scores before he blackballed him for the gun club.

After being turned down for duty at Newport, Spuds asked to be assigned to the Naval Academy. Helen was expecting again. After the Academy duty was promised and Spuds had gone south again, Helen settled in Crabtown. Their second daughter, Mildred Lewis, was born there on 10 April, the day the *South Carolina* left Guantanamo for Philadelphia.

Ellyson expected detachment in Philadelphia at the end of the month. But he was still aboard when the ship left for New England in May. He had lost interest in his job and in the ship and complained to the Bureau of Navigation that others, less deserving, had been relieved, while he was overtime. Washington answered that his relief would not arrive before late June. Spuds asked for ten days' delay in reporting, got it, then did not use it. He was detached in Newport 24 June 1916, and hurried to Annapolis to report for duty.

CHAPTER EIGHTEEN

War in Europe:

Number One Wings

*I*n August 1914 war exploded across Europe. Rear Admiral Bradley Fiske, the Secretary of the Navy's aide for operations, rushed cruisers and transports to help stranded Americans. He sent Jack Towers, Vic Herbster, and B. L. Smith abroad as the Navy's first air attachés. He left the *South Carolina* swinging to her anchor off Cape Haitien from where her gun-boss, Ellyson, wrote:

> ...our interests are not, and cannot become, involved, so there is no chance of the United States being drawn into the war.

Many Americans concurred in this opinion, which Spuds still held unchanged two years later when he went to his Annapolis duty. Disliking his original assignment as a discipline officer, he wangled a teaching billet in the electrical engineering department under Captain Gatewood S. Lincoln, once executive officer of the *South Carolina*. Relaxing with his children and his old shipmates, Spuds raised chickens in his backyard and ignored warring Europe.

In the fall of 1916, Towers wrote from London that he was coming home at last for the sea duty his record needed. Could he visit the Ellysons, with his English wife, for a few days until he received his next assignment? Helen Ellyson disliked Towers; she sent an invitation only because Spuds insisted.

When Towers arrived in America, he found the Democrats campaigning for Wilson's reelection singing "I Didn't Raise My Boy To Be A Soldier" and shouting "Peace at any price," "Too proud to fight," and "He kept us out of war." But Jack was convinced that the United States would go to war, and he was busy telling Congress and the Navy's General Board about the state of European aviation.

Captain Mark L. Bristol had elbowed Chambers into obscurity, then feuded with Mustin until Admiral William S. Benson, the first chief of naval operations, abolished the office of Director of Aeronautics. Limiting Bristol to command of the aviation ship *North Carolina,* Benson personally took over aviation, running it through an aviation desk manned by Lieutenant junior grade C. K. Bronson, naval aviator number fifteen.

The day after Wilson was reelected, a premature bomb explosion blew Bronson and his plane out of the sky. Towers, awaiting assignment, was plunked into Bronson's chair. Before he had a firm hold on that job, Congress decreed a Naval Reserve Flying Corps (NRFC); since he was the only aviator in town, Jack got additional duty as supervisor of the corps.

Heated controversy about preparedness divided the country, Congress, and the Navy Department. Benson had told Congress the Navy was prepared and needed only spotting and scouting planes, but his opinion was bitterly contradicted by Admiral Fiske and others. Towers was caught in the middle of the debate.

In December Bristol went to the War College. Pilots left the *North Carolina* to join Whiting and Chevalier in the *Seattle* to fly under the command of Rear Admiral Albert Gleaves of the Atlantic Torpedo Force. At New Year's, Mustin left Pensacola in the hands of a nonflying commandant and became executive officer of a battleship. The situation was still shifting on 31 March 1917, when Ellyson wrote to Captain Chambers at his Washington home to ask how naval aviation was organized and who was in charge:

> I have seen Towers several times but have not been able to extract much information from him. The reason that I am anxious to find out is that I wish to get back into aviation in case trouble actually comes, and I feel that Towers is not anxious to see me back in the game. If war actually comes, I am going to Washington to see what I can do, but would like a little advance information. I have volunteered my services three times since I left aviation, without any results, and do not intend being turned down a third time so will take anything that comes along unless I find out that I can be of some real use in aviation.

In this letter, written four days after the recalled Atlantic fleet had entered the security of Hampton Roads, the words "if trouble actually comes" and "if war actually comes" indicate Ellyson's uncertainty—and that of the country. Just six days later, Congress declared war on Germany. No doubt Ellyson could not "extract much information" from Towers because, with aviation decisions scattered through several bureaus, neither Towers nor anyone else was sure who was running the shop.

Ellyson's interest in aviation seems to have hit its low ebb about 1916, for he took no interest in the year-long battle Mustin and Whiting fought to replace the bamboo-tailed pushers with safer planes. Nor did he meet with the *North Carolina* fliers who were in Guantanamo at the same time as his *South Carolina*. Ellyson's interest in flying was probably renewed with the publicized expansion of naval air, the Congressional hearings, Towers's tales of European developments, and the work of Ken Whiting.

Whiting may have visited Annapolis in November 1916 on his way from Pensacola to join the *Seattle* in Boston. In the following February and March, his team learned to fly with the Deperdussin controls (the kind used in all later planes), to catapult at sea, and to spot gunfire by radio. In the process, they survived many troublesome events. One plane smashed into the *Dubuque*'s foremast; another crash broke the legs of Robert Alfred Lavender, the staff radio officer. A third nearly drowned Lieutenant junior grade Harold Terry ("Culis") Bartlett.

The prewar recall of ships to the United States stopped the development of the aviation program. Taking leave, Ken visited Washington and invented the 1st Aero Detachment—a Whiting solution for a nonroutine problem, and a way to get himself into the arena of the war. With that arranged, he visited Annapolis in May. Finding Spuds waiting "for anything that comes along," he explained, "Recruiters signed up a lot more would-be pilots than can train in the planes we have. I'm taking 130 of them to Europe, hoping I can arrange their training when I get there. Can't wait to set it up through channels. Jack Towers is getting a new four-stripe boss who'll cancel my orders if he catches me."

Ken sailed uncaught, landing in France three weeks ahead of General John Joseph Pershing, about the time Spuds was embarking with the Annapolis midshipmen for a Chesapeake Bay cruise in third-line battleships.

At least once that summer, Ellyson again considered aviation. Taking midshipmen to inspect the Newport News shipbuilding

Lizzie Walker Ellyson and three of her four sons during Spuds's brief 1917 Richmond visit. *Left to right:* Lieutenant Commander Gordon Ellyson, Douglas Ellyson, and Lieutenant Donald Ellyson.

yard, he visited a Curtiss school for Navy fliers. After arranging flights for the second classmen, he too went up—with Lieutenant junior grade Henry Barton Cecil. Flying with a stranger at the controls made Spuds "nervous as a cat" on this first flight in over four years. The tractor plane handled so much easier than anything he remembered that he wondered how he and Towers had ever gotten the pushers into the air. He found friends from his flying days among the Curtiss group; as he talked of the Early Bird experiences, he thought it would be fun to work with the fliers again. But he wrote no request for aviation duty that night. In his room aboard the *Kansas*, he described the day for Helen, saying, "I believe I have lost my nerve when it comes to flying, for I sure was scared, but maybe it was only because I was not driving." The occasion was a rare one upon which he underestimated himself.

In November, Mamma relayed to Spuds the gripes of his kid brother. Donald beefed because he was in a training camp instead of battle. Still "waiting for anything that comes along," Spuds replied:

> Tell him that he has been in the Army less than six months, whereas I have been in the Navy over sixteen years, and yet I am a school-teacher, whereas my record justifies my right to expect active service in either submarines or aviation, at both of which I was one of the pioneers, and my record shows that I did better than average. I feel sorry for him and his disappointment, but I also feel sorry for myself.

At year's end, learning that the Department planned to issue each pilot a pair of gold wings engraved with his name and designation number, Ellyson wrote a plea for the number one pair. He mentioned nothing about flying duty. In January 1918, Jack Towers, still trapped at a Washington desk, made sure that Spuds got the number one wings.

Subchasers:

A Pioneer Once More

A few days after Spuds pinned on the wings, he was a pioneer again, ordered to the 110-foot wooden subchasers. The subchasers were being commissioned at New London almost as fast as the ninety-day-wonder ensigns who commanded them. Designed as the latest anti-submarine weapons, the chasers were to patrol coastal waters with depth charges. Tests with the first listening gear offered so much hope that the subchasers could kill submarines before they could attack that some of them were to cross the Atlantic and hunt where the subs hunted, near the ends of the convoy routes.

In this operation, Spuds saw his part in the war he had feared he would miss. Putting himself on the wagon for the duration and mustering his customary new-project energy, he helped Commander Lyman A. Cotton ready the first overseas flotilla. When it sailed in May, Spuds parked his family with his mother-in-law and boarded a troop ship.

The gray vessel, almost hidden under life rafts, steamed through New York's narrows at twilight and anchored in the Lower Bay to await the convoy. Soldiers crowded her weather decks, concerned about submarines, seasickness, and storms. On the horizon, the twinkling lights of Coney Island offered no reassurance. Ellyson, at home again in a sardine can of a cabin, began another series of daily, numbered letters to his wife. After opening with proper regrets at leaving her, his pen slowed. Accustomed to scribbling his thoughts and feelings with frankness, he hesitated to write that his country was now exacting a return for the retainer it had advanced to him during seventeen years and that he was determined to give an honest accounting. It sounded too stagey. He gave up that argument, then realized he was delighted to be sailing.

If he wrote of his pleasure, Helen would think he wanted to desert her. But the excited tingle in his spine at moving onto the sea antedated marriage. He had felt it as the train carried him away from Richmond to begin his career in the Navy. Airplanes, submarines, the dark landing craft at Vera Cruz, and the start of every cruise had brought it on. No matter how many arrivals were anticlimactic, the next departure into the unknown always thrilled him, rousing hopes of great accomplishment. Fearing that Helen would misunderstand, he wrote nothing of his excitement. He filled pages with hollow words, then went on deck to twinkle back at the Coney Island lights.

Nothing happened on the three weeks' voyage that took him to Commander Cotton, who was setting up the American submarine chaser base at Plymouth, England. Soon after his arrival, Spuds was promoted to commander; Cotton was elevated to captain.

Captain Cotton thought it politic to mix socially with nearby allies; his ensign flag secretary thought it was fun to mix. Sharing a bungalow with these two and feeling squeezed between Spud's love of fun and Gordon's black-and-white Richmond code, Ellyson shunned the parties. As Cotton's chief staff officer and operations assistant, he worked around the clock organizing and reorganizing the base. He sent subchasers hunting in groups and supergroups, leading a few of the hunts himself. Sinkings ceased in their area though none of the subchasers heard or attacked a sub.

Unsatisfied, determined to destroy U-boats, Spuds drove himself and subchaser crews until he was viewed as a Simon Legree by their yachtsmen skippers. Competent, but uninterested in naval careers, these youngsters saw the war as a vacation from their regular pursuits. They were looking for fun, not back-breaking labor, as they won it. When their grumblings reached London, orders from Admiral William Sims told Spuds to ease up on the youngsters. He obeyed but never eased up on himself. When associates partied at the bungalow, he found work or sat alone in his room complaining in letters of the party noises below.

A visiting marine who had partied with Spuds in Manila heard

him decline to party with Cotton and said, "You must be a newlywed. When you've been married as long as I have, you'll appreciate
a pretty face, form, and ankle, and forget for the moment that
you're married."

Ellyson turned on his old friend. "Militarily, I've always thought
you were a genius, and I always will. But personally you're a con-
temptible cad, and I want nothing more to do with you."

Near the end of the war when an officer coaxed Ellyson from
the base for an afternoon of golf, he enjoyed his first game in
months. The friend took Spuds to a nineteenth hole tea with
several women he introduced as British officers' wives. Spuds enjoyed the tea until he realized he was expected to spend the night.
He left in a rage. Driving back to the base alone, he scratched
another friend from his list.

In September, hunting out of a base well west of Plymouth, the
subchasers scored probable kills, but they were too far away to
give Spuds any feeling of personal success. About that time, Helen's
letters became sharply critical and irregular. Spuds's showed strain
but did not reveal its cause. Changing pace early in November, he
marked an envelope "to be opened on 15 November." The pre-
dated love letter began:

> Honey, do you realize that six years ago tonight you married a man who
> was more or less a derelict?...what a chance you took...I am afraid that
> I have not made you entirely happy until the last year when I cut out
> the booze, but I have loved you more every second of the time....

Before that letter was opened, the armistice had ended the
shooting on 11 November. Everyone in Plymouth "went wild....I
have never seen such crowds nor such joy as was expressed by all
hands. We anticipated trouble so quadrupled our shore patrol and
had a large number of men standing by at the base, but the night
passed without incident. All the bars evidently expected trouble
for they remained closed of their own free will...," he wrote next
day, saying nothing of his own fun or feelings that night. The
duration was over; did he fall off the wagon?

Spuds relaxed into a time of confusion. Each letter carried new
scuttlebutt about his future, the subchasers, the base, about
Cotton and Bristol. Mark L. Bristol, promoted to rear admiral, had
arrived in the summer to command the base, leaving the subchasers to Captain Cotton. Ellyson worked for both men until
Bristol left early in January to become high commissioner to

Turkey. On the eve of his departure, Cotton gave a farewell dinner, boycotted by Ellyson, who was miffed because he had not
been invited to join the admiral's new staff.

When Cotton departed a few days later, Spuds inherited the
base for decommissioning, a job which lasted until 5 March. He
was soon enjoying the social obligations he had inherited with the
base. He tried, not too successfully, to picture them as a bore
though he filled one letter with a list of the titled aristocracy he
had invited to a formal dinner in the house Lady Astor lent to
American officers.

Captain Lincoln, Ellyson's one-time boss in the *South Carolina*
and at the Academy, invited him to be his executive on the cruiser
St. Louis. Spuds accepted with pleasure, and Sims's staff said he
would be released for that duty in March. Then London remembered that Ellyson had once volunteered his subchaser officers
and men to man one of the German merchantmen being taken
over as transports. Sims ordered him to form crew number 14,
which Ellyson would command. For a moment Spuds wondered
what Captain Lincoln would think of him, then he began organizing.
He reported ready the night he entertained the titles.

With his crew quartered in Victoria wharf for three weeks after
the base was decommissioned, Spuds enjoyed independent command and the hospitality of Plymouth, showing no impatient urge
to get home. Late in March, as Admiral Sims's representative at
Spithead, he met, took over, and put American crews aboard the
squadron of German vessels. The 36 officers and 592 men of crew
number 14 manned the last ship, the *Zeppelin*. This liner's name
has made some people think Ellyson got into lighter-than-air flying
while in command of an ex-German rigid airship. While some other
aviators of that period qualified in both airplanes and dirigibles,
Ellyson never did. The nearest he ever got to a balloon was in res-
cuing a blimp crew who crashed at sea near Plymouth.

Bunkering his U.S.S. *Zeppelin* with Plymouth coal and moving
to Brest, he took aboard 5,000 officers and men of the 35th division and the 129th Field Artillery. Helen was waiting when he
landed them on a Hoboken pier. On the last day of April 1919, in
the Brooklyn Navy Yard, he turned the ship over to his relief.
Helen may have expected him to seek a period of shore duty, but
Spuds did not. The rusty, coal-gulping, old *Zeppelin* had taught
him that command of an American Navy ship could be more re-
warding than anything else he had ever done. He wanted more of
it.

The USS *J. Fred Talbot*, destroyer number 156, at Venice, Italy, under the command of Commander Gordon Ellyson. This type was 314 feet 5 inches long and 31 feet 8 inches beam, and had a mean draft of 8 feet 8 inches and a normal displacement of 1,154 tons. The destroyers carried twelve torpedos and four four-inch guns and had a designed speed of thirty-five knots.

The "four-stackers"—the 1,200-ton, flush-deck destroyers ordered as sub-killer escorts—were still being commissioned. For the next twenty years, they were to be the sweethearts of all who bucked an ocean's fury in one, the envy of all other Navy men. Swift, rough-riding, tough, and seaworthy, they were knifing blue water to perform a variety of chores. Some, under the command of Rear Admiral Philip Andrews in the Adriatic, kept Greeks, Slavs, and Italians from murdering each other over the bones of the Austrian Empire. Under Rear Admiral Bristol, high commissioner to Turkey, others worked in the Aegean and Black seas.

As carriers of mail, money, medicines, and other priority cargos, they also ferried Red Cross, State Department, and military officials, as well as American businessmen and refugees, in and out of ports where the war had destroyed normal transportation. Rumor said their crews found romance in Constantinople, and excitement in outports and made occasional killings gambling on exchange.

When Ellyson landed in New York, naval aviation was booming. The first Fleet Air Detachment was with the Atlantic Fleet. Planes had been launched from sea sleds and battleship turrets. The first carrier, the *Langley*, was pending in Congress, the NC flying boats were poised for the first trans-Atlantic flight. Big air stations, operating on both coasts, might have offered interesting shore jobs, and Spuds had been away from his family longer than ever before. But when he was offered command of the four-stacker *J. Fred Talbot*, destined for the Mediterranean, Spuds grabbed it, saying he needed sea duty, and command, on his record.

For ten days, he enjoyed New York with Helen. Then, after moving his family to the Belmar Apartments in Germantown, he spent the rest of the fiscal year watching Cramp's Shipyard finish his ship and the Philadelphia Navy Yard outfit it. Her commissioning on 30 June 1919, the last day before Prohibition was to begin, gave him cause to celebrate in the bars that were pouring free drinks for everyone as the midnight dry-line approached. Five days later, with Helen settled in their Annapolis house, he sailed for Europe via Newport for torpedoes.

CHAPTER TWENTY

J. Fred Talbot:

Four-Stacker in the Adriatic

As the *J. Fred Talbot* headed for Gibraltar, Spuds's spine began to tingle again. And again he filled his daily letters to Helen with trivialities about the voyage, avoiding mention of his pleasure at leading a division of new four-stackers across the Atlantic.

Reporting to Admiral Andrews, Ellyson took up the Adriatic routine, alternating quick messenger-transport rounds of northern ports with ten-day stints as station ship at one or the other port. He lost a man who picked up an old grenade on a Trieste battle-field, got his ship dented by a pilot who rammed an oil dock. He was drydocked at Venice after another pilot wrapped a buoy's mooring chain around the *J. Fred Talbot*'s port propellor. His steering gear jammed twice as the ship entered Gravesa, but Spuds used the engines to avoid grounding. He stopped Slavs from shooting Italians in Pola, hauled the steamer *Susquehanna* off the beach near Trieste, and fell off a bar stool while making a New Year's speech in Venice's Excelsior Bar. But his letters told only of work, casualties, arguments with seniors—little more.

He shed the tensions that had ridden him in Plymouth, becoming again the genial playmate his companions had known before the war. A few of his juniors remained overawed at his wings and his legend. But his own officers enjoyed many hours of bridge and poker with him in the wardroom of the *J. Fred Talbot*.

In January, Admiral Andrews sent the *J. Fred Talbot* on one of the periodic runs to Constantinople. After landing two English nurses at Corfu, the ship rode out a bora—one of the severe, cold, northerly storms of the Adriatic Sea—in the Corinthian Gulf, then stopped for errands in Piraeus and Salonika. Spuds anchored in the Golden Horn on 2 February 1920.

Spuds never held a grudge. His Plymouth pique was long forgotten, and Admiral Bristol was now an old friend who had a car waiting on the dock to carry Ellyson to the embassy where the admiral, as high commissioner, lived and worked. The admiral pleased Spuds by opening the conversation with regrets "that he had not brought me do'/n here with him to run his organization, and that he had never appreciated what I had really done at Plymouth, until he came down here and found he had no one to depend on."

After talking for a couple of hours, they joined Mrs. Bristol. Spuds had never met her but knew she was a cousin of Helen's father. "She was playing bridge with three men of the American colony, none of whom knew how to play the game," he wrote that night. "I do not like her."

When he lunched with Mrs. Bristol next day, she was so nice to him that he was sure the admiral had "prompted her." They played bridge, and she asked him to stay for dinner, "making me feel like one of the family." Though he had dinner plans with Scott, the two met the Bristols and their friend, Mrs. Baggaley, at the Constantinople Club, where they danced until nearly four o'clock.

When the Bristols dropped Spuds at the landing, a freezing wind from the Black Sea whipped the harbor. Snuggling his chin into his boat cape, he watched the car pull away, then turned to the waiting dory. But as he boarded, he missed his footing and plunged through skim ice between the boat and the dock. His brass hat floated away. Deep in the icy water, he fought free of the heavy cape and kicked to the surface. With waterlogged clothes doubling his weight, he needed the help of two husky sailors to struggle into the boat. Before he recovered his breath, his hair and clothes froze ice hard. "This sounds like I had been drinking," he wrote Helen. "But the admiral is my witness I refused even a cocktail at the embassy." Afterwards? He did not say.

Thawed out, he lunched the next day with Mrs. Baggaley; played bridge with the Bristols and joined them at a tea dance; dined with Sadler of Standard Oil. Spuds kept going until after 2 A.M., but he got safely aboard ship without another dunking.

He begged off sight-seeing with the ladies on his third day. After lunch, the admiral told him the Bolsheviks were closing in on Odessa. "Get up there and take charge until I get Admiral [Newton Alexander] McCully there to relieve you. Use your discretion. Evacuate only Americans. You can continue on the trip we laid out after McCully arrives. I have Ham Bryan up there, but he seems to have gone wild."

Spuds mailed a postdated $90 check to Helen for her "house account" and sailed for Odessa with a mixture of passengers that included a United States Shipping Board man bound for Romania, Standard Oil's Mr. Sadler and his secretary, and a Russian lieutenant who laughed easily and was going to Odessa to marry.

Smoke billowed up the afternoon sky the day the *J. Fred Talbot* anchored in Odessa's crowded inner harbor. Rifle shots sounded nearby, and refugees crowded the waterfront. At dusk, the ship's dory nosed into the tip of a breakwater, and Spuds stepped ashore with the Russian lieutenant. Clambering over the debris in front of looted shops, stepping around occasional bodies, the Russian led Spuds toward the American consulate as the sporadic rifle shots drew nearer and fires glowed in the sky. By twos and threes, people scurried past the two officers toward the harbor.

Near midnight, Ellyson was back aboard his ship with Ham Bryan and a number of refugees logged as a vice consul, an embassy man, three YMCA people, a British girl, two Red Cross workers— man and wife—and George and Mrs. Rossen, a Russian couple— hopefully, the laughing lieutenant and his bride, though the record is unclear.

As the night wore on, the fires and shooting drew closer. Near dawn, an old freighter capsized in her berth under an overload of terrified refugees. Other vessels began moving out to avoid similar trouble. Clinging to his anchorage, Spuds could only pity the desperate waterfront mob he had neither the means nor the authority to help. On the *J. Fred Talbot*'s third day in port, Rear Admiral McCully arrived in the U.S.S. *Biddle.* He moved into the *J. Fred Talbot* and sent Spuds's refugees on their way to Constantinople in the *Biddle.*

Ashore, fires and shooting were widespread when the four-stackers cleared the harbor, abandoning the city they could not assist. At Sevastopol, the admiral moved into another destroyer, releasing Ellyson to complete his voyage. The meeting between Newt McCully and Spuds Ellyson off the Crimea was not pleasant; when they met five years later in Brazil, their reunion was not a happy one.

The officers and some of the men of the *J. Fred Talbot* grouped on her forecastle and bridge while the ship was in Spalato harbor in March 1920, after Pierce was detached. The officers seated in the second row were (*left to right*) Ensign Dixon, Lieutenant Junior Grade Tipping, Commander Gordon Ellyson, Lieutenant Ginder, Gunner Garrison, and Machinist Sullivan. Ginder went to flight training shortly after the *J. Fred Talbot* returned to the United States; he was a flying admiral during World War II.

Swapping two Red Cross personnel for three British soldiers at Novorossiysk, Ellyson landed the soldiers with Sadler's team at Batum. For two nights he granted liberty, then sailed with passengers for Constantinople and two Armenian ports. Seventeen days after entering the Black Sea, he anchored again in the Golden Horn.

With no time for society, he landed his passengers, filled his oil tanks, and was gone again in ten hours. After chores at Smyrna, Piraeus, and Corfu, he reached Spalato on 26 February. Next morning, the force doctor told him his engineer officer had to be returned to the States for treatment.

Making the best of the situation, Ellyson divided the work between his executive, Pierce, and his warrant machinist. Barely an hour after the assignments were arranged, Spuds and Pierce were called to the flagship. Admiral Andrews was braced for a blast when he said, "Pierce, I've decided to order you to my staff as flag secretary."

With his face firecracker red, Ellyson went off like a string of big ones. "That's not fair to me, to the *Talbot,* nor to Pierce...."

"Ellyson! You shut up!" Andrews roared. "You are always thinking of 'I' and 'the *Talbot,*' instead of the good of the force as a whole. I've considered this matter from all angles and have made up my mind. I not only do not want to hear your opinions, I order you not to talk to Pierce about this detail."

"This is a hell of a way to treat a man—and an organization you've credited with being the best you've had in the Adriatic," Spuds shouted. "You are especially unfair to Pierce. He refused a command in order to stay with me. Now, because he's made good, you punish him with a job he doesn't want and doesn't feel fitted to fill."

Spinning on his heel, Spuds stamped out, slamming the cabin door.

Andrews grinned at Pierce. "I like Ellyson. He always stands up for his rights," he said. "But you are coming over here just the same."

While boating back to the *J. Fred Talbot,* Pierce tried to cheer his skipper. "The man said you should relax. The *Talbot* will be ordered home in a couple of weeks. I told him I needed to go with you to take care of some family problems, but I didn't get anywhere."

Deep in the dumps, Spuds grumbled, "I'll bet it's closer to four months."

His guess was good. The Adriatic routine held the ship until June. On 21 June 1920, Spuds nosed her into Philadelphia's back channel and secured alongside the new destroyer *Gilmer*. Helen was waving from the *Gilmer*'s deck. Leaving the children with a nurse in Annapolis, Helen had hit Philadelphia for a week of shows and nightlife with her husband.

Minutes after they had checked in at their hotel, the nurse phoned. Daughter Mildred had fallen. Her broken arm had been set, and she was sleeping comfortably.

Knowing that only time could mend the child, Helen wanted to proceed with her plans for the week. But Spuds, feeling fatherly, grabbed the phone and arranged a week's leave. He and Helen headed south on the next train.

Months earlier, he had requested the War College course, thinking the work would look good on his record, though he had no desire to read books for a year in Newport. He felt reprieved when, after his Annapolis leave, he was ordered instead to command the U.S.S. *Little* and a flotilla of reserve destroyers in Philadelphia's back channel.

Nesting like sardines in a can, his ships lay with cold firerooms and dead machinery. Their crews were too short-handed to keep the ships clean, check for rust, or keep records. Spuds's takeover was never recorded in the *Little*'s log. Each day for a week, he hunted chores to keep himself busy until cocktail time. Then, giving it up as a bad job, he asked for another active destroyer command. Within a week he was fitting out the Camden-built *Brooks*. Nine weeks after he had arrived in the *J. Fred Talbot*, he began a new series of numbered letters to Helen and sailed in the *Brooks*.

CHAPTER TWENTY-ONE

The Destroyer *Brooks:*

Trouble at Kiel Canal

*F*or an hour the destroyer steamed smoothly down the Delaware River. Watching a freighter bucking the tide on the other side of the channel, Spuds congratulated himself on heading for another interesting Adriatic cruise, instead of spending a hot summer among the giant mosquitoes of the Philadelphia back channel. Suddenly his ship swung left toward the approaching merchantman.

The *Brooks*'s helmsman spun the wheel to the right. As the bow kept swinging left, he yelled, "Rudder's jammed, sir!"

Spuds was already leaping. Yanking the starboard engine telegraph handle back to full astern, he lifted it and banged it down a second time. The second ring was the old destroyer emergency signal which meant, "Give it everything you can without taking the steam pressure to zero." The fireroom blower shrilled up several octaves, smoke and soot spurted from the stacks, the bridge shook and rattled. Without looking, Spuds knew white water was boiling under the stern. He watched the bow slowly check its turn, then swing to the right to pass a few yards astern of the freighter.

A jammed rudder was not an uncommon occurrence—Ellyson had handled such an emergency before. After the near collision, he juggled the engines to hold his ship in the channel. Engineers soon freed a salt-crusted steering-engine valve; the helmsman regained normal control.

At the time Spuds considered the rudder incident part of the routine. Only in retrospect did he view it as the first indication that his *Brooks* cruise would be different. As he had in the *J. Fred Talbot,* he took on torpedoes at Newport, then sailed for the Azores, unaware that senior officers in London were dreaming up a Baltic Patrol.

As he neared the islands, orders diverted him from the Adriatic to Lisbon. From there, he was to proceed to Copenhagen, fueling at Brest and calling at Le Havre, Southampton, and Antwerp. Anticipating adventures in new ports, Spuds had his ship fueled and on her way again less than three hours after entering Ponta Delgada.

The deep-throated roar of the blowers which kept the firerooms under air pressure permeated life in a cruising four-stacker. Even when they shouted to be heard above it, the men aboard were conscious of every change in pitch. It sang a steady, ignored, bass as Spuds leaned on the port-bridge rail to watch his ship's nimble shadow glide over the oil-smooth, cobalt-blue water. Inside the furrow of creaming foam that angled from the bow, three porpoises humped smoothly out of and into the blue. Almost within spitting distance, they paced the ship. How did they slip along so effortlessly? He could see only the slightest tail wiggles. Tiring of the game, they flashed ahead at five times the destroyer's speed without any apparent extra effort.Like many another sailor, Spuds marvelled at their efficiency, but only for a moment. He had a good ship, a beautiful afternoon, and interesting work ahead. What more could a skipper want?

Next morning, reflected sunlight flashed through the ports and rippled changing patterns across the wardroom's overhead. Relaxed at the starboard end of the table, Ellyson watched his mess boy refill his cup with steaming coffee as he discussed the ship's destination with Lieutenant Henry Mullinix, the executive, and Lieutenant (jg) Joseph James ("Jock") Clark, the engineer.

Suddenly the blower shrilled up like a screaming siren. Slopping the coffee, the boy straightened, wide-eyed. Overturning his chair, Clark leaped through the door with Spuds on his heels. Jock hit the ladder, three rungs from the bottom, as the blower exploded like a five-inch gun.

Popping out of the hatch, the officers saw a kneeling water tender frantically twisting emergency valve wheels to shut down the fireroom. Steam hissed from the blower intake, greasy black smoke billowed from the forward stacks. The soles of their feet told them the engines were slowing; the ship was dying. Losing all way, she soon rolled like a drifting timber in the long oily swells.

Governor, throttle valve, and overspeed emergency trip had all jammed, letting the turbine speed up until it flew apart. Bits of metal like shrapnel had torn up both the fireroom and Water Tender Lukaseweski.

Was it bad luck or the innate orneriness of inanimate objects? Spuds wondered. Did neglect or incompetence contribute? Such speculation could solve nothing. He wasted little time on it. The damage was done. The ship was dead in the water with half her power wrecked. His immediate problems were to get her going again and arrange for dockyard repairs without cancelling his Baltic cruise.

By early afternoon Clark's engineers isolated the damaged fireroom and raised steam in the other one. As soon as a generator was running, Spuds reported the accident by radio and asked permission to stop at Plymouth for repairs instead of calling at Southhampton. He knew the Royal Dockyard people from his wartime duty; he was sure they would fix his ship quickly.

On Saturday, off Brest, the *Brooks* slowly nosed into steep seas. Every other wave lifted the bow clear of the water until the ship, pivoting like a seesaw, dropped faster than men's stomachs, slamming into the wave's trough with a bone-jarring thud. For an instant her bridge watch saw the next wave tower over them as the bow plunged into it, burying the forecastle in solid water and whipping spume over all. Then, spewing green water overside, the bow shot skyward to ride over the next crest.

With water dripping from his chin and his salt-crusted sou'wester, Spuds gripped a stanchion to steady himself and peered over the windscreen. How far was he seeing into the murk from the crests? A half mile? Probably less. What sort of service would that mean at Brest? French port delays had driven him wild during the *Zeppelin* troop loadings. He expected they would be worse in this weather.

His chain of thought was broken by the double thump-thump of the bow hitting the trough, whipping the ship so that it trembled from end to end. "All engines ahead one third!" Spuds yelled. Across the bridge, a seaman shifted his handhold to yank up the handles of the engineroom telegraph. Four-stacker crews knew their vessels could take that keel-quivering double bang, but they believed a triple one might break a destroyer's back. In rough waters, their skippers slowed on the double, not wishing to test the three-thump theory.

The ship had slowed to single thumps again when Mullinix, who also served as navigator, came onto the bridge. "Henry," Spuds said, "I don't think we can get a French pilot to come out in this weather. If we do, I'll bet he won't take us in until it lets up. Anyway, they won't fuel us on the weekend." Mullinix nodded agreement. "I know Admiral Thursby at Plymouth," Spuds continued. "He'll start them working on us whenever we get in. We'll save time by coming back here for oil after our fireroom is fixed."

"Sounds reasonable, sir," Henry agreed. "I'll pick off a course to Plymouth."

Repairs were nearly complete when a radio message from Rear Admiral Harry McLaren Pinckney Huse cancelled Ellyson's calls at Antwerp and Le Havre. He had permission to use the Kiel Canal and was to go to Copenhagen "without delay."

"Huse seems to want you up there in a hurry," the British admiral said. "You can save time by fueling here. Won't cost any more." Accepting this advice, Ellyson filled the tanks and sailed for Denmark.

He had been on the bridge for hours when shortly after midnight on 20 September 1920 he eased into the Kiel Canal. He was still there at ten in the morning, when, dropping the pilot, he cleared the canal's eastern end. Boosting speed to twenty knots, he stretched out in the emergency cabin at the back of the bridge to catch up on sleep.

Sixty miles beyond Kiel, the officer-of-the-deck roused him with a radiogram from Admiral Huse:

> PITTSBURGH WILL ARRIVE KIEL 0200 21st WAIT KIEL FOR ARRIVAL PITTSBURGH AND COMMANDING OFFICER REPORT ON BOARD

"Hurry up and wait," Spuds grumbled. Turning his ship about, he radioed Kiel for a berth assignment near the harbor entrance. He was entering the harbor when he translated their reply:

> CANNOT BE GIVEN IN ADVANCE MUST BE OBTAINED THROUGH GERMAN GOVERNMENT

Wondering what the message meant, Spuds shackled the *Brooks* to a convenient buoy before a German ensign came aboard. He brought no interpreter and spoke neither French nor English. No one in the destroyer spoke German. Ellyson understood him to be saying, "You cannot remain. We are still at war with the United

States. If you do not immediately move outside the three-mile limit, you will be cannonaded."

Before the Armistice, Spuds had "learned to hate the Hun," but at Kiel he supposed the language problem to be the cause of the young officer's sounding offensive. He went ashore to solve his problem with a responsible senior, finding only a stiffly formal lieutenant commander who also refused to understand English or French.

Even if he had not been bone tired from loss of sleep, Ellyson's redhead's temper would have flashed when he decided the German was belittling the United States, its Navy, and its flag. "Put your order in writing," he snapped. The German understood that. Scribbling German he handed the paper to Spuds who jammed it into his jacket pocket without looking at it. "I'm staying at that buoy until this order is confirmed by higher authority," he said and stamped out.

Spuds felt like a fight. He hoped the Germans *would* "cannonade" him, but the afternoon passed quietly. He was unaware that a wire to Berlin had the foreign office complaining to an American diplomat who cabled a German version of the incident to Washington. The diplomat's message ended:

FOREIGN OFFICE OK BUT GERMAN NAVAL AUTHORITIES IRRITATED BY WHAT THEY CONSIDER HIGH HANDED ACTION ON THE PART OF AMERICAN NAVAL AUTHORITIES

By 3 A.M. when Spuds boarded the flagship, he had simmered down. Having won his point, his spat with the German lieutenant commander seemed unworthy of mention.

Ellyson would be the senior American officer in the Baltic as soon as the armored cruisers *Pittsburgh* and *Frederick* went west through the canal. All Baltic patrol skippers were fresh from the States and unacquainted with local politics. For half an hour Spuds absorbed the admiral's information and instructions. "Go to Riga," Huse said. "The Letts kicked out the Bolsheviks a year and a half ago, but they are in a tough economic spot. We want to keep an eye on them until a trade treaty is signed to help get them on their feet. Keep me informed of goings on there."

Soon after Ellyson left the *Pittsburgh,* she headed into the canal. The *Frederick* waited until daylight, sent her paymaster to pay the *Brooks's* crew, then followed the flagship. Spuds headed for Riga.

Before he arrived, he had experienced the first discipline problems of his career. Submarine and aviation crews had been his friends. He had never had occasion to put anyone on the report in the *South Carolina*. In the *J. Fred Talbot,* only one seaman had appeared regularly at report mast. But the *Brooks*'s crew was different. Spuds was holding mast nearly every day.

At Riga, for offenses ranging from liberty breaking to serious assaults, he ordered more courts-martial than he had ever expected to order in his lifetime, but offenses increased. He had first held mast in the old *Villalobos* after two old hands tested their young skipper by returning aboard drunk and raising hell. Giving them stiff sentences had stopped all future trouble. A week later, before being relieved, Spuds had revoked the punishments, leaving the men's records clear. A similar stiff beginning in the *Brooks* had failed, convincing Spuds he was involved in a test of will. He found some of the *Brooks*'s men far better educated but just as ornery as the bums he had pitied when Captain Staunton had put them in double irons during his duty aboard the *Colorado*.

Spuds wondered how he had failed. Why could he not lead this crew as he had led others? He appreciated the competence of his men; he sympathized with their hardships, understood their temptations, and made allowances for normal weaknesses—but this gang remained sullenly unleadable.

At last he understood that neither he nor, years ago, Captain Staunton in the *Colorado,* nor any other captain, had a choice. A captain had to run his ship. Though irons were no longer a legal punishment, the law was loaded in a skipper's favor. Men who would not follow could be driven. Spuds drove because he must.

He had been in Riga a week when the four-stacker *Kane* swished her tail into a mine in the entrance channel. Rushing the *Brooks* to her aid, Spuds found the *Kane* anchored with the flooding controlled but her engines disabled. Retrieving his liberty party, he put a towline on the *Kane* and began a week-long struggle with the sea, parted towlines, and engine breakdowns. Drydocking the *Kane* at Copenhagen, he presided over a three-day investigation of the explosion. By the time the hearing was over, Rear Admiral Huse had suspended the Baltic patrol for the winter. After wiring Helen, Spuds sailed for the Adriatic via England.

Helen Ellyson had wanted to follow when Spuds sailed in the *J. Fred Talbot,* but the Navy would not send her, and the Ellysons were too broke to buy her ticket. Each time Spuds felt low, he thought of sending for her but never had the cash. When she suggested joining him, he told her that only Venice had a decent hotel, and he was not there often enough to make her journey worthwhile. Writing from Constantinople, he mentioned that Mrs. Baggaley was "the most lonesome soul I have ever seen"; in the four months she had been there she had seen her four-stacker husband only six days. Instead of making Helen want to stay home, his mention of dinners, dances, and bridge confirmed her idea that she would rather be a temporary widow in Europe than in Crabtown.

When Spuds asked for command of the *Brooks,* he appeased Helen by arranging her passage in an Army transport. After he was diverted to the Baltic, he told her to wait in England. When she received his message from Copenhagen, she reached Sheerness before he moored the *Brooks* to buoy 4. She convinced a British admiral to send her out to the *Brooks* in his barge and was lunching with the ship's officers when Spuds returned from his official call aboard the *Pittsburgh.*

He greeted Helen distractedly, missing most of her story of her British barge ride, for he was still concerned with where he stood after his surprising interview with his boss, Admiral Huse. Coming out of the Baltic proud of his work, he had boarded the flagship expecting congratulations for his salvage of the *Kane.* Instead, the admiral had handed him a radiogram, demanding, "What have you to say about this?"

The message from the Navy Department was dated two weeks earlier. It read:

GERMAN FOREIGN OFFICE WANTED 24 HOURS NOTICE TO ARRANGE PASSAGE OF SHIPS THROUGH THE KIEL CANAL STATE OF WAR STILL EXISTS PASSAGE OF CANAL IS DELICATE AND RECENT SHORT NOTICE REQUESTS AND ESPECIALLY ALLEGED ACTION OF DESTROYER BROOKS IN REFUSING TO PROCEED OUT OF KIEL HARBOR WHEN ORDERED TO DO SO BY GERMAN NAVAL AUTHORITIES HAVE INCREASED IRRITATION

Spuds told his story. He went hot all over as he remembered the Germans' haughty insults.

"I'm sure your motives were good," the admiral said coldly. "I'll think it over and frame a reply."

When Spuds told Helen about the interview, she cheered him

up. "You were carrying out the admiral's orders; he has to back you up," she said. "Anyway, the message was mostly about short notice at the canal, wasn't it? You had nothing to do with that."

Spuds was convinced by her argument and relaxed. For five days, the two enjoyed Sheerness together. They visited Cooks, arranging her trip to Venice. All was set on the last day when the admiral sent for Ellyson.

He handed Spuds a message addressed to the Navy Department. "I wanted you to see this before you sail," he said. Spuds read:

FULL REPORT FOLLOWS BY MAIL COMMANDER ELLYSON SHOWED POOR JUDGMENT IN REMAINING WHEN ORDERED IN WRITING TO LEAVE AND SHOWED LACK OF TACT IN A SITUATION WHICH HE SHOULD HAVE RECOGNIZED AS EX- TREMELY DELICATE BAD JUDGMENT WAS SHOWN BY COM- MANDER ELLYSON VERGING ON DISOBEDIENCE OF OR- DERS BY FUELING AT PLYMOUTH WHEN ORDERED TO FUEL AT BREST EXTRA EXPENSE ABOUT FIVE THOUSAND DOL- LARS THESE WERE BOTH SERIOUS ERRORS IN JUDGMENT AND TACT ESSENTIAL QUALITIES IN A NAVAL OFFICER WHO AT ANY TIME MAY BE IN INDEPENDENT COMMAND COMMANDER ELLYSON HAS SHOWN ABSENCE OF THESE TWO QUALITIES I RECOMMEND COMMANDER ELLYSON BE RELIEVED OF HIS COMMAND BY CABLE   HUSE

Too shocked to argue, Spuds went ashore. In the boat he told himself, I thought the guy had guts. I was wrong. The striped-pants boys have him buffaloed. Ashore he told Helen, "I think I'm fired. Don't start for Venice until you hear from me."

Two days out of Sheerness, one of the *Brooks*'s two generators ran wild, flying apart as the blower had. By that time Spuds was sure that the breakdowns and his discipline problem were related, but both, along with the generator replacement, would soon be another's worry. He had intercepted the Navy Department's answer to Huse.

ORDER ELLYSON HOME TO AWAIT ORDERS WHEN HE CAN BE SPARED HIS RELIEF COMMANDER V F HOUSTON SAILING FROM NEW YORK ON ARMY TRANSPORT FIVE NOVEMBER

Flag Secretary Pierce climbed the *Brooks*'s sea ladder as soon as her anchor splashed into Castellini Bay. Together, he and Spuds went to report to Admiral Andrews. The admiral tried to turn the occasion into a happy reunion, but Spuds's pending detachment overshadowed the meeting.

Houston took command of the *Brooks* on 23 November. After borrowing money to pay his bridge debts and transportation costs, Spuds joined Helen at the Hotel Gallias in Antwerp.

Helen told people a bad case of flu had forced Gordon's early detachment. She tried unsuccessfully to make their three-week wait into a happy holiday. But nothing she said or did could make Spuds forget he had been fired or feel that he deserved to be relieved of his command.

On 20 December, the Ellysons sailed into a dirty, storm-rumpled ocean in the transport *Cantigny.* A western gale wallowed the tubby vessel, beating her with sleet and rain. Most of her passengers were too seasick to notice Christmas. Ellyson, sick only at heart, watched foam fly from gray waves. Knowing Huse had ended his destroyer career, he wondered what sort of duty he could hope for.

Legend skips lightly over Ellyson's cruise in the *Brooks,* but it had two long-reaching effects. Two of his officers, Mullinix and Clark, asked for flight training; both served as carrier admirals in World War II.

CHAPTER TWENTY-TWO

Back to Aviation:

Hampton Roads, Brazil, and the *Wright*

*U*ntil 1921, Ellyson's wings, like his campaign ribbons, were evidence of past, not present, activity. His record contains no request to return to aviation duty, and his interest in it was declining.

In 1918, when Captain Cone of Sims's London staff had offered him command of an anti-submarine air station, he had declined, thinking he could harm the enemy more with his Plymouth-based subchasers. Spuds knew that Ken Whiting commanded the air station at Killingholme on the Humber and had intended to visit him but never got around to it. Unlike Ken, he could no longer picture naval air as a future power. He wrote Helen that the planes he saw and heard over Plymouth no longer called to him.

When he had left the *Zeppelin* in New York, he had shown no interest in the aviation activities led by Whiting and Towers; he had wanted a ship's command. Orders to leave the *J. Fred Talbot* temporarily to inspect fifteen Caproni bombers for shipment to the States were pleasant evidence that Washington remembered him as an aviation expert. After enjoying a ten-day junket through Italy and damning the planes as junk, he had been glad to get back

Captain Kenneth Whiting, USN. Whiting was a commander in 1922 when he nudged Ellyson back into aviation. More than any other man, Whiting was responsible for putting aircraft carriers in the United States Navy. He died 24 April 1943, while still serving naval aviation.

to his four-stacker. He had said nothing about flying when his *J. Fred Talbot* cruise ended.

Neither legend nor record fully explains his return to flying in January 1921—three weeks after the *Cantigny* landed him in New York. Probably Ken Whiting was the strongest of several influences. Spuds found Ken behind a desk, in a back office of the ugly, concrete, temporary Navy Building on Constitution Avenue in Washington.

Another man might have talked of his war experience. Ken could have told how he conned the French Navy into making seaplane pilots of his 1st Aero Detachment; of joining Sims's London staff in charge of aviation; of commanding the Killingholme Air Station where he gathered destroyer-towed barges for launching flying boats within bombing range of the Cuxhaven anchorage of the High Seas Fleet. Instead of talking of these things, Ken propped his heels on the hissing radiator, stared at the snow falling into the concrete canyon beyond his window, and listened to Spuds's story.

Flooring his feet, Ken swiveled from the window when Spuds pondered his next move. "Get back into flying," he said. "Someday it's going to be the biggest thing in the Navy." He pointed at a blueprint captioned, "*Langley* (ex-*Jupiter*)." "She's only the beginning."

"Aviation?" said the detail officer. "There's no command open, but the Hampton Roads Air Station rates an exec. Would you like that?"

Spuds would.

The detail officer had read papers that reached Ellyson only a month later. Reading them, Spuds understood why the detail officer had been so unexpectedly accommodating. Huse's final fitness report said in part:

> ...a zealous, efficient, and devoted officer. He deserved what he got, but I should be glad to have him under my command. I have written the Department...he did not commit a fault of *omission*; although he judged wrong, his actions showed courage, decision, and initiative. He is an officer much above the average officer who never gets into trouble....

After explaining why Huse thought it necessary to fire him, the accompanying letter said:

...Commander Ellyson is a very gallant and efficient officer, and I now
intercede in his behalf with the recommendation that he be given
another command at an early date. His detachment has probably served
its purpose as a disciplinary measure and as a disavowal on the part of
the government of his incorrect action. Commander Ellyson is a valuable officer, and it is not desirable that his spirit be broken by too-
severe measures.

When he reported to the air station on 17 January 1921, Ellyson
passed a flight physical examination and moved into the executive's
quarters, one of a row of houses salvaged from the 1907 Jamestown
Exposition.

The station's hangars and seaplane ramps faced Willoughby Bay.
Beyond its fish stakes lay the arc of Willoughby Spit where, ten
years earlier, Eugene Ely had landed after the first takeoff from a
ship. Mastering the Deperdussin controls, Ellyson soon checked
out in the station's assorted seaplane types. More stable and easier
to fly than he had expected, these World War I machines made
flying fun again. Some of the other pilots shunned the HS2L,
calling it "the angle-maker"—a fatal nose-high spin would invariably
follow an engine failure unless the pilot reacted instantly to the
motor's first cough. That hazard was old stuff to Spuds, who saw
this machine as a grown-up model of the C-1 he had flown in 1912.

In front of Ellyson's quarters during the spring of 1921, prospective *Langley* pilots flew landplanes from the recently completed,
grass-covered Chambers Field, catercorner from the unused blimp
hangar on one corner of the field. Lieutenant Alfred Melville
("Mel") Pride flew an Aeromarine at a turntable, developing
arresting gear to stop planes on a carrier deck.

Disregarding Prohibition, especially when Ken came from
Washington to check out a new idea with Pride, the Ellysons enjoyed the station for ten months. Then, the Ellysons moved to
Washington where Spuds joined Ken in the Bureau of Aeronautics,
which had been formed in September 1921. Disliking a desk,
lacking Ken's long view, he was somewhat miscast as head of the
plans division.

Working hard, he found escape in membership on four boards,
bureau liaison with others, and an inspection circuit that took him
regularly to other cities. He added Norfolk to the circuit "in connection with the development of arresting gear" after March
1922, when Ken and Chevy went there to commission the *Langley.*

The USS *Langley*, the first American aircraft carrier, a conversion from the collier *Jupiter*. Ken Whiting was her first executive officer and the senior aviator in her. She served as a test bed for ideas to go into the *Saratoga* and *Lexington* and was used to train people for service in these larger carriers before they were commissioned.

Since 1914, Whiting and Chevalier had collaborated on naval air innovations ranging from tractor trainers through the 1st Aero Detachment to torpedo planes and carriers. Dreaming big, playing rough, shrugging off petty details, they had horsed Mel Pride into building the arresting gear Chevalier used to make the first *Langley* landing in October 1922. They saw the *Langley* as a proving ground for the aviation part of the *Lexington* and *Saratoga*. Leaving carrier plans to them, Spuds concentrated on projects with less lead time, including torpedo seaplanes and a piggyback plane for S-type submarines.

That fall, wanting the Ellyson legend's prestige for the naval mission to Brazil, Captain Charles Theodore Voglegesang, chief of the mission, requested Spuds be assigned as the mission aviator. Seeing a chance to swap his desk for an airplane and adventure in new places, Spuds began cramming Portuguese about the time Chevy first landed on the *Langley*.

At the end of 1922, the Ellysons joined Oscar Spears and Jakey Fitch on the mission in Rio de Janeiro, Brazil. After renting a house in a walled garden on Copacabana Beach, they plunged into the social whirl with Brazilian officials—it was all part of the job. Forty years later, those who served with him recalled Ellyson's delightful hospitality, popularity, and great professional accomplishments for the Brazilian Naval Air.

But Ellyson's final report to the chief of the mission discloses how time and legend influence memories. The facts, apart from legend, reveal two and a half years of hard work, zero progress, and complete professional frustration. His report told of how the Brazilian Naval Air had begun in 1916, two years before the first American naval mission arrived. At least three mission aviators before Ellyson offered flight and technical instruction and urged essential administrative reforms. All were politely declined. Ellyson repeated both the offer and the recommendation but, in spite of his reputation, received similar rebuffs.

Brazilian Air Marshal Neto later remembered his frequent flights, as a lieutenant, with Ellyson, who was tactful, serious, and much respected. Spuds, he said, made serious military pilots of dangerous, undisciplined, sporty stunt fliers. But after some twenty months' effort, Ellyson recorded:

...The order was well executed and carried out in all details except after...the planes had broken formation there was considerable stunt and other erratic flying.

When Ellyson, an advisor without authority, reported such disregard of orders to senior Brazilians, they shrugged answers such as: "I issue the order, that's all I can do;" or, "The pilots did not care to comply;" or, "Young men must show off for their girls."

Another officer recalled that Ellyson "completely reorganized Brazilian Naval Aviation into a very loyal and efficient branch of the Navy." As for loyalty, Spuds's report tells of aviators jailed for taking part in three abortive revolutions. None of the reorganization recommended by him or his predecessors had been instituted when he left the country.

Voglegesang's first fitness report on Ellyson was tops, but as the Brazilians clung to their own ways, he lowered the marks on each succeeding report. In January 1925, Rear Admiral McCully became chief of the mission. Five days later, he told Spuds to stop making new recommendations and gain action on the ones he had already made. While Spuds tried unsuccessfully, all flying stopped while aviation materiel was moved from the old station on Ilha das Enaxadas to a new one on Ilha do Governador.

Perhaps the drop in visible activity displeased McCully. He may have remembered some unpleasantness during his time with Spuds at Odessa. Or, being new to the Brazilian's polite evasions, he may have assumed that in two years Spuds could have gotten greater results. In March, putting bottom marks on Spuds's fitness report, McCully wrote:

> This officer possesses much ability and is capable of excellent work. His last report on Brazilian Aviation is not satisfactory, through causes not under the control of this officer. Work of this officer much improved although Brazilian Naval Aviation is not yet functioning satisfactorily.

Ellyson read this double talk, looked at the accompanying low marks, and asked for Stateside duty. His rebuttal of McCully's opinions, a forty-two-page report dated 28 May 1925, details seven and a half years of frustration for mission aviators.

In June, reporting to the Bureau of Aeronautics, formed while he was in Brazil, Spuds found Whiting, off the *Langley* for nearly a year, deeply involved in the battle-cruiser conversions. "The 'Sara' and 'Lex' will be the biggest ships in this or any other Navy," Ken told him. "I'm promised the exec's billet in one of them. You ought to go after the other."

When Spuds asked for it, the detail officer replied that he lacked at least three prerequisites: command of a fleet air squadron, duty in an aviation ship, and familiarity with the *Langley*'s operations.

Admiral William Adger Moffett, the first chief of the Bureau of Aeronautics, was a consummate politician who appreciated the value of legends. "Never mind," he told Spuds. "There is time to sanitize you. We'll start with the squadron."

In mid-July, the seaplane tender *Wright,* carrying Torpedo Squadron One (VT-1) and Scouting One (VS-1) berthed at the Hampton Roads Naval Base, fresh from a Pacific cruise. Taking command of VT-1, Ellyson moved with it into one of the hangars beside Willoughby Bay. A self-sufficient command of eighteen twin-float torpedo planes, it had its own medical and supply departments as well as flight and ground crews.

The lean-to at the bay end of the hangar served as a general office. Shops and storerooms filled the lean-to at the other end.

None of the VT-1 pilots had been in the Navy in 1913 when Ellyson left aviation for the *South Carolina.* A few had been his students at Annapolis in 1917. Some of these young men lived in the bachelor officer's quarters, others had families living in the naval base's Poverty Row—a group of wooden, war-time barracks converted to transient-family tenements. These quarters were far more reasonably priced than anything a transient officer could rent off the base. Most Norfolk landlords set the rent to match the stripes on a Navy sleeve and insisted on an unbreakable one-year lease. The quarters on the Row were a letdown after a Rio garden on the beach, but the Ellysons moved. Helen soon made pals of her young neighbors, but the Ellyson legend kept them from relaxing with Spuds. One grade senior to and seven years older than any other squadron commander, he had to find his fun with nonflying classmates or Army Early Birds, including Hap Arnold, at nearby Langley Field.

Army pilots were helping General Billy Mitchell's flamboyant agitation to create a separate air force. The flimflam failed to enlist support from naval aviators, though they were told the separate air force was the way to promotion and pay. "Why do you feed reporters these cockeyed stories?" Spuds asked Hap across a lunch table. "You know they're a pack of lies."

Arnold grinned. "Sure, I know it. You know it. The public doesn't. If they swallow enough stories, they may force Congress to give us what we want."

In the fall Spuds's veteran department heads readied VT-1 for

The USS *Wright* and five planes of VT-1 taking off beside her. Ellyson commanded VT-1, then later served as the executive officer of the *Wright*. The *Wright* had been started as a merchant ship at the Hog Island shipyard on the Delaware River during World War I. Before completion she was converted to a balloon ship and tender for seaplanes. She served as a seaplane tender from 1920 into World War II.

a winter in the Caribbean with the fleet. Spuds was not directly involved until his executive officer told him a storekeeper named Amos was nine days and ten hours overleave. "I'll hold mast at ten o'clock," Spuds said.

Before ten, Lieutenant junior grade Edward Peerman ("Country") Moore, the squadron engineer, went to the skipper's desk in the corner of the lean-to office. A big, athletic type, Moore cultivated farmerish ways to hide a razor-sharp mind. In stuttering bursts of words, he begged clemency for Amos.

Spuds listened.

Moore got specific. Amos was his storekeeper and carried the only squadron use-records in his head. He alone knew how much of each spare to stock for the winter cruise. Having memorized hundreds of Liberty engine part numbers, he could type the requisitions without stopping to look them up. Only Amos could get the job done in time. "If I lose him now, the squadron will be grounded for spare parts before we get back," Country ended.

Ellyson sat quiet as a Buddha. He disliked holding punishment mast, had not had to since his days on the *Brooks*. This man, within a few hours of legal desertion, was a serious offender. As a new skipper, he could not afford to become known as soft.

While Ellyson silently pondered, sweat popped onto Moore's forehead. "It's partly my fault," he said. "You were flying. I was working on a plane on the apron. A sailor ran out of the hangar yelling that a woman, waving a pistol, was yelling for Amos to come out so she could kill him. I knew Amos was back in the storeroom typing cruise requisitions, so I sent the top chief to get him out the back door and away for awhile.

"I went into the hangar after seeing them drive off. I think she was pretty drunk. She said she was Amos's wife, lived in Portsmouth. Had found herself in the dependent's clinic waiting beside another Mrs. Amos who lived in Norfolk. I kept her talking until the Marines came and put her off the base."

Country squirmed under Ellyson's steady gaze. "I know I should have told you about it then, but she was gone when you landed, and I thought he would be back in an hour or so. I waited two days, but he didn't show up. The chief said he didn't know where he was, that he dropped him at the Willoughby Spit ferry dock. So I reported him absent. This morning I found him in the storeroom typing requisitions as though nothing had happened."

Ellyson's face never changed.

"I know he deserves a general court, Captain, but please, for the good of the squadron, if you can, keep him working for me—at least until we get the *Wright* loaded for the cruise."

"I'll think it over," Spuds said at last.

At ten, leaning on the stand holding the squadron report book, Ellyson slowly looked over Amos from shined shoes to well-combed hair. "Nine days and ten hours overleave," he read from the book. "What have you to say about it?"

"Well, it was this way, Captain...," he began, and Ellyson recognized the classic beginning of a sailorman's filibuster. Amos had learned that Agnes could be a dangerous drunk shortly after they married in Portsmouth the year before. Did he have another wife? "Well, you know how it is with women, Captain. They nag you till you give them what they want. Betty wanted to get married, so a couple of months ago, when Agnes thought I had the duty..."

Amos rambled on. He had talked himself off the watch list but told his wives he had the duty every other night. He didn't know how Agnes got wise, but when she was drunk and had a gun, he knew distance was safer than conversation.

As Amos talked, Spuds compared him to the bums in the *Brooks*, the drunks in the *Villalobos*. This bird's a slick operator, he told himself. Far more useful than the others. He's worth saving for the service, but I can't condone bigamy even though Moore needs him. Hell! He's up for liberty breaking, not bigamy. That's a crime ashore, but there's nothing in the Articles for the Government of the Navy about it.

He interrupted as Amos began to repeat himself. "You deserve a general court," he said sternly and saw Amos's mouth sag. "But because Mr. Moore says you have done good work, and you have a clear record, I'll let you off easy. You are restricted to the base until the cruise begins. That'll be about a month and a half." He initialed the report book and closed it.

Smothering a relieved smile, Amos stepped back, put on his white hat, and saluted smartly. "Thank you, *Captain*," he said emphatically.

Turning toward the office door Spuds heard Moore, behind him, ask, "Amos, where in hell were you for nine days?"

"Sir, I went to Key West to see my wife who lives there with our two children."

Spuds kept walking toward the door.

Adequate engine spares were stowed in the *Wright*'s balloon well when VT-1 flew south after New Year's, but influenza had

put Ellyson on his back in the Portsmouth hospital instead of in
the pilot's seat of the lead plane.

While Ellyson convalesced from the flu, Admiral Moffett asked
the chief of the Bureau of Navigation—"Mr. Personnel" in those
days—to call Spuds's squadron experience adequate and make him
skipper of the *Wright*. Navigation argued that Ellyson should first
serve as exec for a year, then compromised on six months' executive duty—which they never got. Ellyson joined the *Wright* on 4
April 1926 in the Caribbean.

Before he had been aboard three months, the president signed
a law requiring skippers of aviation ships to either be naval aviators
or aerial observers. No four-striper qualified as either. Rather than
entrust the world's largest warships to commander aviators, Navigation decided to qualify two officers as observers. At Pensacola,
the captains could fly as passengers for the required two hundred
hours while the executive officers organized and trained the nucleus
crews at the building yards. Whiting was with the *Saratoga* at
Camden, but the *Lexington* needed Ellyson at Quincy.

"Speed him up," Moffett said. John Rodgers, in naval aviation
again as assistant bureau chief, requested that Spuds be ordered
west to observe some of the flying on the *Langley*.

Spuds left the *Wright* at Newport in mid-July, one day before
Captain E. J. King took command of her. Reaching North Island
nine days later, he found the Naval Air Station completely unlike
the jackrabbit heaven he remembered. The *Langley* was docked
near the spot where Curtiss had launched the hydro from the barn
workshop. Aboard her were John Dale Price, slated for the *Saratoga*,
and officers Spuds had known in the *Langley* detail at Hampton
Roads. For ten days he partied with these and other old friends,
then sailed. Enroute to Seattle, he observed carrier flying nearly
every day.

The *Langley* pilots, who flew at sea as no other pilots had yet
done, also formed an exclusive club ashore. Finding that rank had
not killed Spuds's love of rough fun, they welcomed him to their
anti-Prohibition headquarters in Seattle's Hotel Butler. When the
Langley sailed for San Francisco after a week, the club established
another beachhead there.

One night Ellyson and several others arrived at the bay end of
Market Street too late to board the last boat to the *Langley*. Only
one boat was still tied up at Crowley's Landing. One of the *Langley*
lieutenants asked the coxswain if he would drop them at the

Langley. The sailor apologized. He had strict orders to return to the fleet flagship *Pennsylvania* without stopping at any other ship.

"Let me try," Spuds volunteered. Looking into the boat's canopied cockpit, he recognized a well-known, socially prominent Navy doctor who sat erect in the stern sheets. His gloved hands capped a thin walking stick which stood between his white-spatted, crossed ankles. Greeting the doctor by his first name, Spuds asked for a ride to the *Langley* and got the same answer the coxswain had given: "Sorry..., orders...."

"Thanks, Old Man. I thought you'd say that," Spuds bellowed, then shouted over his shoulder, "Come on, gang, it's OK!" The pilots jumped past him into the cockpit. Price plopped down on the far side of the doctor. "Shove off, Coxswain. Make the *Langley,*" Spuds ordered, dropping to a seat beside the doctor.

Struggling to countermand the order, the doctor found himself securely pinned by the men beside him. The two eyed the spats, something they had seldom seen outside of a comic strip. Their glances met. Upending the social medico, they yanked off his spats, which waved like pennants from the *Langley*'s gangway next morning.

The commander-in-chief's staff doctor was not amused. Contrite apologies kept his complaints from smearing anyone's record, but Spuds was inconspicuous for the few days before he left for Washington. After spending September in the Bureau of Aeronautics, he reported to the Inspector of Machinery at Boston for the *Lexington* detail.

CHAPTER TWENTY-THREE

Commissioning
the *Lexington:*
World's Largest Warship

*K*en and Spuds met at conferences several times that winter;
they were organizing ships built differently from all others to en-
gage in a war of a sort that had never been fought. Everyone involved wanted the sister ships to share identical arrangements. In
April, Spuds served in Washington, on the second Taylor Board,
which met to revise the five-year old Naval Aeronautical Policy.
He then rejoined the *Langley* while she took part in a fleet problem
that allowed no time for shoreside pranks. When she made port, he
hurried to Quincy and his organization work.

In November, eleven years after her construction had begun,
Ken's *Saratoga* was commissioned at Philadelphia. In Quincy,
Spuds planned the commissioning ceremony for the *Lexington*.
After so many months of helping her mature, the ship had become a
part of him. As soon as he was promoted to captain, he would ask
for command of her.

On 14 December, snow drifted on the *Lexington*'s 888-foot-
long flight deck, but her huge, white-walled hangar was pleasantly
warm when Ellyson paraded her crew in dress uniforms.

The crew members saw the number one naval aviator stand big
and unique—their own living legend. The Navy Cross, recent recognition of his subchaser work nine years before, decorated his

The USS *Lexington,* aircraft carrier number two. Spuds Ellyson was her first executive officer. At that time the *Lexington* and *Saratoga* were the largest vessels in any navy. They were 888 feet long and 105 feet 6 inches wide, displaced some 41,000 tons, and had a top speed of over thirty-four knots.

left breast between the Gold Wings and the campaign medals for Mexico and World War I.

Wakeman, vice president of Bethlehem Shipbuilding Company, stepped forward. Grasping the microphone connected to the ship's loudspeakers, he reviewed the design and building problems peculiar to the ship, then offered the vessel to the Navy.

The district commandant, Rear Admiral Andrews, took over the microphone to formally accept the *Lexington* for the country. Watching him talk, Ellyson wondered why the admiral looked so much older than he had when the two had been together in the Adriatic eight years before. Spuds thought himself unchanged, but an impartial doctor would not have agreed.

Spuds's attention wandered while Andrews read his orders to turn the ship over to Captain Albert W. Marshall. But when he heard the captain speaking, Spuds came back to the business at hand, squaring his shoulders a moment before Marshall faced him, ordering, "Set the watch."

Enjoying the spotlight, Commander T. Gordon Ellyson stepped center stage and gave the necessary orders. The band sounded off, filling hangar and ship with the National Anthem. Standing at salute, Spuds pictured the men topside in the falling snow. Some would be running up the Stars and Stripes, while others would be breaking a fluttering commission pennant at the masthead.

The anthem ended. Dignitaries moved toward Marshall's cabin. "Leave your quarters," Ellyson ordered, and the rigid ranks dissolved into moving knots of officers and men. It was done. The *Lexington* had become part of the Navy—Ellyson's part. He was the executive of one of the two biggest, fastest, most unusual ships in the world. Deep pride glowed in him and lighted his eyes as he joined his wife and daughters, who had been sitting with the relatives of the other ship's officers.

None of the Richmond Ellysons, nearly strangers now, had been invited to the show. The breach between Spuds and his family had widened by 1916 when he and Helen had moved into quarters at 34 Upshur Road. He had written then to Mamma:

> ...I wish you had made the surprise visit you almost did. We are settled now, have two guest rooms, one on the second floor which is the real one and the family one which is a double bed in my den on the third

floor. There is a bath on each floor. We have the prettiest house in the
yard, on the inside, and I do want you and Papa to come up and see
it....About the chickens...

Sister Bessie passed near Annapolis a couple of times, but Spuds
heard of her trips only after they were over. Never admitting, even
to himself, that he had joined the Navy to escape his family, he
maintained that families should stick together. "I do not think
sisters should wait for a special invitation," he wrote Mamma, but
the Richmond Ellysons did not visit Upshur Road.

After he left Annapolis for sea duty during World War I, he apparently did not correspond with the Richmond family. A letter
written from Quincy in 1927 while Spuds was organizing the
Lexington crew covered the intervening years.

Dear Mamma:
    I am well and doing well. I was ordered overseas in December, 1917
[he did not actually sail until May, 1918], served as operations officer
at Subchaser Base 1 [called Base 27 in his other letters] Plymouth,
England (first serving two or three months at the USN Headquarters,
London) [this London duty is unconfirmed by records] until December,
1918, and as commanding officer of the Base until April, 1919, when I
took over and commissioned eleven German merchant ships, coming
home in command of the ex-German merchant ship *Zeppelin* in May,
1919, and bringing some 5,000 troops from Brest, France. I returned
to Europe in command of a division of six destroyers in June, 1919,
and helped carry out the Armistice agreements in the Mediterranean,
Adriatic, Black, and Baltic Seas until Janaury, 1921, when I returned
to the United States. Will write later. With love to all.

                                              Your loving son,
                                              Gordon

This terse letter, filled with inaccuracies, is entirely unlike
Ellyson's other surviving letters. The need to capsulize the history
of several years of his career hints at an unexplained gap in correspondence with Mamma and a big change in attitude since the
letter in which he had urged her to visit Upshur Road.

Three weeks after the commissioning, Helen was home in
Annapolis when Captain Marshall, Ellyson, and a group of shipyard,
harbor, and Navy Yard pilots worked with a herd of tugs to maneuver the *Lexington* slowly through a specially dredged channel

into Boston Harbor. While snuffling tugs puffed the ship toward South Boston's big drydock, a UO-1 plane piloted by Mel Pride made the first takeoff from her flight deck.

Crouching in the shallow cockpit with leather and fur shielding his body and hands and the slipstream turning his face blue, Mel looked down on hurrying men rigging the arresting wires on the frosted deck. When the fox flag fluttered up to the port yard, indicating that the arresting gear was ready, he swung wide around the tugs and hit the deck in a perfect landing. As he climbed from the machine, he commented, "Nobody could miss anything this big."

"Just the same, you put us one up on the 'Sara,' " Spuds said, grinning like a schoolboy. "She hasn't flown a plane yet. Bet Ken never suspected we would try a flight before we drydocked."

Before the *Lexington* undocked, the Department changed her home yard to the West Coast, and Ellyson arranged for his family to ride a transport through the Panama Canal. On 21 February 1928, two days out of Boston on her first voyage, the *Lexington* anchored in Narragansett Bay. Spuds found life good. Both ship and family affairs were going his way. On Washington's Birthday, he went ashore at Newport to lunch with Max DeMott, a War College student, and his wife Margaret.

The "free state of Rhode Island" never ratified nor enforced the Prohibition Amendment, so Max poured a good whiskey from Drury's Grocery Store. The old friends laughed over memories of *South Carolina* days when Max had been Gun-boss Ellyson's top assistant and playmate. They rehashed Spuds's angry go-round with the skipper and exec who broke promises and let Max be transferred just before target practice. "I had the pleasure of telling that exec that he was a damn liar," Spuds said. They talked of Annapolis parties, of Margaret's sponsoring of baby Mildred Ellyson. The pleasant afternoon passed like many they had shared before Helen and Margaret had fallen out with one another.

Max found Spuds unchanged, still the same rugged drinking companion he had known in the Caribbean. If he noticed that Spuds steadied his glass with both hands, he thought Spuds was clowning. He was not. In spite of frequent stops in the long climb to the *Lexington*'s bridge, Spuds always puffed into the pilot house like a winded pup.

While he was in Brazil, the Bureau of Medicine and Surgery regularly called for rechecks after reviewing his annual physical examination. In the *Wright,* after Ellyson's three-months' bout with the flu, Captain John Vincent Babcock complained that Spuds did not take proper care of himself. Shortly before the *Lexington* left Boston, Surgeon General Stitt frowned over Spuds's last examination report: high blood pressure, low Snyder (a test of reserve energy), tremor of the hands, bad eyes, nervous irritation...problems sufficient to ground *two* ordinary pilots. But the legendary Ellyson, the original aviator, was not an ordinary pilot; he was Moffett's untouchable. Stitt recommended more waivers.

From Newport the ship made a fast run to Hampton Roads, anchoring on Saturday afternoon, 25 February. By that time Ellyson had received Helen's message telling him that eleven-year-old daughter Mildred was down with an alarming ear infection.

Her illness affected Spuds as her broken arm had years earlier when he had rushed from Philadelphia to her side. The urge to go to her was stronger this time, for Helen, who had been stoical about the arm, was frightened by this infection. At the same time, he felt duty-bound to his giant ship which had not yet shaken down.

CHAPTER TWENTY-FOUR

The Last Flight:

The Family Calls

*I*n 1928 no airline flew from Norfolk to Annapolis. The trip between the two cities was normally a slow, roundabout journey by train or steamer. With airports, airways, air communciations, the weather service, and sophisticated navigational aids still in the future, cross-country flying was almost as rare an adventure for Navy pilots as Ellyson and Towers' flight down the Chesapeake had been in 1911. Pilots, without flight instruments or voice radio, often arrived at their destinations ahead of their departure reports, and obediently saved Navy money by night-lettering news of their arrival. Planes could still land only on the water at Annapolis, but the *Lexington* had an OL-7, a Loening amphibian, ashore at the Hampton Roads Air Station. It could get Spuds to Annapolis in two hours and back on the job just as fast.

After discussing Spuds's family problem and the transportation facts, Captain Marshall told him, "Go ashore and phone your wife for late news. Then, if you are needed, you have my permission to fly up in the amphibian. Get back when you can."

Ashore, Ellyson sent Lieutenant Rogers Ransehousen, who was in charge of the ship's planes, to ready the amphibian while Spuds called Helen. Something over an hour later, in a day before direct dialing, he got through to her. The roundabout connection was

poor, but she heard him saying, "How's Mildred? I've permission
to fly up. I can start now if you need me."

She had to shout to make him understand. "Getting better.
Doctor just left. Her temperature has dropped a little."

"Shall I come up now?" he yelled back.

Helen hesitated, then said, "No. She seems a lot better, and it
would be dark before you could get here."

Her report relieved him. Probably nothing serious after all. He
had seen the children recover suddenly from frightening ailments
before. "I'll stay ashore over the weekend," he told her. "The
station duty officer will know where to reach me. If she has a re-
lapse, let me know, and I'll come right up."

Calling the hangar, he told Ransehousen, "Postpone the flight,
but don't cancel it yet."

On Sunday, Helen didn't call. Spuds assumed that no news was
good news. That evening he went to a party at the Norfolk Country
Club. A loud orchestra, flasks of corn whiskey, women in the
stylishly short evening gowns, and old shipmates combined to
make a good party. The eve of his forty-third birthday seemed a
time to celebrate—and the club was the place. The club was jumping
when, about ten o'clock, someone handed him an urgent telegram.
Helen wanted him. Mildred's condition was critical. An emergency
mastoid operation had been ordered for early morning.

The message washed party, ship, everything except Mildred,
from his mind. He had to get to her. Fast. Looking around for
help, he spotted Hugo Schmidt, an old friend and a good pilot,
and Ransehousen, who, though he was just out of flight school,
had more amphibian time than anyone else in sight. Both were
flattered to be invited to go along.

At eleven they were at the air station commander's quarters.
Commander Albert Cushing ("Putty") Read had been, as commanding officer of the flying boat "NC-4," the first man to fly
the Atlantic (with a crew of six, including himself, he had flown
from Rockaway, Long Island, to Plymouth, England, with inter-
mediate stops, May 8-31, 1919). He was years junior to Ellyson
in rank and in aviation experience. Spuds told him the three were
leaving in the *Lexington*'s plane and asked the station's help in
getting off.

"My duty officer, Lieutenant Clyde Smith, will break out the
duty crew and give you a hand," Read promised as a courtesy to
a senior. No law or regulation gave him any power to veto Ellyson's
decision.

The OL's big inverted Liberty "V" engine was always tricky to start. On a freezing night, with the amphibian pushed from an unheated hangar, the effort it required was heartbreaking. One after another, the sailors winded themselves as they cranked its inertia starter. Between crankings they tried all of the mechanics' tricks—priming, backing down, and microscopically adjusting the throttle and spark. Nothing worked. The engine stood mute. Exhausted men recovered their breath, warmed their stiff fingers around coffee mugs, then tried again. They all took turns in the cockpit; none had the magic touch.

Midnight passed. Ellyson was forty-three years old.

Occasionally the engine burped, coughed blue smoke, then was still. Coffee lost its kick. Spuds phoned Putty Read. "This clunk won't start," he said. "The station has one of the same type. May I borrow it for the trip?" Read agreed.

Leaving the *Lexington* plane on the ramp, tired sailors hiked down the line of hangars. Manhandling the heavy doors, they pushed out the other OL and began cranking its cold engine. Sometime after 1:30, it coughed and fired tentatively on two or three cylinders. The man in the cockpit cautiously moved throttle and spark while softly pleading, "Come on, you bastard." Suddenly all twelve cylinders roared, and he let the motor race to warm up. The three pilots, buckling helmets and swapping coffee mugs for gloves, moved stiffly toward the machine.

"I'm sending a couple of men to get the battery and the landing flares from the other plane," Clyde Smith told Ellyson. Planes of that day were wired for lights but had no generators; their batteries were kept on charge in a shop except when installed for scheduled night flying.

"How long will that take?" Ellyson demanded.

"Ten or fifteen minutes, if everything fits."

"We'll go without them. I've waited too long now," Spuds decided. "All we have to do is follow the lighted buoys of the Baltimore ship channel. We don't need lights for that." His reaction was normal for the times. Most night flights were made with little more preparation or equipment than Spuds had had in July 1911, on Lake Keuka.

The duty officer told the men, "Never mind the battery." After all, he told himself, I'm just the helper. I don't like anything about this flight, but I can't stop him.

Spuds normally preferred to take the controls himself, but that night, without explanation, he put Ransehousen in the pilot's seat and climbed into the lower compartment which had no controls. Schmidt took the second pilot's seat.

The unlighted plane rolled down the ramp. The duty crew watched it idle, while Ransehousen cranked up the wheels. Then the engine spurted long red flames, and the keel slashed a white wake into Willoughby Bay that chopped off at 1:58 A.M. when the machine left the water. Moments later, the exhaust flames faded beyond Willoughby Spit. Dismissing the tired men, the duty officer phoned the naval base radio, told them to send a departure report to radio Annapolis, and hoped he was through for the night.

In Monday's gray dawn, attendants wheeled Mildred Ellyson into an Annapolis operating room. "Your father is coming to make everything all right," Helen assured the child. "The doctor will put you to sleep, so nothing will hurt you. When you wake up, you'll feel better, and your father will be with us."

Helen knew telegrams sometimes took a day for delivery. Maybe Spuds had not yet started. She had been an aviator's wife long enough to know that balky engines often delayed takeoffs or caused forced landings in isolated spots. Possibly he had to stop for repairs. Certainly she had no cause for alarm just because he had not arrived before daylight.

While surgeons worked over Mildred, Commander Read, a hundred and fifty miles to the south, worried because he had heard nothing of Ellyson's arrival. A midmorning query to radio Annapolis brought an afternoon answer that Ellyson was not there.

Read immediately began an air search. He also broadcast the alarm over the police and Coast Guard communication networks. The plane was probably down in some out-of-the-way Chesapeake cove, drifting with a dead engine, as often happened in those days.

Across the country, the afternoon papers headlined the story of the missing plane with the Navy's first aviator aboard. They reported that the Thimble Shoal lightkeeper had seen the plane pass two minutes after takeoff. Forty minutes later and a dozen miles east of the shoal, crewmen on the railroad ferry *Salisbury* saw the OL fly close aboard. They said it was low over the water heading south. At 4 A.M. the Thomas Point lightkeeper, nearly as far north as Annapolis, saw it fly north. Two army blimps and twenty-three Navy planes reported to be searching northward from Thomas Point were expected to find the missing plane before dark.

A Loening amphibian plane, similar to the one Spuds Ellyson used on his last flight. His was equipped with an inverted twelve-cylinder "V" Liberty engine; this later model uses a radial engine. The black square indicated by the arrow is the window of the lower observer's cockpit in which Ellyson took off.

"Don't let Mrs. Ellyson see a paper or hear any mention of this," ordered the senior surgeon. "No telling what it might do to her with the child on the critical list." Workers in the intensive-care room guarded their tongues. Helen did not leave the room; she sat all night and half the next day at Mildred's side.

Tuesday afternoon color tinged the child's face. She spoke rationally for the first time, then slept normally. "She'll be all right now," the doctor assured Helen. "But you must get some rest."

Nurses coaxed her to a sofa. Rousing after a short nap, she said she was going home to change clothes and to wire Gordon. As gently as they could, the staff told her that Gordon had been missing for nearly two days. Feigning confidence, they assured her the searching planes would soon find him in good shape. To cover all the Chesapeake's likely coves and islands just took time.

Helen said little. Maybe she was too tired to respond. Perhaps she had been bracing herself for such news ever since she married an Early Bird. She probably told herself that since Gordon was the oldest and the best aviator, no airplane could do him in. He would be found OK.

For two more days she expected good news, while others grew pessimistic. Editors rehashed stories of Ellyson's early flying exploits as they reported the widening search with still-negative results. Then, on Friday, they announced that wreckage found in the entrance of Chesapeake Bay had been identified as part of Ellyson's plane. No sign of the personnel had been found.

At last Helen admitted to herself that her husband was gone. He had died answering her call for help. She knew the size of her loss; she knew a hero had loved her dearly. But she wanted to hide her tears and jeer at fate as her Early Bird had always done.

That afternoon she gave a cocktail party. "Gordon sent it to me," she explained when guests admired the orchid on her shoulder. Some Annapolitans thought her odd. Her Poverty Row neighbors, young fliers who also regularly rolled death's dice, understood, recognizing her gallant gesture for what it was.

Editors revived the old legends and published them as obituaries, then dropped the story. Brief notices appeared forty days later when the body of Commander Theodore Gordon Ellyson washed up on Willoughby Spit. Helen's wire calling him to Annapolis was still in his pocket.

Epilogue

In history's view, Spuds Ellyson may have overvalued some of the "firsts" which fate handed him. Accidents of timing made him the first naval aviator, the first naval flight instructor, the first naval test pilot, the first to fly a float plane from a catapult, and more. He was the first to advocate a designation for naval fliers and wrote the first qualification for it. Some of his requirements continued in use for more than twenty years, so long as the Navy continued elementary flight training in float planes.

On the other hand, Ellyson undervalued his most far-reaching contributions to naval aviation. His most important achievements for naval aviation may have been to teach Lieutenant junior grade John Henry Towers to fly and to start Naval Constructor Holden Chester Richardson's flight instruction, for these two men worked continually to improve naval aviation until they retired after World War II. The power stall landing which Ellyson invented, unintentionally, on his first night flight above Lake Keuka has been used by seaplane pilots ever since for landings in black nights or on glossy water. His many forced landings and accidents helped men like Curtiss and Richardson to see ways to improve the early planes. Unintentionally he inspired many younger shipmates in the *South Carolina* and in the destroyers to take up flying. At least five of these fliers were flying admirals in World War II.

Even his death indirectly led to aviation progress. Because he
was so well known, the report of the Board of Investigation, con-
vened to determine the facts of his crash, was not quietly interred
in Washington file cabinets. For several years the report passed
over Washington desks, heckling bureaucrats and officials. Eventually they laid the ghost to rest by starting the first system of
formal flight clearances and prompt departure and arrival reports
and by establishing reponsibility for the positive guarding of all
flights. Like most of Spuds Ellyson's other important contributions to the art of aviation, this final contribution was, of course,
unplanned.

Bibliography

Unpublished material

1. *National Archives, Navy Section, Washington, D.C.*

   Files:
   Ellyson correspondence
   Ellyson fitness reports
   Ellyson orders
   Navy Department general correspondence
   Investigation of the death of Commander T. G. Ellyson

   Ships' Logs:
   USS *Bailey* (1911)
   USS *Brooks*
   USS *Colorado* (1907)
   USS *Chesapeake*
   USS *Iowa*
   USS *Iris*
   USS *J. Fred Talbot*
   USS *Langley*
   USS *Lexington* (1927)
   USS *Missouri* (1905)
   USS *Pennsylvania*
   USS *Porpoise*

USS *Rainbow*
USS *Shark*
USS *South Carolina*

2. *Navy Department, Washington, D.C.*

Aviation log, Curtiss Hydroaeroplane, Navy Number A-1
Aviation log, Curtiss Hydroaeroplane, Navy Number A-2
Aviation log, Wright hydroaeroplane, Navy Number B-1
Aviation record files
Welborn, Mary Catherine, *History of the technical development of Naval Aircraft.* Unpublished manuscript with source notes.

3. *Library of Congress, Washington, D.C.*

Bristol, Mark L., Personal papers
Chambers, W.I., Personal papers
Loening, Grover, Personal papers
Wright, Wilbur and Orville, Personal papers
Whiting, K., Personal papers

4. *Miscellaneous*

BELLINGER, P. N. I. Filmed interview held at Navy Photographic Center, Washington, D.C.
_____ *Memoirs.* Unpublished manuscript, Office of the Technical Historian, Naval Air Systems Command.
TOWERS, John H. Talk before the Institute of Aeronautical Sciences. New York, Janaury 26, 1954, as recorded (held by Mrs. Towers).
WRIGHT, C. Q. *History of the Washington Navy Yard.* Unpublished manuscript in the Navy History section of the National Archives.
ZOGBAUM, R. Filmed interview held by Navy Photographic Center, Washington, D.C.

Magazines

Anonymous articles in issues during 1910-1913
   Aero
   Aeronautics
   Aircraft
   Flying

Scientific American
Bellinger, P. N. L. "Sailors in the Sky," *National Geographic,* Vol. 120, No. 2 (August, 1961), 277 ff.

Books

Chandler, Charles D. & Frank P. Lahm. *How Our Army Grew Wings.* New York: Ronald Press, 1943.

Fiske, Bradley A. *From Midshipman to Rear Admiral.* New York: Century Company, 1919.

Furlong, William Rea (ed). *The First Twenty-Five Years.* Annapolis: U.S. Naval Academy, 1930.

Halsey, William F., & J. Bryan III. *Admiral Halsey's Story.* New York & London: McGraw Hill Book Company, 1947.

Howeth, L. S. *History of Communications—Electronic—in the U. S. Navy.* Washington, D.C.: Government Printing Office, 1963.

Loening, Grover. *Our Wings Grow Faster.* Garden City, New York: Doubleday Doran Company, 1935.

Magoun, F. A., & E. Hodgins. *History of Aircraft.* New York & London: McGraw Hill, 1931.

Miller, Harold Blaine. *Navy Wings* (revised edition). New York: Dodd, Meade & Company, 1943.

New International Yearbook. New York: Dodd, Meade & Company.

Sullivan, Mark. *Our Times: The United States 1900-1925, Vol. II.* New York and London: Charles Scribner & Sons, 1927.

Turnbull, A. D., & C. L. Lord. *History of U. S. Naval Aviation.* New Haven: Yale University Press, 1949.

U. S. Naval Aviation 1898-1956. Washington, D.C.: Bureau Aeronautics, Navy Department, 1956.

U. S. Naval Aviation, 1910-1960. Washington, D.C.: Government Printing Office, 1961.

van Deurs, George. *Wings for the Fleet.* Annapolis: U. S. Naval Institute, 1966.

Zogbaum, Rufus Fairchild. *From Sail to Saratoga.* Rome: Tipografia Italo-Oriental S. Nilo. Grottaferrata, 1961.

Index

Rear Admiral GEORGE VAN DEURS,
U.S.N. retired, was himself one of the first
of the naval aviators, earning his wings in
1923 after graduation from the U.S. Naval
Academy. Currently a free-lance author and
photographer, he has written *Wings for the
Fleet* (Naval Institute Press, 1966) and *The
Battleship Oregon Influence* (Albert M.
Lewis, 1978).